CHEKHOV'S
THE CHERRY ORCHARD

EDITED BY Herbert Goldstone, University of Connecticut

ALLYN AND BACON, INC. • BOSTON, 1965

ALLYN AND BACON CASEBOOK SERIES

GENERAL EDITOR • LEONARD F. DEAN

PREFACE

For a number of reasons *The Cherry Orchard*, probably more than any other Chekhov play, lends itself effectively to a casebook study in depth and variety of perspectives.

First, there is considerable material to draw upon for such a casebook. We have illuminating letters by Chekhov both about the play itself and more general questions of art and morality that provide a valuable context in which to study the play. Chekhov's letters are candid, precise, and toughly perceptive. If Chekhov does not, like Shaw, favor us with marvellous discursive prefaces to his plays, he has written some very incisive comments about them in various personal letters. Besides the letters, we have immediate secondary materials in the rich reminiscences of Chekhov by theatre contemporaries such as Gorki, his good friend and fellow dramatist, and Stanislavski, the famous Moscow Art Theatre director, whose productions of Chekhov's plays have been so celebrated and moving, if also open to some question in interpretation. These reminiscences may not be models of objective fact—David Magarshack in *Chekhov: a Life* suggests that both men sentimentalized Chekhov—but they still provide valuable personal insights and judgments. At a somewhat greater distance, we have significant books and articles both about the play and Chekhov's literary achievement to draw upon, including biography, literary history, cultural history, and literary criticism. While these books and articles differ considerably, fortunately, they also seem to build upon one another so that to read them together both clarifies and perhaps also resolves some of the differences. Last, but by no means least, we have many fine reviews of various celebrated productions of the play from Stanislavski to the present which help us experience the play in dramatic terms as a work of theatrical art. What is more, they bring into sharper focus some of the comments in the books and articles and raise other crucial questions about the meaning, form, and impact of the play.

A second reason results from the play's great popularity. If frequency of inclusion in anthologies is any criterion, then *The Cherry Orchard* seems to be Chekhov's best known play and for many the *only* Chekhov play they know. This popularity almost in itself makes a casebook study of the play useful, especially when it seems connected with what some critics call "Chekhovism"—a series of widespread impressions about the characters and the form of his plays. Among other things, these impressions include the idea that Chekhov's plays concern themselves with ineffectual, decadent characters who waste themselves on trifles and have almost nothing significant ever happen to them, and that the mood of the plays is melancholy and sombre, certainly nearer to tragedy than comedy. However, the question is: how accurate is "Chekhovism?" Does it adequately reflect Chekhov's dramatic vision or grossly distort it? And is there any particular connection between The Cherry Orchard as the best known Chekhov play and "Chekhovism?" Furthermore, what is the play's form, especially when Stanislavski insisted the play was tragic and Chekhov termed The Cherry Orchard, as well as The Sea Gull and Uncle Vanya, comedies? Just what does comedy mean for Chekhov and how does this compare to more traditional ideas of the form? I mention these questions not only because they can enlighten us about The Cherry Orchard, but because they present some interesting implications for many other literary works, especially in the last fifty years, to which conventional definitions of tragedy and comedy may not apply. To study The Cherry Orchard in depth then is to immerse ourselves not only in the play itself but in many significant questions about modern literature and thought.

A third reason for a casebook on The Cherry Orchard is that we can better understand one of the play's major themes, the impact of change upon a society in transition from one social, economic, and perhaps cultural order to another. I do not mean to imply that Chekhov in The Cherry Orchard portrays change so complexly and allusively as to defy interpretation without elaborate glosses, but only that we can more fully appreciate his insight and delicacy when we realize what he has done with his materials. In part we can do so by knowing something about the particular society upon which presumably he bases his presentation and in part by realizing just what Chekhov does not do—the easy ways out he avoids. Chekhov does not present such a wide panorama that he can only scratch the surface and so avoid any depth. He does not settle for oversimplified explanations in depth, such as that of hero and villain, victim and victimizer, or oversimplified results, such as a change from darkness to light or vice versa. Or, to put it differently, he does not herald the 1917 revolution and he does not nostalgically recall the good old days. Nor does he go to opposite extremes of presenting so many explanations and results as to avoid meaning and to abdicate his responsibility for selection and discrimination. Rather, he shows how variously the change affects individuals at the same time that it unites them in various ways, and he selects a moment when he can convey maximum suggestiveness of implication without sacrificing rich concreteness of character, situation, and mood.

In fact, he suggests so much because he does remain so concrete, as we can see more clearly when we bring to the play the perceptions of critics and scholars about the treatment of change.

While we could certainly mention other reasons that make a casebook appropriate—such as the orchestration of emotion in a variety of ways—I think the point is clear enough: how many avenues we can explore and need to explore in order to try to do justice to this beautiful and evocative play, so effervescent and yet so haunting, so full of life, and yet written, as we know from the biographies, so close to death when Chekhov as a doctor knew he was fatally ill but tried to conceal this as much as he could to spare his intimates, if not himself.

Herbert Goldstone

CONTENTS

PART FOUR: THE CHERRY ORCHARD IN
THE THEATRE: Selected Reviews

PART ONE

THE CHERRY ORCHARD

THE CHERRY ORCHARD:
A Comedy in Four Acts

Translated by Stark Young*

CHARACTERS

Ranevskaya, Lyuboff Andreevna (Lyuba), a landowner
Anya (Anitchka), her daughter, 17 years old
Varya (Varvara Mikhailovna), her adopted daughter, 24 years old
Gayeff, Leonid Andreevich (Lenya or Lyonya), her brother
Lopahin, Yermolay Alexeevich, a merchant
Trofimoff, Pyotr Sergeevich (Petya), a student, about 30 years old
Semyonoff-Pishtchik, Boris Borisovich, a landowner
Charlotta Ivanovna, a governess
Epihodoff, Semyon Panteleevich, a clerk
Dunyasha (Avdotya Feodorovna), a maid
Fiers, valet to Gayeff; 87 years old
Yasha, a young valet
A Stranger Passing Through The Estate
Station-Master
A Post-office Clerk
Visitors, Servants

The action takes place on the estate of Ranevskaya.

The time is the beginning of the twentieth century, about forty years after the Emancipation of the Serfs (1861) and the end of the Russian feudal system.

ACT ONE

A room that is still called the nursery. One of the doors leads into Anya's room. Dawn, the sun will soon be rising. It is May, the cherry trees are in blossom but in the orchard it is cold, with a morning frost. The windows in the room are closed. Enter Dunyasha with a candle and Lopahin with a book in his hand.

Lopahin   The train got in, thank God! What time is it?

Dunyasha   It's nearly two. (Blows out her candle) It's already daylight.

Lopahin   But how late was the train? Two hours at least. (Yawning and stretching) I'm a fine one, I am, look what a fool thing I did! I drove here on purpose just to meet them at the station, and then all of a sudden I'd overslept myself! Fell asleep in my chair. How provoking!—You could have waked me up.

Dunyasha   I thought you had gone. (Listening) Listen, I think they are coming now.

Lopahin (Listening)   No—No, there's the luggage and one thing and another. (A pause) Lyuboff Andreevna has been living abroad five years. I don't know what she is like now. She is a good woman. An easy-going, simple woman. I remember when I was a boy about fifteen, my father, who is at rest—in those days he ran a shop here in the village—hit me in the face with his fist, my nose was bleeding. We'd come to the yard together for something or other, and he was a little drunk. Lyuboff Andreevna, I can see her now, still so young, so slim, led me to the washbasin here in this very room, in the nursery. "Don't cry," she says, "little peasant, it will be well in time for your wedding"—(A pause) Yes, "little peasant"—my father was a peasant truly, and here I am in a white waistcoat and yellow shoes. Like a pig rooting in a pastry shop—I've got this rich, lots of money, but if you really stop and think of it, I'm just a peasant—(Turning the pages of a book) Here I was reading a book and didn't get a thing out of it. Reading and went to sleep. (A pause)

Dunyasha   And all night long the dogs were not asleep, they know their masters are coming.

Lopahin   What is it, Dunyasha, you're so—

Dunyasha   My hands are shaking. I'm going to faint.

Lopahin   You're just so delicate, Dunyasha. And all dressed up like a lady, and your hair all done up! Mustn't do that. Must know your place.

  (Enter *Epihodoff*, with a bouquet: he wears a jacket and highly polished boots with a loud squeak. As he enters he drops the bouquet.)

Epihodoff (Picking up the bouquet)   Look, the gardener sent these, he says to put them in the dining room.

  (Giving the bouquet to *Dunyasha*)

Lopahin   And bring me some *kvass*.

Dunyasha   Yes, sir. (Goes out)

Epihodoff   There is a morning frost now, three degrees of frost (Sighing) and the cherries all in bloom. I cannot approve of your climate—I cannot. Our climate can never quite rise to the occasion. Listen, Yermolay Alexeevich, allow me to acquaint you with the fact that I bought myself, day before yesterday, some boots and they, I venture to assure you, squeak so that they are, well, impossible. What could I grease them with?

Lopahin Go on. You annoy me.

Epihodoff Every day some misfortune happens to me. But I don't complain, I am used to it, and I even smile.

(*Dunyasha* enters, serves *Lopahin* the kvass)

Epihodoff I'm going. (Stumbling over a chair and upsetting it) There (As if triumphant) there, you see, pardon the expression, a circumstance like that, among others—It is simply quite remarkable. (Goes out)

Dunyasha And I must tell you, Yermolay Alexeevich, that Epihodoff has proposed to me.

Lopahin Ah!

Dunyasha I don't know really what to—He is a quiet man but sometimes when he starts talking, you can't understand a thing he means. It's all very nice, and full of feeling, but just doesn't make any sense. I sort of like him. He loves me madly. He's a man that's unfortunate, every day there's something or other. They tease him around here, call him "twenty-two misfortunes—"

Lopahin (Cocking his ear) Listen, I think they are coming—

Dunyasha They are coming! But what's the matter with me—I'm cold all over.

Lopahin They're really coming. Let's go meet them. Will she recognize me? It's five years we haven't seen each other.

Dunyasha (Excitedly) I'm going to faint this very minute. Ah, I'm going to faint!

(Two carriages can be heard driving up to the house. *Lopahin* and *Dunyasha* hurry out. The stage is empty. In the adjoining rooms a noise begins. *Fiers* hurries across the stage, leaning on a stick; he has been to meet *Lyuboff Andreevna*, and wears an old-fashioned livery and a high hat; he mutters something to himself, but one cannot understand a word of it. The noise offstage gets louder and louder. A voice: "Look! Let's go through here—" *Lyuboff Andreevna*, *Anya* and *Charlotta Ivanovna*, with a little dog on a chain, all of them dressed for traveling, *Varya*, in a coat and kerchief, *Gayeff*, *Semyonoff-Pishtchik*, *Lopahin*, *Dunyasha*, with a bundle and an umbrella, servants with pieces of luggage—all pass through the room.)

Anya Let's go through here. Mama, do you remember what room this is?

Lyuboff (Happily, through her tears) The nursery!

Varya How cold it is, my hands are stiff. (To *Lyuboff*) Your rooms, the white one and the violet, are just the same as ever, Mama.

Lyuboff The nursery, my dear beautiful room—I slept here when I was little—(Crying) And now I am like a child—(Kisses her brother and *Varya*, then her brother again) And Varya is just the same as ever, looks like a nun. And I knew Dunyasha—(Kisses *Dunyasha*)

Gayeff The train was two hours late. How's that? How's that for good management?

Charlotta (To *Pishtchik*) My dog—he eats nuts, too.

Pishtchik (Astonished) Think of that!

(Everybody goes out except *Anya* and *Dunyasha*.)

Dunyasha We waited so long—(Taking off *Anya's* coat and hat.)

Anya I didn't sleep all four nights on the way. And now I feel so chilly.

Dunyasha It was Lent when you left, there was some snow then, there was frost, and now? My darling (Laughing and kissing her), I waited so long for you, my joy, my life—I'm telling you now, I can't keep from it another minute.

Anya (Wearily) There we go again—

Dunyasha The clerk, Epihodoff, proposed to me after Holy Week.

Anya You're always talking about the same thing—(Arranging her hair) I've lost all my hairpins—(She is tired to the point of staggering)

Dunyasha I just don't know what to think. He loves me, loves me so!

Anya (Looks in through her door, tenderly) My room, my windows, it's just as if I had never been away. I'm home! Tomorrow morning I'll get up, I'll run into the orchard—Oh, if I only could go to sleep! I haven't slept all the way, I was tormented by anxiety.

Dunyasha Day before yesterday, Pyotr Sergeevich arrived.

Anya (Joyfully) Petya!. . . .

Dunyasha He's asleep in the bathhouse, he lives there. I am afraid, he says, of being in the way. (Taking her watch from her pocket and looking at it) Somebody ought to wake him up. It's only that Varvara Mikhailovna told us not to. Don't you wake him up, she said.

(Enter *Varya* with a bunch of keys at her belt)

Varya Dunyasha, coffee, quick—Mama is asking for coffee.

Dunyasha This minute. (Goes out)

Varya Well, thank goodness, you've come back. You are home again. (Caressingly) My darling is back! My precious is back!

Anya I've had such a time.

Varya I can imagine!

Anya I left during Holy Week, it was cold then. Charlotta talked all the way and did her tricks. Why did you fasten Charlotta on to me—?

Varya But you couldn't have traveled alone, darling; not at seventeen!

Anya We arrived in Paris, it was cold there and snowing. I speak terrible French. Mama lived on the fifth floor; I went to see her; there were some French people in her room, ladies, an old priest with his prayer book, and the place was full of tobacco smoke—very dreary. Suddenly I began to feel sorry for Mama, so sorry, I drew her to me, held her close and couldn't let her go. Then Mama kept hugging me, crying—yes—

Varya (Tearfully) Don't—oh, don't—

Anya Her villa near Mentone she had already sold, she had nothing left, nothing. And I didn't have a kopeck left. It was all we could do to get here. And Mama doesn't understand! We sit dówn to dinner at a station and she orders, insists on the most expensive things and gives the waiters rouble tips. Charlotta does the same. Yasha too demands his share; it's simply dreadful. Mama has her butler, Yasha, we've brought him here—

Varya I saw the wretch.

Anya Well, how are things? Has the interest on the mortgage been paid?

Varya How could we?

Anya Oh, my God, my God—!

Varya In August the estate is to be sold—

Anya My God—!

Lopahin (Looking in through the door and mooing like a cow) Moo-o-o —(Goes away)

Varya (Tearfully) I'd land him one like that—(Shaking her fist)

Anya (Embracing *Varya* gently) Varya, has he proposed? (*Varya* shakes her head) But he loves you—Why don't you have it out with him, what are you waiting for?

Varya I don't think anything will come of it for us. He is very busy, he hasn't any time for me—And doesn't notice me. God knows, it's painful for me to see him—Everybody talks about our marriage, everybody congratulates us, and the truth is, there's nothing to it—it's all like a dream—(In a different tone) You have a brooch looks like a bee.

Anya (Sadly) Mama bought it. (Going toward her room, speaking gaily, like a child) And in Paris I went up in a balloon!

Varya My darling is back! My precious is back! (*Dunyasha* has returned with the coffee pot and is making coffee. *Varya* is standing by the door) Darling, I'm busy all day long with the house and I go around thinking things. If only you could be married to a rich man, I'd be more at peace, too. I would go all by myself to a hermitage—then to Kiev—to Moscow, and I'd keep going like that from one holy place to another—I would go on and on. Heavenly!

Anya The birds are singing in the orchard. What time is it now?

Varya It must be after two. It's time you were asleep, darling. (Going into *Anya's* room) Heavenly!

Yasha (*Yasha* enters with a lap robe and a traveling bag. Crossing the stage airily) May I go through here?

Dunyasha We'd hardly recognize you, Yasha; you've changed so abroad!

Yasha Hm—And who are you?

Dunyasha When you left here, I was like that—(Her hand so high from the floor) I'm Dunyasha, Fyodor Kozoyedoff's daughter. You don't remember!

Yasha Hm—You little peach!

(Looking around before he embraces her; she shrieks and drops a saucer; *Yasha* hurries out)

Varya (At the door, in a vexed tone) And what's going on here?

Dunyasha (Tearfully) I broke a saucer—

Varya That's good luck.

Anya (Emerging from her room) We ought to tell Mama beforehand: Petya is here—

Varya I told them not to wake him up.

Anya (Pensively) Six years ago our father died, a month later our brother Grisha was drowned in the river. Such a pretty little boy, just seven. Mama couldn't bear it, she went away, went away without ever looking back—(Shuddering) How I understand her, if she only knew I did. (A pause) and Petya Trofimoff was Grisha's tutor, he might remind—

(Enter *Fiers*; he is in a jacket and white waistcoat)

Fiers (Going to the coffee urn, busy with it) The mistress will have her breakfast here—(Putting on white gloves) Is the coffee ready? (To *Dunyasha*, sternly) You! What about the cream?

Dunyasha Oh, my God—(Hurrying out)

Fiers (Busy at the coffee urn) Oh, you good-for-nothing—!¹ (Muttering to himself) Come back from Paris—And the master used to go to Paris by coach—(Laughing)

Varya Fiers, what are you—?

Fiers At your service (Joyfully) My mistress is back! It's what I've been waiting for! Now I'm ready to die—(Crying for joy)

(*Lyuboff, Gayeff* and *Semyonoff-Pishtchik* enter; *Semyonoff-Pishtchik* wears a full-length short-waisted peasant coat of fine cloth [podyovka] and wide, full trousers designed to be worn tucked inside high boots [sharovary]. *Gayeff* enters, making gestures with his hands and body as if he were playing billiards.)

Lyuboff How is it? Let me remember—Yellow into the corner! Duplicate in the middle!²

Gayeff I cut into the corner. Sister, you and I slept here in this very room once, and now I am fifty-one years old, strange as that may seem—

Lopahin Yes, time passes.

Gayeff What?

Lopahin Time, I say, passes.

---

¹ No translator of Chekhov has ever found an adequate English equivalent for Chekhov's phrase here, *nedotyopa*. It was originally a brilliant creation by Chekhov, a term given wide currency because of its effective use in this play. Literally, it means "half-chopped." In English, "daffy" and "wooly-headed" are close approximations, but these terms do not convey the overtone of "mediocre" or "unpromising" also found in the Russian word.

² The terms from billiards used throughout the play usually refer to difficult, if not impossible shots, classic problems in billiards the avid player might spend his life trying to master.

Gayeff And it smells like patchouli here.[3]
Anya I'm going to bed. Good night, Mama. (Kissing her mother)
Lyuboff My sweet little child. (Kissing her hands) You're glad you are home? I still can't get myself together.
Anya Good-by, Uncle.
Gayeff (Kissing her face and hands) God be with you. How like your mother you are! (To his sister) Lyuba, at her age you were exactly like her.

    (*Anya* shakes hands with *Lopahin* and *Pishtchik,* goes out and closes the door behind her)

Lyuboff She's very tired.
Pishtchik It is a long trip, I imagine.
Varya (To *Lopahin* and *Pishtchik*) Well, then, sirs? It's going on three o'clock, time for gentlemen to be going.
Lyuboff (Laughing) The same old Varya. (Drawing her to her and kissing her) There, I'll drink my coffee, then we'll all go. (*Fiers* put a small cushion under her feet) Thank you, my dear. I am used to coffee. Drink it day and night. Thank you, my dear old soul.
    (Kissing *Fiers*)
Varya I'll go see if all the things have come. (Goes out).
Lyuboff Is it really me sitting here? (Laughing) I'd like to jump around and wave my arms. (Covering her face with her hands) But I may be dreaming! God knows I love my country, I love it deeply, I couldn't look out of the car window, I just kept crying. (Tearfully) However, I must drink my coffee. Thank you, Fiers, thank you, my dear old friend. I'm so glad you're still alive.
Fiers Day before yesterday.
Gayeff He doesn't hear well.
Lopahin And I must leave right now for Kharkov. It's nearly five o'clock in the morning. What a nuisance! I wanted to look at you—talk—You are as beautiful as ever.
Pishtchik (Breathing heavily) Even more beautiful—In your Paris clothes—It's a feast for the eyes—
Lopahin Your brother, Leonid Andreevich here, says I'm a boor, a peasant money grubber, but that's all the same to me, absolutely. Let him say it. All I wish is you'd trust me as you used to, and your wonderful, touching eyes would look at me as they did. Merciful God! My father was a serf; belonged to your grandfather and your father; but you, your own self, you did so much for me once that I've forgotten all that and love you like my own kin—more than my kin.
Lyuboff I can't sit still—I can't. (Jumping up and walking about in great excitement) I'll never live through this happiness—Laugh at me, I'm

[3] A strong mentholated perfume frequently used by men as shaving lotion. Lopahin apparently applies it too copiously.

silly—My own little bookcase—! (Kissing the bookcase) My little table!

Gayeff And in your absence the nurse here died.

Lyuboff (Sitting down and drinking coffee) Yes, may she rest in Heaven! They wrote me.

Gayeff And Anastasy died. Cross-eyed Petrushka left me and lives in town now at the police officer's. (Taking out of his pocket a box of hard candy and sucking a piece)

Pishtchik My daughter, Dashenka—sends you her greetings—

Lopahin I want to tell you something very pleasant, cheerful. (Glancing at his watch) I'm going right away. There's no time for talking. Well, I'll make it two or three words. As you know, your cherry orchard is to be sold for your debts; the auction is set for August 22nd, but don't you worry, my dear, you just sleep in peace, there's a way out of it. Here's my plan. Please listen to me. Your estate is only thirteen miles from town. They've run the railroad by it. Now if the cherry orchard and the land along the river were cut up into building lots and leased for summer cottages, you'd have at the very lowest twenty-five thousand roubles per year income.

Gayeff Excuse me, what rot!

Lyuboff I don't quite understand you, Yermolay Alexeevich.

Lopahin At the very least you will get from the summer residents twenty-five roubles per year for a two-and-a-half acre lot and if you post a notice right off, I'll bet you anything that by autumn you won't have a single patch of land free, everything will be taken. In a word, my congratulations, you are saved. The location is wonderful, the river's so deep. Except, of course, it all needs to be tidied up, cleared—For instance, let's say, tear all the old buildings down and this house, which is no good any more, and cut down the old cherry orchard.

Lyuboff Cut down? My dear, forgive me, you don't understand at all. If there's one thing in the whole province that's interesting—not to say remarkable—it's our cherry orchard.

Lopahin The only remarkable thing about this cherry orchard is that it's very big. There's a crop of cherries once every two years and even that's hard to get rid of. Nobody buys them.

Gayeff This orchard is even mentioned in the encyclopedia.

Lopahin (Glancing at his watch) If we don't cook up something and don't get somewhere, the cherry orchard and the entire estate will be sold at auction on the twenty-second of August. Do get it settled then! I swear there is no other way out. Not a one!

Fiers There was a time, forty-fifty years ago when the cherries were dried, soaked, pickled, cooked into jam and it used to be—

Gayeff Keep quiet, Fiers.

Fiers And it used to be that the dried cherries were shipped by the wagon-load to Moscow and to Kharkov. And the money there was! And the dried cherries were soft then, juicy, sweet, fragrant—They had a way of treating them then—

Lyuboff And where is that way now?

Fiers They have forgotten it. Nobody remembers it.

Pishtchik (To *Lyuboff*) What's happening in Paris? How is everything? Did you eat frogs?

Lyuboff I ate crocodiles.

Pishtchik Think of it—!

Lopahin Up to now in the country there have been only the gentry and the peasants, but now in summer the villa people too are coming in. All the towns, even the least big ones, are surrounded with cottages. In about twenty years very likely the summer resident will multiply enormously. He merely drinks tea on the porch now, but it might well happen that on this two-and-a-half acre lot of his, he'll go in for farming, and then your cherry orchard would be happy, rich, splendid—

Gayeff (Getting hot) What rot!

(Enter *Varya* and *Yasha*)

Varya Here, Mama. Two telegrams for you. (Choosing a key and opening the old bookcase noisily) Here they are.

Lyuboff From Paris. (Tearing up the telegrams without reading them) Paris, that's all over—

Gayeff Do you know how old this bookcase is, Lyuba? A week ago I pulled out the bottom drawer and looked, and there the figures were burned on it. The bookcase was made exactly a hundred years ago. How's that? Eh? You might celebrate its jubilee. It's an inanimate object, but all the same, be that as it may, it's a bookcase.

Pishtchik (In astonishment) A hundred years—! Think of it—!

Gayeff Yes—quite something—(Shaking the bookcase) Dear, honored bookcase! I saluted your existence, which for more than a hundred years has been directed toward the clear ideals of goodness and justice; your silent appeal to fruitful endeavor has not flagged in all the course of a hundred years, sustaining (Tearfully) through the generations of our family, our courage and our faith in a better future and nurturing in us ideals of goodness and of a social consciousness.

(A pause)

Lopahin Yes.

Lyuboff You're the same as ever, Lenya.

Gayeff (Slightly embarrassed) Carom to the right into the corner pocket. I cut into the side pocket!

Lopahin (Glancing at his watch) Well, it's time for me to go.

Yasha (Handing medicine to *Lyuboff*) Perhaps you'll take the pills now—

Pishtchik You should never take medicaments, dear madam—They do neither harm nor good—Hand them here, dearest lady. (He takes the pillbox, shakes the pills out into his palm, blows on them, puts them in his mouth and washes them down with kvass) There! Now!

Lyuboff (Startled)   Why, you've lost your mind!

Pishtchik   I took all the pills.

Lopahin   Such a glutton!

(Everyone laughs)

Fiers   The gentleman stayed with us during Holy Week, he ate half a bucket of pickles—(Muttering)

Lyuboff   What is he muttering about?

Varya   He's been muttering like that for three years. We're used to it.

Yasha   In his dotage.

(*Charlotta Ivanovna* in a white dress—she is very thin, her corset laced very tight—with a lorgnette at her belt, crosses the stage)

Lopahin   Excuse me, Charlotta Ivanova, I haven't had a chance yet to welcome you. (Trying to kiss her hand)

Charlotta (Drawing her hand away)   If I let you kiss my hand, 'twould be my elbow next, then my shoulder—

Lopahin   No luck for me today. (Everybody laughs) Charlotta Ivanovna, show us a trick!

Charlotta   No. I want to go to bed. (Exit)

Lopahin   In three weeks we shall see each other. (Kissing *Lyuboff's* hand) Till then, good-by. It's time. (To *Gayeff*) See you soon. (Shaking *Varya's* hand, then *Fiers'* and *Yasha's*) I don't feel like going. (To *Lyuboff*) If you think it over and make up your mind about the summer cottages, let me know and I'll arrange a loan of something like fifty thousand roubles. Think it over seriously.

Varya (Angrily)   Do go on, anyhow, will you!

Lopahin   I'm going, I'm going—(Exit)

Gayeff   Boor. However, pardon—Varya is going to marry him, it's Varya's little fiancé.

Varya   Don't talk too much, Uncle.

Lyuboff   Well, Varya, I should be very glad. He's a good man.

Pishtchik   A man, one must say truthfully—A most worthy—And my Dashenka—says also that—she says all sorts of things—(Snoring but immediately waking up) Nevertheless, dearest lady, oblige me— with a loan of two hundred and forty rubles—Tomorrow the interest on my mortgage has got to be paid—

Varya (Startled)   There's not any money, none at all.

Lyuboff   Really, I haven't got anything.

Pishtchik   I'll find it, somehow. (Laughing) I never give up hope. There, I think to myself, all is lost, I am ruined and lo and behold—a railroad is put through my land and—they paid me. And then, just watch, something else will turn up—if not today, then tomorrow—Dashenka will win two hundred thousand—She has a ticket.

Lyuboff We've finished the coffee, now we can go to bed.

Fiers (Brushing *Gayeff's* clothes, reprovingly) You put on the wrong trousers again. What am I going to do with you!

Varya (Softly) Anya is asleep. (Opening the window softly) Already the sun's rising—it's not cold. Look, Mama! What beautiful trees! My Lord, what air! The starlings are singing!

Gayeff (Opening another window) The orchard is all white. You haven't forgotten, Lyuba? That long lane there runs straight—as a strap stretched out. It glistens on moonlight nights. Do you remember? You haven't forgotten it?

Lyuboff (Looking out of the window on to the orchard) Oh, my childhood, my innocence! I slept in this nursery and looked out on the orchard from here, every morning happiness awoke with me, it was just as it is now, then—nothing has changed. (Laughing with joy) All, all white! Oh, my orchard! After a dark, rainy autumn and cold winter, you are young again and full of happiness. The heavenly angels have not deserted you—If I only could lift the weight from my breast, from my shoulders, if I could only forget my past!

Gayeff Yes, and the orchard will be sold for debt, strange as that may seem.

Lyuboff Look, our dear mother is walking through the orchard—in a white dress! (Laughing happily) It's she.

Gayeff Where?

Varya God be with you, Mama!

Lyuboff There's not anybody, it only seemed so. To the right, as you turn to the summerhouse, a little white tree is leaning there, looks like a woman—(Enter *Trofimoff*, in a student's uniform, well worn, and glasses) What a wonderful orchard! The white masses of blossoms, the sky all blue.

Trofimoff Lyuboff Andreevna! (She looks around at him) I will just greet you and go immediately. (Kissing her hand warmly) I was told to wait until morning, but I hadn't the patience—

(*Lyuboff* looks at him puzzled)

Varya (Tearfully) This is Petya Trofimoff—

Trofimoff Petya Trofimoff, the former tutor of your Grisha—have I really changed so?

(*Lyuboff* embraces him; and crying quietly)

Gayeff (Embarrassed) There, there, Lyuba.

Varya (Crying) I told you, Petya, to wait till tomorrow.

Lyuboff My Grisha—My boy—Grisha—Son—

Varya What can we do, Mama? It's God's will.

Trofimoff (In a low voice tearfully)   There, there—

Lyuboff (Weeping softly)   My boy was lost, drowned—Why? Why, my friend? (More quietly) Anya is asleep there, and I am talking so loud —Making so much noise—But why, Petya? Why have you lost your looks? Why do you look so much older?

Trofimoff   A peasant woman on the train called me a mangy-looking gentleman.

Lyuboff   You were a mere boy then, a charming young student, and now your hair's not very thick any more and you wear glasses. Are you really a student still? (Going to the door)

Trofimoff   Very likely I'll be a perennial student.

Lyuboff (Kissing her brother, then *Varya*)   Well, go to bed—You've grown older too, Leonid.

Pishtchik (Following her)   So that's it, we are going to bed now. Oh, my gout! I'm staying here—I'd like, Lyuboff Andreevna, my soul, tomorrow morning—Two hundred and forty roubles—

Gayeff   He's still at it.

Pishtchik   Two hundred and forty roubles—To pay interest on the mortgage.

Lyuboff   I haven't any money, my dove.

Pishtchik   I'll pay it back, my dear—It's a trifling sum—

Lyuboff   Oh, very well, Leonid will give—You give it to him, Leonid.

Gayeff   Oh, certainly, I'll give it to him. Hold out your pockets.

Lyuboff   What can we do, give it, he needs it—He'll pay it back.

(*Lyuboff*, *Trofimoff*, *Pishtchik* and *Fiers* go out. *Gayeff*, *Varya* and *Yasha* remain)

Gayeff   My sister hasn't yet lost her habit of throwing money away. (To *Yasha*) Get away, my good fellow, you smell like hens.

Yasha (With a grin)   And you are just the same as you used to be, Leonid Andreevich.

Gayeff   What? (To *Varya*) What did he say?

Varya (To *Yasha*)   Your mother has come from the village, she's been sitting in the servants' hall ever since yesterday, she wants to see you—

Yasha   The devil take her!

Varya   Ach, shameless creature!

Yasha   A lot I need her! She might have come tomorrow.

(Goes out)

Varya   Mama is just as she was, she hasn't changed at all. If she could, she'd give away everything she has.

Gayeff   Yes—If many remedies are prescribed for an illness, you may know the illness is incurable. I keep thinking, I wrack my brains, I have many remedies, a great many, and that means, really, I haven't any at all. It would be fine to inherit a fortune from somebody, it would be fine to marry off our Anya to a very rich man, it would be fine to go to Yaroslavl and try our luck with our old aunt, the Countess. Auntie is very, very rich.

Varya (Crying) If God would only help us!

Gayeff Don't bawl, Auntie is very rich but she doesn't like us. To begin with, Sister married a lawyer, not a nobleman—(*Anya* appears at the door) Married not a nobleman and behaved herself, you could say, not very virtuously. She is good, kind, nice, I love her very much, but no matter how much you allow for the extenuating circumstances, you must admit she's a depraved woman. You feel it in her slightest movement.

Varya (Whispering) Anya is standing in the door there.

Gayeff What? (A pause) It's amazing, something got in my right eye. I am beginning to see poorly. And on Thursday, when I was in the District Court—

(*Anya* enters)

Varya But why aren't you asleep, Anya?

Anya I don't feel like sleeping. I can't.

Gayeff My little girl—(Kissing *Anya's* face and hands) My child—(Tearfully) You are not my niece, you are my angel, you are everything to me. Believe me, believe—

Anya I believe you, Uncle. Everybody loves you, respects you—But dear Uncle, you must keep quiet, just keep quiet—What were you saying, just now, about my mother, about your own sister? What did you say that for?

Gayeff Yes, yes—(Putting her hand up over his face) Really, it's terrible! My God! Oh, God, save me! And today I made a speech to the bookcase—So silly! And it was only when I finished it that I could see it was silly.

Varya It's true, Uncle, you ought to keep quiet. Just keep quiet. That's all.

Anya If you kept quiet, you'd have more peace.

Gayeff I'll keep quiet. (Kissing *Anya's* and *Varya's* hands) I'll keep quiet. Only this, it's about business. On Thursday I was in the District Court; well, a few of us gathered around and a conversation began about this and that, about lots of things; apparently it will be possible to arrange a loan on a promissory note to pay the bank the interest due.

Varya If the Lord would only help us!

Gayeff Tuesday I shall go and talk it over again. (To *Varya*) Don't bawl! (To *Anya*) Your mother will talk to Lopahin; of course, he won't refuse her . . . And as soon as you rest up, you will go to Yaroslavl to your great-aunt, the Countess. There, that's how we will move from three directions, and the business is in the bag. We'll pay the interest. I am convinced of that—(Putting a hard candy in his mouth) On my honor I'll swear, by anything you like, that the estate shall not be sold! (Excitedly) By my happiness, I swear! Here's my hand, call me a worthless, dishonorable man, if I allow it to come up for auction! With all my soul I swear it!

Anya (A quieter mood returns to her; she is happy) How good you are, Uncle, how clever! (Embracing her uncle) I feel easy now! I feel easy! I'm happy!

(*Fiers* enters)

Fiers (Reproachfully) Leonid Andreevich, have you no fear of God! When are you going to bed?

Gayeff Right away, right away. You may go, Fiers. For this once I'll undress myself. Well, children, beddy bye—More details tomorrow, and now, go to bed (Kissing *Anya* and *Varya*) I am a man of the eighties— It is a period that's not admired, but I can say, nevertheless, that I've suffered no little for my convictions in the course of my life. It is not for nothing that the peasant loves me. One must know the peasant! One must know from what—

Anya Again, Uncle!

Varya You, Uncle dear, keep quiet.

Fiers (Angrily) Leonid Andreevich!

Gayeff I'm coming, I'm coming—Go to bed. A double bank into the side pocket! A clean shot—

(Goes out, *Fiers* hobbling after him)

Anya I feel easy now. I don't feel like going to Yaroslavl; I don't like Great-aunt, but still I feel easy. Thanks to Uncle. (Sits down)

Varya I must get to sleep. I'm going. And there was unpleasantness here during your absence. In the old servants' quarters, as you know, live only the old servants: Yephemushka, Polya, Yevstignay, well, and Karp. They began to let every sort of creature spend the night with them—I didn't say anything. But then I hear they've spread the rumor that I'd given orders to feed them nothing but beans. Out of stinginess, you see—And all that from Yevstignay—Very well, I think to myself. If that's the way it is, I think to myself, then you just wait. I call in Yevstignay—(Yawning) He comes—How is it, I say, that you, Yestignay—You're such a fool—(Glancing at *Anya*) Anitchka!—(A pause) Asleep! (Takes *Anya* by her arm) Let's go to bed—Come on!— (Leading her) My little darling fell asleep! Come on—(They go. Far away beyond the orchard a shepherd is playing on a pipe. *Trofimoff* walks across the stage and, seeing *Varya* and *Anya*, stops) Shh—She is asleep—asleep—Let's go, dear.

Anya (Softly, half dreaming) I'm so tired—All the bells!—Uncle—dear —And Mama and Uncle—

Varya Come on, my dear, come on. (They go into *Anya's* room)

Trofimoff (Tenderly) My little sun! My spring!

Curtain

ACT TWO

A field. An old chapel, long abandoned, with crooked walls, near it a well, big stones that apparently were once tombstones, and an old bench. A road to the estate of *Gayeff* can be seen. On one side poplars rise, casting their shadows, the cherry orchard begins there. In the distance a row of telegraph poles; and far, far away, faintly traced on the horizon, is a large town, visible only in the clearest weather. The sun will soon be down. *Charlotta, Yasha* and *Dunyasha* are sitting on the bench; *Epihodoff* is standing near and playing the guitar; everyone sits lost in thought. *Charlotta* wears a man's old peaked cap (fourrage); she has taken a rifle from off her shoulders and is adjusting the buckle on the strap.

Charlotta (Pensively) I have no proper passport, I don't know how old I am—it always seems to me I'm very young. When I was a little girl, my father and mother traveled from fair to fair and gave performances, very good ones. And I did *salto mortale*[1] and different tricks. And when Papa and Mama died, a German lady took me to live with her and began teaching me. Good. I grew up. And became a governess. But where I came from and who I am I don't know—Who my parents were, perhaps they weren't even married—I don't know. (Taking a cucumber out of her pocket and beginning to eat it) I don't know a thing. (A pause) I'd like so much to talk but there's not anybody. I haven't anybody.

Epihodoff (Playing the guitar and singing) "What care I for the noisy world, what care I for friends and foes."—How pleasant it is to play the mandolin!

Dunyasha That's a guitar, not a mandolin. (Looking into a little mirror and powdering her face)

Epihodoff For a madman who is in love this is a mandolin—(Singing) "If only my heart were warm with the fire of requited love."

(Yasha sings with him)

Charlotta How dreadfully these people sing—Phooey! Like jackals.

Dunyasha (To Yasha) All the same what happiness to have been abroad.

Yasha Yes, of course. I cannot disagree with you.

(Yawning and then lighting a cigar)

Epihodoff That's easily understood. Abroad everything long since attained its complete development.

Yasha That's obvious.

Epihodoff I am a cultured man. I read all kinds of remarkable books, but the trouble is I cannot discover my own inclinations, whether to

[1] A "death-defying" jump or leap.

live or to shoot myself. But nevertheless, I always carry a revolver on me. Here it is—(Showing a revolver)

Charlotta That's done. Now I am going. (Slinging the rifle over her shoulder) You are a very clever man, Epihodoff, and a very terrible one; the women must love you madly. Brrrr-r-r-r! (Going) These clever people are all so silly, I haven't anybody to talk with. I'm always alone, alone, I have nobody and—Who I am, why I am, is unknown—(Goes out without hurrying)

Epihodoff Strictly speaking, not touching on other subjects, I must state about myself, in passing, that fate treats me mercilessly, as a storm does a small ship. If, let us suppose, I am mistaken, then why, to mention one instance, do I wake up this morning, look and there on my chest is a spider of terrific size—There, like that. (Showing the size with both hands) And also I take some *kvass* to drink and in it I find something in the highest degree indecent, such as a cockroach. (A pause) Have you read Buckle?[2] (A pause) I desire to trouble you, Avdotya Feodorovna, with a couple of words.

Dunyasha Speak.

Epihodoff I have a desire to speak with you alone—(Sighing)

Dunyasha (Embarrassed) Very well—But bring me my cape first—by the cupboard—It's rather damp here—

Epihodoff Very well—I'll fetch it—Now I know what I should do with my revolver—(Takes the guitar and goes out playing)

Yasha "Twenty-two misfortunes!" Between us he's a stupid man, it must be said. (Yawning)

Dunyasha God forbid he should shoot himself. (A pause) I've grown so uneasy, I'm always fretting. I was only a girl when I was taken into the master's house, and now I've lost the habit of simple living—and here are my hands white, white as a lady's. I've become so delicate, fragile, ladylike, afraid of everything—Frightfully so. And, Yasha, if you deceive me, I don't know what will happen to my nerves.

Yasha (Kissing her) You little cucumber! Of course every girl must behave properly. What I dislike above everything is for a girl to conduct herself badly.

Dunyasha I have come to love you passionately, you are educated, you can discuss anything. (A pause)

Yasha (Yawning) Yes, sir—To my mind it is like this: If a girl loves someone, it means she is immoral. (A pause) It is pleasant to smoke a cigar in the clear air—(Listening) They are coming here—It is the ladies and gentlemen—(Dunyasha impulsively embraces him) Go to the house, as though you had been to bathe in the river, go by this path, otherwise, they might meet you and suspect me of making a rendezvous with you. That I cannot tolerate.

[2] Henry Thomas Buckle (1821–1862), a nineteenth century historian.

Dunyasha (With a little cough) Your cigar has given me the headache. (Goes out)

    (*Yasha* remains, sitting near the chapel. *Lyuboff, Gayeff* and *Lopahin* enter)

Lopahin We must decide definitely, time doesn't wait. Why, the matter's quite simple. Are you willing to lease your land for summer cottages or are you not? Answer in one word, yes or no? Just one word!

Lyuboff Who is it smokes those disgusting cigars out here—? (Sitting down)

Gayeff The railroad running so near is a great convenience. (Sitting down) We made a trip to town and lunched there—Yellow in the side pocket! Perhaps I should go in the house first and play one game—

Lyuboff You'll have time.

Lopahin Just one word! (Imploringly) Do give me your answer!

Gayeff (Yawning) What?

Lyuboff (Looking in her purse) Yesterday there was lots of money in it. Today there's very little. My poor Varya! For the sake of economy she feeds everybody milk soup, and in the kitchen the old people get nothing but beans, and here I spend money—senselessly—(Dropping her purse and scattering gold coins) There they go scattering! (She is vexed)

Yasha Allow me, I'll pick them up in a second. (Picking up the coins)

Lyuboff If you will, Yasha. And why did I go in town for lunch—? Your restaurant with its music is trashy, the tablecloths smell of soap— Why drink so much, Lyonya? Why eat so much? Why talk so much? Today in the restaurant you were talking a lot again, and all of it beside the point. About the seventies, about the decadents. And to whom? Talking to waiters about the decadents!

Lopahin Yes.

Gayeff (Waving his hand) I am incorrigible, that's evident—(To *Yasha* irritably) What is it?—You are forever swirling around in front of us?

Yasha (Laughing) I cannot hear your voice without laughing.

Gayeff (To his sister) Either I or he—

Lyuboff Go away, Yasha. Go on—

Yasha (Giving *Lyuboff* her purse) I am going right away. (Barely suppressing his laughter) This minute. (Goes out)

Lopahin The rich Deriganoff intends to buy your estate. They say he is coming personally to the auction.

Lyuboff And where did you hear that?

Lopahin In town they are saying it.

Gayeff Our Yaroslavl aunt promised to send us something, but when and how much she will send, nobody knows—

Lopahin How much will she send? A hundred thousand? Two hundred?

Lyuboff Well—maybe ten, fifteen thousand—we'd be thankful for that.

Lopahin Excuse me, but such light-minded people as you are, such odd, unbusinesslike people, I never saw. You are told in plain Russian that your estate is being sold up and you just don't seem to take it in.

Lyuboff But what are we to do? Tell us what?

Lopahin I tell you every day. Every day I tell you the same thing. Both the cherry orchard and the land have got to be leased for summer cottages, it has to be done right now, quick—The auction is right under your noses. Do understand! Once you finally decide that there are to be summer cottages, you will get all the money you want, and then you'll be saved.

Lyuboff Summer cottages and summer residents—it is so common, excuse me, but that's what it is.

Gayeff I absolutely agreed with you.

Lopahin I'll either burst out crying, or scream, or faint. I can't bear it! You are torturing me! (To *Gayeff*) You're a perfect old woman!

Gayeff What?

Lopahin A perfect old woman! (About to go)

Lyuboff (Alarmed) No, don't go, stay, my lamb, I beg you. Perhaps we will think of something!

Lopahin What is there to think about?

Lyuboff Don't go, I beg you. With you here it is more cheerful anyhow—(A pause) I keep waiting for something, as if the house were about to tumble down on our heads.

Gayeff (Deep in thought) Double into the corner pocket—Bank into the wide pocket—

Lyuboff We have sinned so much—

Lopahin What sins have you—?

Gayeff (Puts a hard candy into his mouth) They say I've eaten my fortune up in hard candies—(Laughing)

Lyuboff Oh, my sins—I've always thrown money around like mad, recklessly, and I married a man who accumulated nothing but debts. My husband died from champagne—he drank fearfully—and to my misfortune I fell in love with another man. I lived with him, and just at that time—it was my first punishment—a blow over the head: right here in the river my boy was drowned and I went abroad—went away for good, never to return, never to see this river again—I shut my eyes, ran away, beside myself, and he after me—mercilessly, brutally. I bought a villa near Mentone, because he fell ill there, and for three years I knew no rest day or night, the sick man exhausted me, my soul dried up. And last year when the villa was sold for debts, I went to Paris and there he robbed me of everything, threw me over, took up with another woman; I tried to poison myself—so stupid, so shameful—And suddenly I was seized with longing for

Russia, for my own country, for my little girl—(Wiping away her tears) Lord, Lord, have mercy, forgive me my sins! Don't punish me any more! (Getting a telegram out of her pocket) I got this today from Paris, he asks forgiveness, begs me to return—(Tears up the telegram) That sounds like music somewhere.
(Listening)

Gayeff It is our famous Jewish orchestra. You remember, four violins, a flute and double bass.

Lyuboff Does it still exist? We ought to get hold of it sometime and give a party.

Lopahin (Listening) Can't hear it—(Singing softly) "And for money the Germans will frenchify a Russian." (Laughing) What a play I saw yesterday at the theatre, very funny!

Lyuboff And most likely there was nothing funny about it. You shouldn't look at plays, but look oftener at yourselves. How gray all your lives are, what a lot of idle things you say!

Lopahin That's true. It must be said frankly this life of ours is idiotic— (A pause) My father was a peasant, an idiot, he understood nothing, he taught me nothing, he just beat me in his drunken fits and always with a stick. At bottom I am just as big a dolt and idiot as he was. I wasn't taught anything, my handwriting is vile, I write like a pig— I am ashamed for people to see it.

Lyuboff You ought to get married, my friend.

Lopahin Yes—that's true.

Lyuboff To our Varya, perhaps. She is a good girl.

Lopahin Yes.

Lyuboff She comes from simple people, and she works all day long, but the main thing is she loves you. And you, too, have liked her a long time.

Lopahin Why not? I am not against it—She's a good girl. (A pause)

Gayeff They are offering me a position in a bank. Six thousand a year—Have you heard that?

Lyuboff Not you! You stay where you are—
(Fiers enters, bringing an overcoat)

Fiers (To *Gayeff*) Pray, Sir, put this on, it's damp.

Gayeff (Putting on the overcoat) You're a pest, old man.

Fiers That's all right—This morning you went off without letting me know. (Looking him over)

Lyuboff How old you've grown, Fiers!

Fiers At your service.

Lopahin She says you've grown very old!

Fiers I've lived a long time. They were planning to marry me off before your papa was born. (Laughing) And at the time the serfs were freed I was already the head footman. I didn't want to be freed then, I stayed with the masters—(A pause) And I remember, everybody was happy, but what they were happy about they didn't know themselves.

Lopahin In the old days it was fine. At least they flogged.

Fiers (Not hearing) But, of course. The peasants stuck to the masters, the masters stuck to the peasants, and now everything is all smashed up, you can't tell about anything.

Gayeff Keep still, Fiers. Tomorrow I must go to town. They have promised to introduce me to a certain general who might make us a loan.

Lopahin Nothing will come of it. And you can rest assured you won't pay the interest.

Lyuboff He's just raving on. There aren't any such generals.

(*Trofimoff, Anya* and *Varya* enter)

Gayeff Here they come.

Anya There is Mama sitting there.

Lyuboff (Tenderly) Come, come—My darlings—(Embracing *Anya* and *Varya*) If you only knew how I love you both! Come sit by me—there —like that.

(Everybody sits down)

Lopahin Our perennial student is always strolling with the young ladies.

Trofimoff It's none of your business.

Lopahin He will soon be fifty and he's still a student.

Trofimoff Stop your stupid jokes.

Lopahin But why are you so peevish, you queer duck?

Trofimoff Don't you pester me.

Lopahin (Laughing) Permit me to ask you, what do you make of me?

Trofimoff Yermolay Alexeevich, I make this of you; you are a rich man, you'll soon be a millionaire. Just as it is in the metabolism of nature, a wild beast is needed to eat up everything that comes his way; so you, too, are needed.

(Everyone laughs)

Varya Petya, you'd better tell us about the planets.

Lyuboff No, let's go on with yesterday's conversation.

Trofimoff What was it about?

Gayeff About the proud man.

Trofimoff We talked a long time yesterday, but didn't get anywhere. In a proud man, in your sense of the word, there is something mystical. Maybe you are right, from your standpoint, but if we are to discuss it in simple terms, without whimsy, then what pride can there be, is there any sense in it, if man physiologically is poorly constructed, if in the great majority he is crude, unintelligent, profoundly miserable. One must stop admiring oneself. One must only work.

Gayeff All the same, you will die.

Trofimoff Who knows? And what does it mean—you will die? Man may have a hundred senses, and when he dies only the five that are known to us may perish, and the remaining ninety-five go on living.

Lyuboff How clever you are, Petya!

Lopahin (Ironically) Terribly!

Trofimoff Humanity goes forward, perfecting its powers. Everything that's unattainable now will some day become familiar, understandable; it is only that one must work and must help with all one's might those who seek the truth. With us in Russia so far only a very few work. The great majority of the intelligentsia that I know are looking for nothing, doing nothing, and as yet have no capacity for work. They call themselves intelligentsia, are free and easy with the servants, treat the peasants like animals, educate themselves poorly, read nothing seriously, do absolutely nothing; about science they just talk and about art they understand very little. Every one of them is serious, all have stern faces; they all talk of nothing but important things, philosophize, and all the time everybody can see that the workmen eat abominably, sleep without any pillows, thirty or forty to a room, and everywhere there are bedbugs, stench, dampness, moral uncleanness—And apparently with us, all the fine talk is only to divert the attention of ourselves and of others. Show me where we have the day nurseries they are always talking so much about, where are the reading rooms? They only write of these in novels, for the truth is there are not any at all. There is only filth, vulgarity, orientalism— I am afraid of very serious faces and dislike them. I'm afraid of serious conversations. Rather than that let's just keep still.

Lopahin You know I get up before five o'clock in the morning and work from morning till night. Well, I always have money, my own and other people's, on hand, and I see what the people around me are. One has only to start doing something to find out how few honest and decent people there are. At times when I can't go to sleep, I think: Lord, thou gavest us immense forests, unbounded fields and the widest horizons, and living in the midst of them we should indeed be giants—

Lyuboff You feel the need for giants—They are good only in fairy tales; anywhere else they only frighten us.

(At the back of the stage *Epihodoff* passes by, playing the guitar)

Lyuboff (Lost in thought) Epihodoff is coming—

Anya (Lost in thought) Epihodoff is coming.

Gayeff The sun has set, ladies and gentlemen.

Trofimoff Yes.

Gayeff (Not loud and as if he were declaiming) Oh, Nature, wonderful, you gleam with eternal radiance, beautiful and indifferent, you, whom we call Mother, combine in yourself both life and death, you give life and you take it away.

Varya (Beseechingly) Uncle!

Anya Uncle, you're doing it again!

Trofimoff You'd better bank the yellow into the side pocket.

Gayeff I'll be quiet, quiet.

(All sit absorbed in their thoughts. There is only the silence. *Fiers* is heard muttering to himself softly. Suddenly a distant sound is heard, as if from the sky, like the sound of a snapped string, dying away, mournful)

Lyuboff What's that?

Lopahin I don't know. Somewhere far off in a mine shaft a lift cable must have broken. But somewhere very far off.

Gayeff Or it may be some bird—like a heron.

Trofimoff Or an owl—

Lyuboff (Shivering) It's unpleasant, somehow. (A pause)

Fiers Before the disaster it was like that. The owl hooted and the samovar hummed without stopping, both.

Gayeff Before what disaster?

Fiers Before the emancipation.

(A pause)

Lyuboff You know, my friends, let's go. Twilight is falling. (To *Anya*) You have tears in your eyes—What is it, my dear little girl? (Embracing her)

Anya It's just that, Mama. It's nothing.

Trofimoff Somebody is coming.

(A *Stranger* appears in a shabby white cap, and an overcoat; he is a little drunk)

The Stranger Allow me to ask you, can I go straight through here to the station?

Gayeff You can. Go by that road.

The Stranger I am heartily grateful to you. (Coughing) The weather is splendid—(Declaiming) "Brother of mine, suffering brother—Go out to the Volga, whose moans—" (To *Varya*) Mademoiselle, grant a hungry Russian man some thirty kopecks—

(*Varya* is frightened and gives a shriek)

Lopahin (Angrily) There's a limit to everything.

Lyuboff (Flustered) Take this—Here's this for you—(Searching in her purse) No silver—It's all the same, here's a gold piece for you—

The Stranger I am heartily grateful to you. (Goes out. Laughter)

Varya (Frightened) I'm going—I'm going—Oh, Mama, you poor little Mama! There's nothing in the house for people to eat, and you gave him a gold piece.

Lyuboff What is to be done with me, so silly? I shall give you all I have in the house. Yermolay Alexeevich, you will lend me some this once more!—

Lopahin Agreed.

Lyuboff Let's go, ladies and gentlemen, it's time. And here, Varya, we have definitely made a match for you, I congratulate you.

Varya (Through her tears) Mama, that's not something to joke about.

Lopahin Achmelia, get thee to a nunnery.[3]

Gayeff And my hands are trembling; it is a long time since I have played billiards.

Lopahin Achmelia, Oh nymph, in thine orisons be all my sins remember'd—

Lyuboff Let's go, my dear friends, it will soon be suppertime.

Varya He frightened me. My heart is thumping so!

Lopahin I remind you, ladies and gentleman: August 22nd the cherry orchard will be auctioned off. Think about that!—Think!—

(All go out except *Trofimoff* and *Anya*)

Anya (Laughing) My thanks to the stranger, he frightened Varya. Now we are alone.

Trofimoff Varya is afraid we might begin to love each other and all day long she won't leave us to ourselves. With her narrow mind she cannot understand that we are above love. To sidestep the petty and illusory, which prevent our being free and happy, that is the aim and meaning of our life. Forward! We march on irresistibly toward the bright star that burns there in the distance. Forward! Do not fall behind, friends!

Anya (Extending her arms upward) How well you talk! (A pause) It's wonderful here today!

Trofimoff Yes, the weather is marvelous.

Anya What have you done to me, Petya? Why don't I love the cherry orchard any longer the way I used to? I loved it so tenderly, it seemed to me there was not a better place on earth than our orchard.

Trofimoff All Russia is our orchard. The earth is immense and beautiful, and on it are many wonderful places. (A pause) Just think, Anya: your grandfather, great-grandfather and all your ancestors were slave owners, in possession of living souls, and can you doubt that from every cherry in the orchard, from every leaf, from every trunk, human beings are looking at you. Can it be that you don't hear their voices? To possess living souls, well, that depraved all of you who lived before and who are living now, so that your mother and you, and your uncle no longer notice that you live by debt, at somebody else's expense, at the expense of those very people whom you wouldn't let past your front door—We are at least two hundred years behind the times, we have as yet absolutely nothing, we have no definite attitude toward the past, we only philosophize, complain of our sadness or drink vodka. Why, it is quite clear that to begin to live in the present time we must first atone for our past, must be done with it; and we can atone for it only through suffering, only through uncommon, incessant labor. Understand that, Anya.

---

[3] Here and below Lopahin is quoting somewhat distortedly Hamlet's advice to Ophelia (Act III, Scene 1).

Anya   The house we live in ceased to be ours long ago, and I'll go away, I give you my word.

Trofimoff   If you have the household keys, throw them in the well and go away. Be free as the wind.

Anya (Transported) How well you said that!

Trofimoff   Believe me, Anya, believe me! I am not thirty yet, I am young, I am still a student, but I have already borne so much! Every winter I am hungry, sick, anxious, poor as a beggar, and—where has destiny not chased me, where haven't I been! And yet, my soul has always, every minute, day and night, been full of inexplicable premonitions. I have a premonition of happiness, Anya, I see it already—

Anya   (Pensively) The moon is rising.

(Epihodoff is heard playing on the guitar, always the same sad song. The moon rises. Somewhere near the poplars Varya is looking for Anya and calling: "Anya! Where are you?")

Trofimoff   Yes, the moon is rising. (A pause) Here is happiness, here it comes, comes always nearer and nearer, I hear its footsteps now. And if we shall not see it, shall not come to know it, what does that matter? Others will see it!

Varya   (Off) Anya! Where are you?

Trofimoff   Again, that Varya! (Angrily) It's scandalous!

Anya   Well, let's go to the river. It's lovely there.

Trofimoff   Let's go. (They go out)

Varya   (Off) Anya! Anya!

Curtain

ACT THREE

The drawing room, separated by an arch from the ballroom. A chandelier is lighted. A Jewish orchestra is playing—the same that was mentioned in Act Two. Evening. In the ballroom they are dancing grand rond. The voice of Semyonoff-Pishtchik: "Promenade à une paire!" They enter the drawing room; in the first couple are Pishtchik and Charlotta Ivanovna; in the second, Trofimoff and Lyuboff Andreevna; in the third, Anya with the Post-Office Clerk; in the fourth, Varya with the Stationmaster, et cetera—Varya is crying softly and wipes away her tears while she is dancing. Dunyasha is in the last couple through the drawing room, Pishtchik shouts: "Grand rond, balancez!" and "Les Cavaliers à genoux et remerciez vos dames!" [1]

_____

[1] The pattern of the Grand Rond is close to the familiar American square dances. The last of Pishtchik's calls signalizes the end of the full set: "Gentlemen, on your knees and thank your ladies."

Fiers in a frock coat goes by with seltzer water on a tray. *Pishtchik* and *Trofimoff* come into the drawing room.

Pishtchik I am full-blooded, I have had two strokes already, and dancing is hard for me, but as they say, if you are in a pack of dogs, you may bark and bark, but you must still wag your tail. At that, I have the health of a horse. My dear father—he was a great joker—may he dwell in Heaven—used to talk as if our ancient line, the Semyonoff-Pishtchiks, were descended from the very horse that Caligula made a Senator—(Sitting down) But here's my trouble: I haven't any money. A hungry dog believes in nothing but meat—(Snoring but waking at once) And the same way with me—I can't talk about anything but money.

Trofimoff Well, to tell you the truth, there *is* something horsy about your figure.

Pishtchik Well—a horse is a fine animal—You can sell a horse—
(The sound of playing billards comes from the next room. *Varya* appears under the arch to the ballroom)

Trofimoff (Teasing) Madam Lopahin! Madam Lopahin!

Varya (Angrily) A mangy-looking gentleman!

Trofimoff Yes, I am a mangy-looking gentleman, and proud of it!

Varya (In bitter thought) Here we have gone and hired musicians and what are we going to pay them with? (Goes out)

Trofimoff (To *Pishtchik*) If the energy you have wasted in the course of your life trying to find money to pay the interest had gone into something else, you could very likely have turned the world upside down before you were done with it.

Pishtchik Nietzsche—the philosopher—the greatest—the most celebrated—a man of tremendous mind—says in his works that one may make counterfeit money.

Trofimoff And have you read Nietzsche?

Pishtchik Well—Dashenka told me. And I'm in such a state now that I could make counterfeit money myself—Day after tomorrow three hundred and ten roubles must be paid—one hundred and thirty I've on hand—(Feeling in his pockets, alarmed) The money is gone! I have lost the money! (Tearfully) Where is the money? (Joyfully) Here it is, inside the lining—I was in quite a sweat—
(*Lyuboff* and *Charlotta Ivanovna* come in)

Lyuboff (Humming the "Lezginka," a Georgian dance) Why does Leonid take so long? What's he doing in town? (To *Dunyasha*) Dunyasha, offer the musicians some tea—

Trofimoff In all probability the auction did not take place.

Lyuboff And the musicians came at an unfortunate moment and we planned the ball at an unfortunate moment—Well, it doesn't matter. (Sitting down and singing softly)

Charlotta (Gives *Pishtchik* a deck of cards) Here is a deck of cards for you, think of some one card.

Pishtchik I have thought of one.

Charlotta Now, shuffle the deck. Very good. Hand it here; oh, my dear Monsieur Pishtchik. *Ein, zwei, drei!* Now look for it, it's in your coat pocket—

Pishtchik (Getting a card out of his coat pocket) The eight of spades, that's absolutely right! (Amazed) Fancy that!

Charlotta (Holding a deck of cards in her palm; to *Trofimoff*) Tell me quick now, which card is on top?

Trofimoff What is it? Well—the Queen of Spades.

Charlotta Right! (To *Pishtchik*) Well? Which card's on top?

Pishtchik The Ace of Hearts.

Charlotta Right! (Strikes the deck against her palm; the deck of cards disappears) And what beautiful weather we are having today!

(A mysterious feminine voice answers her, as if from under the floor)

Voice Oh, yes. The weather is splendid, madam.

Charlotta You are so nice, you're my ideal—

Voice—Madam, you too please me greatly.

The Stationmaster (Applauding) Madam Ventriloquist, bravo!

Pishtchik (Amazed) Fancy that! Most charming Charlotta Ivanovna— I am simply in love with you.

Charlotta In love? (Shrugging her shoulders) Is it possible that you can love? *Guter mensch aber schlechter musikant.*[2]

Trofimoff (Slapping *Pishtchik* on the shoulder) You horse, you—

Charlotta I beg your attention, one more trick. (Taking a lap robe from the chair) Here is a very fine lap robe—I want to sell it—(Shaking it out) Wouldn't somebody like to buy it?

Pishtchik (Amazed) Fancy that!

Charlotta *Ein, zwei, drei!*

(She quickly raises the lowered robe, behind it stands *Anya*, who curtseys, runs to her mother, embraces her and runs back into the ballroom amid the general delight)

Lyuboff (Applauding) Bravo, bravo—!

Charlotta Now again! *Ein, zwei, drei!*

(Lifting the robe: behind it stands *Varya*, who bows)

Pishtchik (Amazed) Fancy that!

Charlotta That's all. (Throwing the robe at *Pishtchik*, curtseying and running into the ballroom)

Pishtchik (Hurrying after her) You little rascal—What a girl! What a girl! (Goes out)

Lyuboff And Leonid is not here yet. What he's doing in town so long, I don't understand! Everything is finished there, either the estate is

---

[2] Literally, "a good man but a poor music-maker." Its modern equivalent would be "a nice guy but a lousy lover."

sold by now, or the auction didn't take place. Why keep it from us so long?

Varya (Trying to comfort her) Uncle has bought it, I am sure of that.

Trofimoff (Mockingly) Yes.

Varya Great-aunt sent him power of attorney to buy it in her name and transfer the debt. She did this for Anya. And I feel certain, God willing, that Uncle will buy it.

Lyuboff Our great-aunt in Yaroslavl has sent fifteen thousand to buy the estate in her name—She doesn't trust us, but that wouldn't be enough to pay the interest even—(Covering her face with her hands) Today my fate will be decided, my fate—

Trofimoff (Teasing *Varya*) Madam Lopahin!

Varya (Angrily) Perennial student! You have already been expelled from the University twice.

Lyuboff But why are you angry, Varya? He teases you about Lopahin, what of it? Marry Lopahin if you want to, he is a good man, interesting. If you don't want to, don't marry him; darling, nobody is making you do it.

Varya I look at this matter seriously, Mama, one must speak straight out. He's a good man, I like him.

Lyuboff Then marry him. What there is to wait for I don't understand!

Varya But I can't propose to him myself, Mama. It's two years now; everyone has been talking to me about him, everyone talks, and he either remains silent or jokes. I understand. He's getting rich, he's busy with his own affairs, and has no time for me. If there were money, ever so little, even a hundred roubles, I would drop everything, and go far away. I'd go to a nunnery.

Trofimoff How saintly!

Varya (To *Trofimoff*) A student should be intelligent! (In a low voice, tearfully) How homely you have grown, Petya, how old you've got. (To *Lyuboff*, no longer crying) It is just that I can't live without working, Mama. I must be doing something every minute.

(Yasha enters)

Yasha (Barely restraining his laughter) Epihodoff has broken a billiard cue!—(Goes out)

Varya But why is Epihodoff here? Who allowed him to play billiards? I don't understand these people—(Goes out)

Lyuboff Don't tease her, Petya; you can see she has troubles enough without that.

Trofimoff She is just too zealous. Sticking her nose into things that are none of her business. All summer she gave us no peace, neither me nor Anya; she was afraid a romance would spring up between us. What business is that of hers? And besides I haven't shown any signs of it. I am so remote from triviality. We are above love!

Lyuboff Well, then, I must be beneath love. (Very anxiously) Why isn't Leonid here? Just to tell us whether the estate is sold or not? Calamity seems to me so incredible that I don't know what to think, I'm lost—I could scream this minute—I could do something insane. Save me, Petya. Say something, do say. . . .

Trofimoff Whether the estate is sold today or is not sold—is it not the same? There is no turning back, the path is all grown over. Calm yourself, my dear, all that was over long ago. One mustn't deceive oneself; one must for once at least in one's life look truth straight in the eye.

Lyuboff What truth? You see where the truth is and where the untruth is, but as for me, it's as if I had lost my sight, I see nothing. You boldly decide all important questions, but tell me, my dear boy, isn't that because you are young and haven't had time yet to suffer through any one of your problems? You look boldly ahead, and isn't that because you don't see and don't expect anything terrible, since life is still hidden from your young eyes? You are braver, more honest, more profound than we are, but stop and think, be magnanimous, have a little mercy on me, just a little. Why, I was born here. My father and mother lived here and my grandfather. I love this house, I can't imagine my life without the cherry orchard and if it is very necessary to sell it, then sell me along with the orchard—(Embracing *Trofimoff* and kissing him on the forehead) Why, my son was drowned here—(Crying) Have mercy on me, good, kind man.

Trofimoff You know I sympathize with you from the bottom of my heart.

Lyuboff But that should be said differently, differently—(Taking out her handkerchief; a telegram falls on the floor) My heart is heavy today, you can't imagine how heavy. It is too noisy for me here, my soul trembles at every sound, I tremble all over and yet I can't go off by myself. When I am alone the silence frightens me, Petya—I love you as one of my own. I should gladly have given you Anya's hand, I assure you, only, my dear, you must study and finish your course. You do nothing. Fate simply flings you about from place to place, and that's so strange—Isn't that so? Yes? And you must do something about your beard, to make it grow somehow—(Laughing) You look funny!

Trofimoff (Picking up the telegram) I do not desire to be beautiful.

Lyuboff This telegram is from Paris. I get one every day. Yesterday and today too. That wild man has fallen ill again, something is wrong again with him—He asks forgiveness, begs me to come, and really I ought to make a trip to Paris and stay awhile near him. Your face looks stern, Petya, but what is there to do, my dear, what am I to do, he is ill, he is alone, unhappy and who will look after him there, who will keep him from doing the wrong thing, who will give him his medicine on time? And what is there to hide or keep still about? I love him, that's plain. I love him, love him—It's a stone about my neck, I'm sinking to the bottom with it, but I love that stone and live without it I cannot. (Pressing *Trofimoff's* hand) Don't think harshly of me, Petya, don't say anything to me, don't—

Trofimoff (Tearfully) Forgive my frankness, for God's sake! Why, he picked your bones.

Lyuboff No, no, no, you must not talk like that. (Stopping her ears)

Trofimoff But he is a scoundrel. Only you, you are the only one that doesn't know it. He is a petty scoundrel, a nonentity—

Lyuboff (Angry but controlling herself) You are twenty-six years old or twenty-seven, but you are still a schoolboy in the second grade!

Trofimoff Very well!

Lyuboff You should be a man—at your age you should understand people who love. And you yourself should love someone—you should fall in love! (Angrily) Yes, yes! And there is no purity in you; you are simply smug, a ridiculous crank, a freak—

Trofimoff (Horrified) What is she saying!

Lyuboff "I am above love!" You are not above love, Petya. You are, as our Fiers would say, just a good-for-nothing. Imagine, at your age, not having a mistress—!

Trofimoff (Horrified) This is terrible! What is she saying! (Goes quickly into the ballroom, clutching his head) This is horrible—I can't bear it, I am going—(Goes out but immediately returns) All is over between us. (Goes out into the hall)

Lyuboff (Shouting after him) Petya, wait! You funny creature, I was joking! Petya! (In the hall you hear someone running up the stairs and suddenly falling back down with a crash. You hear *Anya* and *Varya* scream but immediately you hear laughter) What's that?

(*Anya* runs in)

Anya (Laughing) Petya fell down the stairs! (Runs out)

Lyuboff What a funny boy that Petya is—! (The *Stationmaster* stops in the center of the ballroom and begins to recite "The Sinner" by A. Tolstoi.[3] They listen to him but he has recited only a few lines when the strains of a waltz are heard from the hall and the recitation is broken off. They all dance. *Trofimoff, Anya, Varya* and *Lyuboff* come in from the hall) But, Petya—but, dear soul—I beg your forgiveness—Let's go dance.

(She dances with *Trofimoff*. *Anya* and *Varya* dance. *Fiers* enters, leaving his stick by the side door. *Yasha* also comes into the drawing room and watches the dancers)

Yasha What is it, Grandpa?

Fiers I don't feel very well. In the old days there were generals, barons, admirals dancing at our parties, and now we send for the post-office clerk and the stationmaster, and even they are none too anxious to

[3] Alexei Tolstoi (1817–1875), a popular poet.

come. Somehow I've grown feeble. The old master, the grandfather, treated everybody with sealing-wax for all sicknesses. I take sealing-wax every day, have done so for twenty-odd years or more; it may be due to that that I'm alive.

Yasha You are tiresome, Grandpa. (Yawning) Why don't you go off and die?

Fiers Aw, you—good-for-nothing!—(Muttering)

(Trofimoff and Lyuboff dance in the ballroom and then in the drawing room)

Lyuboff Merci. I'll sit down awhile—(Sitting down) I'm tired.

(Anya enters)

Anya (Agitated) And just now in the kitchen some man was saying that the cherry orchard had been sold today.

Lyuboff Sold to whom?

Anya He didn't say. He's gone.

(Dancing with Trofimoff, they pass into the ballroom)

Yasha It was some old man babbling there. A stranger.

Fiers And Leonid Andreevich is still not here, he has not arrived. The overcoat he has on is light, midseason—let's hope he won't catch cold. Ach, these young things!

Lyuboff I shall die this minute. Go, Yasha, find out who it was sold to.

Yasha But he's been gone a long time, the old fellow.

(Laughing)

Lyuboff (With some annoyance) Well, what are you laughing at? What are you so amused at?

Yasha Epihodoff is just too funny. An empty-headed man. "Twenty-two misfortunes!"

Lyuboff Fiers, if the estate is sold, where will you go?

Fiers Wherever you say, there I'll go.

Lyuboff Why do you look like that? Aren't you well? You know you ought to go to bed—

Fiers Yes—(With a sneer) I go to bed and without me who's going to serve, who'll take care of things? I'm the only one in the whole house.

Yasha Lyuboff Andreevna, let me ask a favor of you, do be so kind! If you ever go back to Paris, take me with you, please do! It's impossible for me to stay here. (Looking around him, and speaking in a low voice) Why talk about it? You can see for yourself it's an uncivilized country, an immoral people and not only that, there's the boredom of it. The food they give us in that kitchen is abominable and there's that Fiers, too, walking about and muttering all kinds of words that are out of place. Take me with you, be so kind!

Pishtchik (Entering) Allow me to ask you—for a little waltz, most beautiful lady—(Lyuboff goes with him) Charming lady, I must borrow a hundred and eighty roubles from you—will borrow—(Dancing) a hundred and eighty roubles—(They pass into the ballroom)

Yasha (Singing low) "Wilt thou know the unrest in my soul!"
(In the ballroom a figure in a gray top hat and checked trousers waves both hands and jumps about; there are shouts of "Bravo, Charlotta Ivanovna!")

Dunyasha (Stopping to powder her face) The young lady orders me to dance—there are a lot of gentlemen and very few ladies—but dancing makes my head swim and my heart thump. Fiers Nikolaevich, the post-office clerk said something to me just now that took my breath away.
(The music plays more softly)

Fiers What did he say to you?

Dunyasha You are like a flower, he says.

Yasha (Yawning) What ignorance—! (Goes out)

Dunyasha Like a flower—I am such a sensitive girl, I love tender words awfully.

Fiers You'll be getting your head turned.
(Epihodoff enters)

Epihodoff Avdotya Feodorovna, you don't want to see me—It's as if I were some sort of insect. (Sighing) Ach, life!

Dunyasha What do you want?

Epihodoff Undoubtedly you may be right. (Sighing) But of course, if one considers it from a given point of view, then you—I will allow myself so to express it, forgive my frankness—absolutely led me into such a state of mind. I know my fate, every day some misfortune happens to me, but I have long since become accustomed to that, and so I look on my misfortunes with a smile. You gave me your word and, although I—

Dunyasha I beg you, we'll talk later on, but leave me now in peace. I'm in a dream now. (Playing with her fan)

Epihodoff I have something wrong happen every day—I will allow myself so to express it—I just smile, I even laugh.

Varya (Entering from the ballroom) You are not gone yet, Semyon? What a really disrespectful man you are! (To Dunyasha) Get out of here, Dunyasha. (To Epihodoff) You either play billiards and break a cue or you walk about the drawing room like a guest.

Epihodoff Allow me to tell you, you cannot make any demands on me.

Varya I'm not making any demands on you, I'm talking to you. All you know is to walk from place to place but not do any work. We keep a clerk, but what for, nobody knows.

Epihodoff (Offended) Whether I work, whether I walk, whether I eat, or whether I play billiards are matters to be discussed only by people of understanding and my seniors.

Varya You dare to say that to me! (Flying into a temper) You dare? So I don't understand anything? Get out of here! This minute!

Epihodoff (Alarmed) I beg you to express yourself in a delicate manner.

Varya (Beside herself) This very minute, get out of here! Get out! (He goes to the door; she follows him) "Twenty-two misfortunes!" Don't you dare breathe in here! Don't let me set eyes on you! (*Epihodoff* has gone out, but his voice comes from outside the door: "I shall complain about you.") Ah, you are coming back? (Grabbing the stick that *Fiers* put by the door) Come on, come—come on, I'll show you— Ah, you are coming? You are coming? Take that then—!

(She swings the stick, at the very moment when *Lopahin* is coming in)

Lopahin Most humbly, I thank you.

Varya (Angrily and ironically) I beg your pardon!

Lopahin It's nothing at all. I humbly thank you for the pleasant treat.

Varya It isn't worth your thanks. (Moving away, then looking back and asking gently) I haven't hurt you?

Lopahin No, it's nothing. (Pause) There's a great bump coming, though. (Voices in the ballroom: "Lopahin has come back." "Yermolay Alexeevich!")

Pishtchik (Enters) See what we see, hear what we hear—! (He and *Lopahin* kiss one another) You smell slightly of cognac, my dear, my good old chap. And we are amusing ourselves here too.

Lyuboff (Entering) Is that you, Yermolay Alexeevich? Why were you so long? Where is Leonid?

Lopahin Leonid Andreevich got back when I did, he's coming.

Lyuboff (Agitated) Well, what happened? Was there an auction? Do speak!

Lopahin (Embarrassed, afraid of showing the joy he feels) The auction was over by four o'clock—We were late for the train, had to wait till half-past nine. (Sighing heavily) Ugh, my head's swimming a bit! (*Gayeff* enters; with his right hand he carries his purchases, with his left he wipes away his tears)

Lyuboff Lyona, what? Lyona, eh? (Impatiently, with tears in her eyes) Quick, for God's sake—

Gayeff (Not answering her, merely waving his hand; to *Fiers,* crying) Here, take it—There are anchovies, some Kertch herrings—I haven't eaten anything all day—What I have suffered! (The door into the billiard room is open; you hear the balls clicking and *Yasha's* voice: "Seven and eighteen!" *Gayeff's* expression changes, he is no longer crying) I'm terribly tired. You help me change, Fiers. (Goes to his room through the ballroom, *Fiers* behind him)

Pishtchik What happened at the auction? Go on, tell us!

Lyuboff Is the cherry orchard sold?

Lopahin It's sold.

Lyuboff Who bought it?

Lopahin I bought it. (A pause. *Lyuboff* is overcome. She would have fallen had she not been standing near the chair and table. *Varya* takes the keys from her belt, throws them on the floor in the middle of the drawing room and goes out) I bought it. Kindly wait a moment, ladies and gentlemen, everything is muddled up in my head, I can't speak—(Laughing) We arrived at the auction, Deriganoff was already there. Leonid Andreevich had only fifteen thousand and Deriganoff right off bids thirty over and above indebtedness. I see how things are, I match him with forty thousand. He forty-five. I fifty-five. That is to say he raises it by fives, I by tens— So it ended. Over and above the indebtedness, I bid up to ninety thousand, it was knocked down to me. The cherry orchard is mine now. Mine! (Guffawing) My God, Lord, the cherry orchard is mine! Tell me I'm drunk, out of my head, that I'm imagining all this—(Stamps his feet) Don't laugh at me! If only my father and grandfather could rise from their graves and see this whole business, see how their Yermolay, beaten, half-illiterate Yermolay, who used to run around barefoot in winter, how that very Yermolay has bought an estate that nothing in the world can beat. I bought the estate where grandfather and father were slaves, where you wouldn't even let me in the kitchen. I am asleep, it's only some dream of mine, it only seems so to me—That's nothing but the fruit of my imagination, covered with the darkness of the unknown—(Picking up the keys, with a gentle smile) She threw down the keys, wants to show she is not mistress any more—(Jingling the keys) Well, it's all the same. (The orchestra is heard tuning up) Hey, musicians, play, I want to hear you! Come on, everybody, and see how Yermolay Lopahin will swing the ax in the cherry orchard, how the trees will fall to the ground! We are going to build villas and our grandsons and great-grandsons will see a new life here—Music, play! (The music is playing. Lyuboff has sunk into a chair, crying bitterly. Lopahin reproachfully) Why, then, didn't you listen to me? My poor dear, it can't be undone now. (With tears) Oh, if this could all be over soon, if somehow our awkward, unhappy life would be changed!

Pishtchik (Taking him by the arm, in a low voice) She is crying. Come on into the ballroom, let her be by herself—Come on—(Taking him by the arm and leading him into the ballroom)

Lopahin What's the matter? Music, there, play up! (Ironically) Everything is to be as I want it! Here comes the new squire, the owner of the cherry orchard. (Quite accidentally, he bumps into the little table, and very nearly upsets the candelabra) I can pay for everything! (Goes out with Pishtchik)

(There is nobody left either in the ballroom or the drawing room but Lyuboff who sits all huddled up and crying bitterly. The music plays softly. Anya and Trofimoff enter hurriedly. Anya comes up to her mother and kneels in front of her. Trofimoff remains at the ballroom door)

Anya Mama—! Mama, you are crying? My dear, kind, good Mama, my beautiful, I love you—I bless you. The cherry orchard is sold, it's not ours any more, that's true, true; but don't cry, Mama, you've your life ahead of you, you've your good, pure heart still left you—Come with me, come on, darling, away from here, come on—We will plant a new orchard, finer than this one, you'll see it, you'll understand; and joy, quiet, deep joy will sink into your heart, like the sun at evening, and you'll smile, Mama! Come, darling, come on!

Curtain

ACT FOUR

The same setting as in Act One. There are no curtains on the windows or any pictures on the walls. Only a little furniture remains piled up in one corner as if for sale. A sense of emptiness is felt. Near the outer door, at the rear of the stage, is a pile of suitcases, traveling bags, and so on. The door on the left is open, and through it *Varya's* and *Anya's* voices are heard. *Lopahin* stands waiting. *Yasha* is holding a tray with glasses of champagne. In the hall *Epihodoff* is tying up a box, offstage at the rear there is a hum of voices. It is the peasants who have come to say good-by. *Gayeff's* voice: "Thanks, friends, thank you."

Yasha The simple folk have come to say good-by. I am of the opinion, Yermolay Alexeevich, that the people are kind enough but don't understand anything.
(The hum subsides. *Lyuboff* enters through the hall with *Gayeff;* she is not crying, but is pale, her face quivers, she is not able to speak)

Gayeff You gave them your purse, Lyuba. Mustn't do that! Mustn't do that!

Lyuboff I couldn't help it! I couldn't help it!
(Both go out)

Lopahin (Calling through the door after them) Please, I humbly beg you! A little glass at parting. I didn't think to bring some from town, and at the station I found just one bottle. Please! (A pause) Well, then, ladies and gentlemen! You don't want it? (Moving away from the door) If I'd known that, I wouldn't have bought it. Well, then I won't drink any either. (*Yasha* carefully sets the tray down on a chair) At least, you have some, Yasha.

Yasha To those who are departing! Pleasant days to those who stay behind! (Drinking) This champagne is not the real stuff, I can assure you.

Lopahin Eight roubles a bottle. (A pause) It's devilish cold in here.

Yasha They didn't heat up today. We are leaving anyway. (Laughing)

Lopahin What are you laughing about?

Yasha For joy.

Lopahin   Outside it's October, but it's sunny and still, like summer. Good for building. (Looking at his watch, then through the door) Ladies and gentlemen, bear in mind we have forty-six minutes in all till train time! Which means you have to go to the station in twenty minutes. Hurry up a little.

Trofimoff   (In an overcoat, entering from outside) Seems to me it is time to go. The carriages are ready. The devil knows where my rubbers are. They've disappeared. (In the door) Anya, my rubbers are not here! I can't find them.

Lopahin   And I have to go to Kharkov. I'm going on the same train with you. I'm going to live in Kharkov all winter. I've been dilly-dallying along with you, I'm tired of doing nothing. I can't be without work; look, I don't know what to do with my hands here. See, they are dangling somehow, as if they didn't belong to me.

Trofimoff   We are leaving right away, and you'll set about your useful labors again.

Lopahin   Here, drink a glass.

Trofimoff   I shan't.

Lopahin   It's to Moscow now?

Trofimoff   Yes. I'll see them off to town, and tomorrow to Moscow.

Lopahin   Yes—Maybe the professors are not giving their lectures. I imagine they are waiting till you arrive.

Trofimoff   That's none of your business.

Lopahin   How many years is it you've been studying at the University?

Trofimoff   Think of something newer. This is old and flat. (Looking for his rubbers) You know, perhaps, we shall not see each other again; therefore, permit me to give you one piece of advice at parting! Don't wave your arms! Cure yourself of that habit—of arm waving. And also of building summer cottages, figuring that the summer residents will in time become individual landowners; figuring like that is arm-waving too—Just the same, however, I like you. You have delicate soft fingers like an artist, you have a delicate soft heart—

Lopahin   (Embracing him) Good-by, my dear boy. Thanks for everything. If you need it, take some money from me for the trip.

Trofimoff   Why should I? There's no need for it.

Lopahin   But you haven't any!

Trofimoff   I have. Thank you. I got some for a translation. Here it is my pocket. (Anxiously) But my rubbers are gone.

Varya   (From another room) Take your nasty things! (Throws a pair of rubbers on to the stage)

Trofimoff   But what are you angry about, Varya? Hm—Why, these are not my rubbers.

Lopahin   In the spring I planted twenty-seven hundred acres of poppies and now I've made forty thousand clear profit. And when my poppies were in bloom, what a picture it was! So look, I say, I've made forty thousand, which means I'm offering you a loan because I can afford to. Why turn up your nose? I'm a peasant—I speak straight out.

Trofimoff Your father was a peasant, mine—an apothecary—and from that absolutely nothing follows. (*Lopahin* takes out his wallet) Leave it alone, leave it alone—If you gave me two hundred thousand even, I wouldn't take it. I am a free man. And everything that you—you rich men and beggars—all value so highly and dearly, has not the slightest power over me, it's like a mere feather in the air. I can get along without you, I can pass you by, I am strong and proud. Humanity is moving toward the loftiest happiness that is possible on earth and I am in the front ranks.

Lopahin Will you get there?

Trofimoff I'll get there. (A pause) I'll get there, or I'll show the others the way to get there.

(In the distance is heard the sound of an ax on a tree)

Lopahin Well, good-by, my dear boy. It's time to go. We turn up our noses at one another, but life keeps on passing. When I work a long time without stopping, my thoughts are clearer, and it seems as if I, too, know what I exist for. And, brother, how many people are there in Russia who exist, nobody knows for what! Well, all the same, it's not that that keeps things circulating. Leonid Andreevich, they say, has accepted a position—he'll be in a bank, six thousand a year—the only thing is, he won't stay there, he's very lazy—

Anya (In the doorway) Mama begs you not to cut down the orchard until she's gone.

Trofimoff Honestly, haven't you enough tact to—(Goes out through the hall)

Lopahin Right away, right away—What people, really!

(Goes out after him)

Anya Has Fiers been sent to the hospital?

Yasha I told them to this morning. They must have sent him.

Anya (To *Epihodoff,* who is passing through the room) Semyon Pante-leevich, please inquire whether or not they have taken Fiers to the hospital.

Yasha (Huffily) This morning, I told Igor. Why ask ten times over!

Epihodoff The venerable Fiers, in my opinion, is not worth mending, he ought to join his forefathers. And I can only envy him. (Putting a suitcase on a hatbox and crushing it) Well, there you are, of course. I knew it. (Goes out)

Yasha (Mockingly) "Twenty-two misfortunes—"

Varya (On the other side of the door) Have they taken Fiers to the hospital?

Anya They have.

Varya Then why didn't they take the letter to the doctor?

Anya We must send it on after them—(Goes out)

Varya (From the next room) Where is Yasha? Tell him his mother has come, she wants to say good-by to him.

Yasha (Waving his hand) She merely tries my patience.

(Dunyasha has been busying herself with the luggage; now when Yasha is left alone, she goes up to him)

Dunyasha If you'd only look at me once, Yasha. You are going away—leaving me—(Crying and throwing herself on his neck)

Yasha Why are you crying? (Drinking champagne) In six days I'll be in Paris again. Tomorrow we will board the express train and dash off out of sight; somehow, I can't believe it. *Vive la France!* It doesn't suit me here—I can't live here—Can't help that. I've seen enough ignorance—enough for me. (Drinking champagne) Why do you cry? Behave yourself properly, then you won't be crying.

Dunyasha (Powdering her face, looking into a small mirror) Send me a letter from Paris. I loved you, Yasha, you know, loved you so! I am a tender creature, Yasha!

Yasha They are coming here. (Bustling about near the suitcases, humming low)

(Lyuboff, Gayeff, Anya and Charlotta Ivanovna enter)

Gayeff We should be going. There is very little time left. (Looking at Yasha) Who is it smells like herring!

Lyuboff In about ten minutes let's be in the carriage—(Glancing around the room) Good-by, dear house, old Grandfather. Winter will pass, spring will be here, but you won't be here any longer, they'll tear you down. How much these walls have seen! (Kissing her daughter warmly) My treasure, you are beaming, your eyes are dancing like two diamonds. Are you happy? Very?

Anya Very! It's the beginning of a new life, Mama!

Gayeff (Gaily) Yes, indeed, everything is fine now. Before the sale of the cherry orchard, we all were troubled, distressed, and then when the question was settled definitely, irrevocably, we all calmed down and were even cheerful—I'm a bank official. I am a financier now—Yellow ball into the side pocket. Anyway, Lyuba, you look better, no doubt about that.

Lyuboff Yes. My nerves are better, that's true. (They hand her her hat and coat) I sleep well. Carry out my things, Yasha. It's time. (To Anya) My little girl, we shall see each other again soon—I am going to Paris, I shall live there on the money your Yaroslavl great-aunt sent for the purchase of the estate—long live Great-aunt! But that money won't last long.

Anya Mama, you'll come back soon, soon—Isn't that so? I'll prepare myself, pass the examination at high school, and then I'll work, I will help you. We'll read all sorts of books together. Mama, isn't that so? (Kissing her mother's hands) We'll read in the autumn evenings, read lots of books, and a new, wonderful world will open up before us—(Daydreaming) Mama, do come—

Lyuboff I'll come, my precious. (Embracing her daughter)

(*Lopahin* enters with *Charlotta* who is softly humming a song)

Gayeff Lucky Charlotta: she's singing!

Charlotta (Taking a bundle that looks like a baby wrapped up) My baby, bye, bye—(A baby's cry is heard: Ooah, ooah—!) Hush, my darling, my dear little boy. (Ooah, ooah—!) I am so sorry for you! (Throwing the bundle back) Will you please find me a position? I cannot go on like this.

Lopahin We will find something, Charlotta Ivanovna, don't worry.

Gayeff Everybody is dropping us, Varya is going away—All of a sudden we are not needed.

Charlotta I have no place in town to live. I must go away. (Humming) It's all the same—

(*Pishtchik* enters)

Lopahin The freak of nature—!

Pishtchik (Out of breath) Ugh, let me catch my breath—I'm exhausted —My honored friends—Give me some water—

Gayeff After money, I suppose? This humble servant will flee from sin! (Goes out)

Pishtchik It's a long time since I was here—Most beautiful lady— (To *Lopahin*) You here—? Glad to see you—a man of the greatest intellect—Here—take it—(Giving *Lopahin* some money) Four hundred roubles—That leaves eight hundred and forty I still owe you—

Lopahin (With astonishment, shrugging his shoulders) I must be dreaming. But where did you get it?

Pishtchik Wait—I'm hot—Most extraordinary event. Some Englishmen came and found on my land some kind of white clay—(To *Lyuboff*) And four hundred for you—Beautiful lady—Wonderful lady—(Handing over the money) The rest later. (Taking a drink of water) Just now a young man was saying on the train that some great philosopher recommends jumping off roofs—"Jump!" he says, "and that settles the whole problem." (With astonishment) You don't say! Water!

Lopahin And what Englishmen were they?

Pishtchik I leased them the parcel of land with the clay for twenty-four years—And now, excuse me, I haven't time—I must run along—I'm going to Znoykoff's—To Kardamonoff's—I owe everybody—(Drinking) I wish you well—I'll drop in on Thursday—

Lyuboff We are moving to town right away, and tomorrow I'm going abroad—

Pishtchik What? (Alarmed) Why to town? That's why I see furniture —suitcases—Well, no matter—(Tearfully) No matter—Men of the greatest minds—those Englishmen—No matter—Good luck! God will

help you—No matter—Everything in this world comes to an end—
(Kissing *Lyuboff's* hand) And should the report reach you that my
end has come, think of that well-known horse and say: "There was
once on earth a so and so—Semyonoff Pishtchik—The kingdom of
Heaven be his." Most remarkable weather—yes—(Going out greatly
disconcerted, but immediately returning and speaking from the door)
Dashenka sends her greetings!

(Goes out)

Lyuboff   And now we can go. I am leaving with two worries. First,
that Fiers is sick. (Glancing at her watch) We still have five minutes—

Anya   Mama, Fiers has already been sent to the hospital. Yasha sent
him off this morning.

Lyuboff   My second worry—is Varya. She is used to getting up early
and working, and now without any work she is like a fish out of water.
She has grown thin, pale and she cries all the time, poor thing—(A
pause) You know this, Yermolay Alexeevich: I dreamed—of marrying her to you. And there was every sign of your getting married.
(Whispering to *Anya,* who beckons to *Charlotta;* both go out) She
loves you, you are fond of her, and I don't know, I just don't know
why it is you seem to avoid each other—I don't understand it!

Lopahin   I don't understand it either, I must confess. It's all strange
somehow—If there's still time, I am ready right now even—Let's
settle it now—and get it over and done with. (Pause) But without you,
I doubt if I would ever propose to her.

Lyuboff   But that's excellent. Surely it takes only a minute. I'll call her
at once.

Lopahin   And to fit the occasion there's the champagne. (Looking at
the glasses) Empty, somebody has already drunk them. (*Yasha* coughs)
That's what's called lapping it up—

Lyuboff   (Vivaciously) Splendid! We'll go out—Yasha, *allez!* I'll call her
—(Through the door) Varya, drop everything and come here. Come
on! (Goes out with *Yasha*)

Lopahin   (Looking at his watch) Yes—

(A pause. Behind the door you hear smothered laughter, whispering, finally *Varya* enters)

Varya   (Looking at the luggage a long time) That's strange, I just
can't find it—

Lopahin   What are you looking for?

Varya   I packed it myself and don't remember where. (A pause)

Lopahin   Where do you expect to go now, Varvara Mikhailovna?

Varya   I? To the Regulins. I agreed to go there to look after the house—
As a sort of housekeeper.

Lopahin   That's in Yashnevo? It's nigh on to seventy miles. (A pause)
And here ends life in this house—

Varya (Examining the luggage) But where is it? Either I put it in the trunk, perhaps—Yes, life in this house is ended—it won't be any more—

Lopahin And I am going to Kharkov now—by the next train. I've a lot to do. And I am leaving Epihodoff—on the ground here—I've hired him.

Varya Well!

Lopahin Last year at this time it had already been snowing, if you remember, and now it's quiet, it's sunny. It's only that it's cold, about three degrees of frost.

Varya I haven't noticed. (A pause) And besides—our thermometer is broken—

(A pause. A voice is heard from the yard beyond the door: Yermolay Alexeevich!)

Lopahin (As if he had been expecting this call for a long time) This minute! (Goes out quickly)

(*Varya*, sitting on the floor, puts her head on a bundle of clothes and sobs quietly. The door opens and *Lyuboff* enters cautiously.)

Varya (Stops crying and wipes her eyes) Yes, it's time, Mama. (Pause) I can get to the Regulins today—if we are just not too late for the train!

Lyuboff (Calling through the door) Anya, put your things on! (*Anya*, then *Gayeff* and *Charlotta Ivanovna* enter. *Gayeff* has on a warm overcoat, with a hood. The servants gather, also the drivers. *Epihodoff* busies himself with the luggage) Now we can be on our way.

Anya (Joyfully) On our way!

Gayeff My friends, my dear, kind friends! Leaving this house forever, can I remain silent, can I restrain myself from expressing, as we say, farewell, those feelings that fill now my whole being—

Anya (Beseechingly) Uncle!

Varya Dear Uncle, don't!

Gayeff (Dejectedly) Bank the yellow into the side pocket—I am silent—

(*Trofimoff* and then *Lopahin* enter)

Trofimoff Well, ladies and gentlemen, it's time to go!

Lopahin Epihodoff, my coat!

Lyuboff I'll sit here just a minute more. It's as if I had never seen before what the walls in this house are like, what kind of ceilings, and now I look at them greedily, with such tender love—

Gayeff I remember when I was six years old, on Trinity Day, I sat in this window and watched my father going to Church—

Lyuboff Are all the things taken out?

Lopahin Everything, I think. (Putting on his overcoat. To *Epihodoff*) Epihodoff, you see that everything is in order.

Epihodoff (Talking in a hoarse voice) Don't worry, Yermolay Alexeevich!

Lopahin Why is your voice like that?

Epihodoff Just drank some water, swallowed something.

Yasha (With contempt) The ignorance—

Lyuboff We are going and there won't be a soul left here—

Lopahin Till spring.

Varya (She pulls an umbrella out from a bundle; it looks as if she were going to hit someone; *Lopahin* pretends to be frightened) What do you, what do you—I never thought of it.

Trofimoff Ladies and gentlemen, let's get in the carriage—It's time! The train is coming any minute.

Varya Petya, here they are, your rubbers, by the suitcase. (Tearfully) And how dirty yours are, how old—!

Trofimoff (Putting on the rubbers) Let's go, ladies and gentlemen!

Gayeff (Greatly embarrassed, afraid he will cry) The train—The station—Cross into the side, combination off the white into the corner—

Lyuboff Let's go!

Lopahin Everybody here? Nobody there? (Locking the side door on the left) Things are stored here, it must be locked up. Let's go!

Anya Good-by, house! Good-by, the old life!

Trofimoff Long live the new life!

(Goes out with *Anya*. *Varya* casts a glance around the room and, without hurrying, goes out. *Yasha* and *Charlotta*, with her dog, go out)

Lopahin And so, till spring. Come along, ladies and gentlemen—Till we meet. (Goes out)

(*Lyuboff* and *Gayeff* are left alone. As if they had been waiting for this, they throw themselves on one another's necks sobbing, but smothering their sobs as if afraid of being heard)

Gayeff (In despair) Oh, Sister, Sister—

Lyuboff Oh, my dear, my lovely, beautiful orchard! My life, my youth, my happiness, good-by!

Anya's voice [Gaily, appealingly] Mama!

Trofimoff's voice (Gaily, excitedly) Aaooch!

Lyuboff For the last time, just to look at the walls, at the window— My dear mother used to love to walk around in this room—

Gayeff Oh, Sister, Sister—!

Anya's voice Mama—!

Trofimoff's voice Aaooch—!

Lyuboff We are coming! (They go out.)

(The stage is empty. You hear the keys locking all the doors, then the carriages drive off. It grows quiet. In the silence you hear the dull thud of an ax on a tree, a lonely, mournful sound. Footsteps are heard. From the door on the right *Fiers* appears. He is dressed as usual, in a jacket and a white waistcoat, slippers on his feet. He is sick)

Fiers (Going to the door and trying the knob) Locked. They've gone. (Sitting down on the sofa) They forgot about me—No matter—I'll sit here awhile—And Leonid Andreevich, for sure, didn't put on his fur coat, he went off in his topcoat— (Sighing anxiously) And I didn't see to it—The young saplings! (He mutters something that cannot be understood) Life has gone by, as if I hadn't lived at all—(Lying down) I'll lie down awhile—You haven't got any strength, nothing is left, nothing— Ach, you—good-for-nothing—(He lies still)

(There is a far-off sound as if out of the sky, the sound of a snapped string, dying away, sad. A stillness falls, and there is only the thud of an ax on a tree, far away in the orchard)

PART TWO

SELECTED LETTERS

SELECTED LETTERS*

AUTOBIOGRAPHICAL SKETCHES

1. TO V. A. TIHONOV.

Moscow, *February* 22, 1892.

. . . You are mistaken in thinking you were drunk at Shtcheglov's name-day party. You had had a drop, that was all. You danced when they all danced, and your jigitivka on the cabman's box excited nothing but general delight. As for your criticism, it was most likely far from severe, as I don't remember it. I only remember that Vvedensky and I for some reason roared with laughter as we listened to you.

Do you want my biography? Here it is. I was born in Taganrog in 1860. I finished the course at Taganrog high school in 1879. In 1884 I took my degree in medicine at the University of Moscow. In 1888 I gained the Pushkin prize. In 1890 I made a journey to Sahalin across Siberia and back by sea. In 1891 I made a tour in Europe, where I drank excellent wine and ate oysters. In 1892 I took part in an orgy in the company of V. A. Tihonov at a name-day party. I began writing in 1879. The published collections of my works are: "Motley Tales," "In the Twilight," "Stories," "Surly People," and a novel, "The Duel." I have sinned in the dramatic line too, though with moderation. I have been translated into all the languages with the exception of the foreign ones, though I have indeed long ago been translated by the Germans. The Czechs and the Serbs approve of me also, and the French are not indifferent. The mysteries of love I fathomed at the age of thirteen. With my colleagues, doctors, and literary men alike, I am on the best of terms. I am a bachelor. I should like to receive a pension. I practice medicine, and so much so that sometimes in the summer I perform

* Letters # 1,2,3, and 6 are from *The Letters of Anton Chekhov*, translated by Constance Garnett (New York: Macmillan, 1920), pp. 295–296, 368–369, 51–54, and 127 respectively. Reprinted by permission of Chatto and Windus Ltd., London.

Letters # 4,7,8,9,11,12,13,14,16,18,19, and 21 are from *The Life and Letters of Anton Tchekhov*, translated and edited by S. S. Koteliansky and Philip Tomlinson, (London: Casell and Company, 1925), pp. 282–283, 283, 283–284, 286, 288, 289, 289–290, 290–291, 292–293, 293, 293–294, and 294–295 respectively. Reprinted by permission of Casell and Company, London, and Benjamin Blom, New York.

Letters # 5,10,15,17, and 20 are from Anton Chekhov, *Letters on the Short Story, the Drama, and Other Literary Topics* (London: Geoffrey Bles, 1924), pp. 59–60, 158, 159, 161–162, and 162 respectively. Reprinted by permission of Geoffry Bles, London.

post-mortems, though I have not done so for two or three years. Of authors my favourite is Tolstoy, of doctors Zaharin.

All that is nonsense though. Write what you like. If you haven't facts make up with lyricism.

2. TO G. I. ROSSOLIMO.

Yalta, *October* 11, 1899.

. . . Autobiography? I have a disease—Autobiographophobia. To read any sort of details about myself, and still more to write them for print, is a veritable torture to me. On a separate sheet I send a few facts, very bald, but I can do no more . . .

I, A. P. Chekhov, was born on the 17th of January, 1860, at Taganrog. I was educated first in the Greek School near the church of Tsar Constantine; then in the Taganrog high school. In 1879 I entered the Moscow University in the Faculty of Medicine. I had at the time only a slight idea of the Faculties in general, and chose the Faculty of Medicine I don't remember on what grounds, but did not regret my choice afterwards. I began in my first year to publish stories in the weekly journals and newspapers, and these literary pursuits had, early in the eighties, acquired a permanent professional character. In 1888 I took the Pushkin prize. In 1890 I travelled to the Island of Sahalin, to write afterwards a book upon our penal colony and prisons there. Not counting reviews, feuilletons, paragraphs, and all that I have written from day to day for the newspapers, which it would be difficult now to seek out and collect, I have, during my twenty years of literary work, published more than three hundred signatures of print, of tales, and novels. I have also written plays for the stage.

I have no doubt that the study of medicine has had an important influence on my literary work; it has considerably enlarged the sphere of my observation, has enriched me with knowledge the true value of which for me as a writer can only be understood by one who is himself a doctor. It has also had a guiding influence, and it is probably due to my close association with medicine that I have succeeded in avoiding many mistakes.

Familiarity with the natural sciences and with scientific method has always kept me on my guard, and I have always tried where it was possible to be consistent with the facts of science, and where it was impossible I have preferred not to write at all. I may observe in passing that the conditions of artistic creation do not always admit of complete harmony with the facts of science. It is impossible to represent upon the stage a death from poisoning exactly as it takes place in reality. But harmony with the facts of science must be felt even under those conditions —i.e., it must be clear to the reader or spectator that this is only due to the conditions of art, and that he has to do with a writer who understands.

I do not belong to the class of literary men who take up a sceptical attitude towards science; and to the class of those who rush into everything with only their own imagination to go upon, I should not like to belong. . . .

ON CULTURE

3. TO HIS BROTHER NIKOLAY.

Moscow, 1886.

. . . You have often complained to me that people "don't understand you"! Goethe and Newton did not complain of that . . . Only Christ complained of it, but He was speaking of His doctrine and not of Himself. . . . People understand you perfectly well. And if you do not understand yourself, it is not their fault.

I assure you as a brother and as a friend I understand you and feel for you with all my heart. I know your good qualities as I know my five fingers; I value and deeply respect them. If you like, to prove that I understand you, I can enumerate those qualities. I think you are kind to the point of softness, magnanimous, unselfish, ready to share your last farthing; you have no envy nor hatred; you are simple-hearted, you pity men and beasts; you are trustful, without spite or guile, and do not remember evil. . . . You have a gift from above such as other people have not: you have talent. This talent places you above millions of men, for on earth only one out of two millions is an artist. Your talent sets you apart: if you were a toad or a tarantula, even then, people would respect you, for to talent all things are forgiven.

You have only one failing, and the falseness of your position, and your unhappiness and your catarrh of the bowels are all due to it. That is your utter lack of culture. Forgive me, please, but *veritas magis amicitiae.* . . . You see, life has its conditions. In order to feel comfortable among educated people, to be at home and happy with them, one must be cultured to a certain extent. Talent has brought you into such a circle, you belong to it, but . . . you are drawn away from it, and you vacillate between cultured people and the lodgers *vis-à-vis.*

Cultured people must, in my opinion, satisfy the following conditions:

1. They respect human personality, and therefore they are always kind, gentle, polite, and ready to give in to others. They do not make a row because of a hammer or a lost piece of india-rubber; if they live with anyone they do not regard it as a favour and, going away, they do not say "nobody can live with you." They forgive noise and cold and dried-up meat and witticisms and the presence of strangers in their homes.

2. They have sympathy not for beggars and cats alone. Their heart aches for what the eye does not see. . . . They sit up at night in order to help P. . . . , to pay for brothers at the University, and to buy clothes for their mother.

3. They respect the property of others, and therefor pay their debts.

4. They are sincere, and dread lying like fire. They don't lie even in small things. A lie is insulting to the listener and puts him in a lower position in the eyes of the speaker. They do not pose, they behave in the street as they do at home, they do not show off before their humbler comrades. They are not given to babbling and forcing their uninvited confidences on others. Out of respect for other people's ears they more often keep silent than talk.

5. They do not disparage themselves to rouse compassion. They do not play on the strings of other people's hearts so that they may sigh and make much of them. They do not say "I am misunderstood," or "I have become second-rate," because all this is striving after cheap effect, is vulgar, stale, false. . . .

6. They have no shallow vanity. They do not care for such false diamonds as knowing celebrities, shaking hands with the drunken P.,* listening to the raptures of a stray spectator in a picture show, being renowned in the taverns. . . . If they do a pennyworth they do not strut about as though they had done a hundred roubles' worth, and do not brag of having the entry where others are not admitted. . . . The truly talented always keep in obscurity among the crowd, as far as possible from advertisement. . . . Even Krylov has said that an empty barrel echoes more loudly than a full one.

7. If they have a talent they respect it. They sacrifice to it rest, women, wine, vanity. . . . They are proud of their talent. . . . Besides, they are fastidious.

8. They develop the aesthetic feeling in themselves. They cannot go to sleep in their clothes, see cracks full of bugs on the walls, breathe bad air, walk on a floor that has been spat upon, cook their meals over an oil stove. They seek as far as possible to restrain and ennoble the sexual instinct. . . . What they want in a woman is not a bed-fellow . . . they do not ask for the cleverness which shows itself in continual lying. They want especially, if they are artists, freshness, elegance, humanity, the capacity for motherhood. . . . They do not swill vodka at all hours of the day and night, do not sniff at cupboards, for they are not pigs and know they are not. They drink only when they are free, on occasion. . . . For they want *mens sana in corpore sano.*

And so on. This is what cultured people are like. In order to be cultured and not to stand below the level of your surroundings it is not enough to have read "The Pickwick Papers" and learnt a monologue from "Faust." . . .

* Probably Palmin, a minor poet.—*Translator's Note.*

What is needed is constant work, day and night, constant reading, study, will. . . . Every hour is precious for it. . . . Come to us, smash the vodka bottle, lie down and read. . . . Turgenev, if you like, whom you have not read.

You must drop your vanity, you are not a child . . . you will soon be thirty. It is time!

I expect you. . . . We all expect you.

4. TO S. P. DIAGUILEV.

Yalta, *December* 30, 1902.

You write that we talked about a serious religious movement in Russia. We talked not of a Russian but of an intellectual movement. About Russia I won't say anything, and as for the intellectuals, they are at present only playing at religion, chiefly from lack of anything else to do. Of the cultured part of our public, it may be said that it has moved away from religion and is moving further and further away from it, whatever else may be said and whatever religious and philosophic societies may be formed. Whether that is a good or a bad thing I cannot decide; I will only say that the religious movement of which you write is one thing, and all modern culture is another, and it is impossible to place the latter in causal dependence on the former. Modern culture is but the beginning of a work for a great future, a work which will go on, perhaps for tens of thousands of years, in order that mankind may, even in the remote future, come to know the truth of a real God— that is, not by guessing, not by seeking in Dostoevsky, but by perceiving clearly, as one perceives that twice two is four. Modern culture is only the beginning of a work, but the religious movement of which we spoke is a survival, almost the end of what has ceased, or is ceasing to exist. But it is a long story; one can't put it all into a letter. . . .

5. TO A. S. SOUVORIN.

Moscow, *October* 27, 1888.

In conversation with my literary colleagues I always insist that it is not the artist's business to solve problems that require a specialist's knowledge. It is a bad thing if a writer tackles a subject he does not understand. We have specialists for dealing with special questions: it is their business to judge of the commune, of the future, of capitalism, of the evils of drunkenness, of boots, of the diseases of women. An artist must judge only of what he understands, his field is just as limited as that of any other specialist—I repeat this and insist on it always. That in his sphere there are no questions, but only answers, can be maintained only by those who have never written and have had no experience of thinking in images. An artist observes, selects, guesses, combines—and this in itself presupposes a problem: unless he had set himself a problem from the very first there would be nothing to conjecture and nothing to select. To put it briefly, I will end by using the language of psychiatry: if one denies that creative work involves problems and purposes, one must admit that an artist creates without premeditation or intention, in a state of aberration; therefore, if an author boasted to me of having written a novel without a preconceived design, under a sudden inspiration, I should call him mad.

You are right in demanding that an artist should take an intelligent attitude to his work, but you confuse two things: *solving a problem* and *stating a problem correctly*. It is only the second that is obligatory for the artist. In "Anna Karenina" and "Evgeni Onegin" not a single problem is solved, but they satisfy you completely because all the problems in these works are correctly stated. It is the business of the judge to put the right questions, but the answers must be given by the jury according to their own lights.

6. TO A. N. PLESCHTCHEYEV.

October, 1889.

I am afraid of those who look for a tendency between the lines, and who are determined to regard me either as a liberal or as a conservative. I am not a liberal, not a conservative, not a believer in gradual progress, not a monk, not an indifferentist. I should like to be a free artist and nothing more, and I regret that God has not given me the power to be one. I hate lying and violence in all their forms, and am equally repelled by the secretaries of consistories and by Notovitch and Gradovsky. Pharisaism, stupidity and despotism reign not in merchants' houses and prisons alone. I see them in science, in literature, in the younger generation. . . . That is why I have no preference either for gendarmes, or for butchers, or for scientists, or for writers, or for the younger generation. I regard trade-marks and labels as a superstition. My holy of holies is the human body, health, intelligence, talent, inspiration, love, and the most absolute freedom—freedom from violence and lying, whatever forms they may take. This is the programme I would follow if I were a great artist.

ON *THE CHERRY ORCHARD**

7. TO MME. V. F. KOMMISSARZHEVSKY.

Yalta, January 27, 1903.

. . . I am very glad that you are feeling well. About the play I will say this: (1) It is true my play is planned, and that I already have a title for it (*The Cherry Orchard*—but it is still a secret), and I shall settle down to write it not later, probably, than the end of February, if, of course, I am well; (2) the central character in the play is an old woman

* Compare letters 7ff. with Stanislavsky and Meyerhold, pp. 63–74.

—to the great regret of the author; and (3) if I let the Art Theatre have the play, then, according to its conditions and rules, it has the exclusive disposal of the play both for Moscow as well as for Petersburg—and there is no getting out of it. If the Art Theatre does not go to Petersburg in 1904* (which is quite likely; are they going this year?), there can be no doubt that, if the play suits you, I will let you have it with pleasure. Or perhaps this will do. Shall I write a play *for you?* Not for this or that theatre, but for you. This has long, long been my dream. Well, as God wills it. If I had my former health I would not be talking about it, but would simply sit down to write the play at once. Since December I have had pleurisy—fancy that!—and to-morrow I can go out of the house after a long imprisonment.

Anyhow, I have written to Moscow asking to know definitely whether the Art Theatre is going to Petersburg. I shall get an answer in about a week or ten days, and will write to you then.

You have seen my wife, but I shall not see her till the spring. Either she is ill or I am away, and so nothing happens as to other people.

You write . . . "I give myself to the theatre with such faith that were it broken it would kill me," and so on. Just so, you are right, but for the love of God don't let your faith depend on the new theatre. You are a real actress, and that is the same as being a good sailor: in whatever ship, government or private, he may sail, everywhere and in all circumstances he remains a good sailor. . . .

8. TO MME. M. P. ALEXEYEV†

Yalta, *February* 11, 1903.
. . . I have not been well but have now recovered, though to-day I am again coughing and feeling lazy. I have not yet begun to write the play. I'll begin after February 20th in the full hope that *you* are going to act in the play. I do not know what it will be like, whether it will come off successfully—that is to be seen—but however it may be I shall not give it to the theatre if you refuse to play. Keep that in mind, and don't ruin the author. I am almost without money now, and should you refuse to act I shall be, as they say, completely lost. I'll make such a row! I thought in the autumn that you were not well, but it is clear now that you are perfectly well and able to act, so let there be no talk about it! My play will be ready in the spring and I'll bring it. . . .

9. TO N. E. EFROS.

Nara, *June* 17, 1903.
Alas! I haven't yet even begun the play, let alone finished it, as you write. As regards my participation in the *Russkaya Mysl*, from the

* The Art Theatre usually went to Petersburg at Easter time.
† Actress, wife of Stanislavsky, producer for the Moscow Art Theatre.

autumn I shall probably edit or manage the fiction section, having nothing to do with the rest. But I will use all my efforts to have you attached to *Russkaya Mysl*. I have valued you highly as a dramatic critic for a long while, and I remember urging ardently that you should work for the *Russkaya Mysl*. I shall be in Moscow in about a couple of weeks and will talk over the matter, and send you an answer.

10. TO K. S. STANISLAVSKY.

Yalta, *July* 28, 1903.

My play "The Cherry Orchard" is not yet finished; it makes slow progress, which I put down to laziness, fine weather, and the difficulty of the subject. . . .

I think your part is all right, though I can't undertake to decide, as I can judge very little of a play by reading it. . . .

11. TO VL. I. NEMIROVICH-DANCHENKO.

Yalta, *August* 22, 1903.

. . . About my own play, *The Cherry Orchard*. For the time being everything is well. I am working slowly. If I be a bit late it is no great matter. The stagey part of the play I have reduced to a minimum; no special kind of decorations will be needed, nor will the actors have to strain their wits. For the moment my health is excellent; it couldn't be better, so I can work.

The chairman of the Committee of Ministers is more of an honourable office, which is usually occupied by those ministers who have finished their careers (Bunge, Durnovo). There can be no mention of a dictatorship, about which you write.

I propose to stay in Moscow for the winter as well. I will come about November. I shall be glad to see *The Lower Depths*, which I have not seen yet, as well as *Julius Caesar*, which I foretaste with pleasure. In Act II of my play instead of a river I have an old shrine and a well. It is better so. But in Act II you must give me a genuine green field and a road, and a perspective unusual on the stage. . . .

12. TO VL. I. NEMIROVICH-DANCHENKO.

Yalta, *September* 2, 1903.

Thank you for your letter. It is a great pity we should disagree about Naydionov's play. There is some resemblance to *The Lonely* in Act II and Kouporossov is not well-formed, but surely those things are not very important. What is important is that there should be a play and that the author should be felt in it. In the modern plays one has to read there is no author, as though they were all made in the same factory by one machine; but there is an author in Naydionov's plays. . . .

My play you may be sure (if I continue working so as I have done till to-day) will be ready soon. It was difficult, very difficult, to write the second Act, but, I believe, it comes off tolerably. I will call the play a comedy.

My health is tolerable; I don't grumble; and I dream of the winter which I count upon spending in Moscow.

Keep safe and well. The role of the mother in my play will be taken by Olga, but I cannot undertake to decide who is to act the daughter of 17 or 18, a young, slim, little girl. Well, we shall see.

13. TO MME. M. P. ALEXEYEV*.

September 15, 1903.

Don't believe anyone, not one living soul, has read my play yet. I have written for you not a "hypocrite," but a very lovely girl, with whom, I hope, you will be satisfied. The play is almost finished, but eight or ten days ago I fell ill and began to cough and get weak—in a word, last year's story began over again. Now, that is to-day, it is warm and my health is better, yet I cannot work, as my head aches. Olga will not bring the play, so I will send all the four acts as soon as there is a possibility of writing for a whole day. The play has turned out not a drama, but a comedy, in parts even a farce, and I fear I am in for it from Vladimir Ivanovich. Konstantin Serguevich [Mme. A.'s husband] has a big part. There are few parts altogether.

I can't come for the opening. I shall sit in Yalta till November. Olga, who has grown plumper and healthier after the summer, will arrive in Moscow probably on Sunday. I shall remain alone and, of course, shall not fail to avail myself of that. As a writing man I have to observe as many women as possible; I have to study them, and therefore, unhappily, I cannot be a faithful husband. As I have to study women chiefly for my plays, the Art Theatre, in my opinion, ought to increase my wife's salary or give her a pension.

You gave me no address in your letter, so I am sending this to Kamerhersky Lane. You are probably going to rehearsals and will therefore receive it early. For having remembered me and written me a letter I am boundlessly grateful to you. To Igor and Kira I send a low bow, and I thank them also for remembering me, but Kira will hardly delight in the St. Bernard; it is a good dog, but uncomfortable and perfectly useless. Such is not the case with my friend Gypsy. The other day I bought for myself a mongrel, an extraordinarily silly one.

When you see Vishnevsky, tell him that he should try to grow thin —it is necessary for my play. . . .

14. TO NEMIROVICH-DANCHENKO.

Yalta, *October* 23, 1903.

When I let your theatre have my *Three Sisters*, and when a review appeared in . . ., *we both*, you and I, were indignant; I spoke to N. and

* Mme. Alexeyev, actress of the Moscow Art Theatre and wife of Stanislavsky, the producer and director. Her stage name was Mme. Lilina.

he gave me his word that it would never occur again. Now I suddenly read that Ranievskaya lives with Anya abroad, has an affair with a Frenchman, that Act III takes place in a hotel, that Lopakhin is a profiteer and a son of a ——, etc. etc. What could I think? How could I suspect your interference? In my telegram I had no one in view but N., and I accused N. alone, and it was very strange to me, I could not even believe my eyes when I read your telegram in which you take all the blame on yourself. It is sad you should have understood me like that; it is sadder still that such a misunderstanding should have occurred. But the whole story should be speedily forgotten. Tell N. that I no longer want to know him, and please forgive me if I oversalted my telegram— and basta! . . .

For a long time I have been having stomach trouble and a cough. The stomach seems to be recovering, but my cough doesn't improve. I don't know what to do, whether to go to Moscow or not. And I should so very much like to see the rehearsals. I am afraid lest Anya's tone is too tearful (for some reason you find her similar to Irene). I fear that a young actress might not be given the part. Anya doesn't once shed tears; nowhere does she speak in a weeping tone; in Act II, though she has tears in her eyes, her tone is cheerful and lively. Why do you say in your telegram that there are many tearful people in the play? Where are they? Varya is the only one, and that is because she is a cry-baby by nature, and her tears should not provoke depression in the spectator. Frequently one meets. the remark "through tears," but that merely denotes the mood of the character, not tears. There is no cemetery in Act II.

I live in loneliness, keep to a diet, cough, get furious at times, am tired of reading—such is my life. . . .

15. TO K. S. STANISLAVSKY.

Yalta, *October* 30, 1903.

When I was writing Lopakhin, I thought of it as a part for you. If for any reason you don't care for it, take the part of Gaev. Lopakhin is a merchant, of course, but he is a very decent person in every sense. He must behave with perfect decorum, like an educated man, with no petty ways or tricks of any sort, and it seemed to me this part, the central one of the play, would come out brilliantly in your hands. . . . In choosing an actor for the part you must remember that Varya, a serious and religious girl, is in love with Lopakhin; she wouldn't be in love with a mere money-grubber. . . .

16. TO VLADIMIR I. NEMIROVICH-DANCHENKO.

Yalta, *November* 2, 1903.

In one day two letters from you! Many thanks! I don't drink beer; the last I had was in July; and I may not eat honey, as the stomach aches from it. Now, about the play:

(1) Anya can be acted by anyone, even by a quite unknown actress, provided she is young and looks like a girl, and speaks in a young, ringing voice. This is not one of the important parts.

(2) Varya's is a more serious part, if only Marie Petrovna can take it. Without M. P. the part may turn out a little flat and crude; I will have to re-make it and soften it down. M. P. can't repeat herself, firstly because she is a talented person, and secondly, because Varya is not like Sonia and Natasha; she is a figure in a black dress, nun-like, a silly, a cry-baby, etc. etc.

(3) Gayev and Lopakhin—let Konstantin Serguevich choose and try these parts. If he took Lopakhin and succeeded in that, the play would have a success. Indeed, if Lopakhin were to be dim, played by a feeble actor, both the part and play would be lost.

(4) Pischik—for Gribunin. God forbid the part be given to N.

(5) Charlotte—a question mark . . . it certainly can't be given to . . . Mlle. Muratov would perhaps be good, but she is not amusing. It is Mme. Knipper's part.

(6) Epikhodov—if Moskvin wants it, be it so. He would be a splendid Epikhodov. I thought Luzhsky was going to act the part.

(7) Feers—Artiom.

(8) Duniasha—Mme. Khaliutin.

(9) Yasha—if the Alexandrov of whom you write, your assistant producer, let him take Yasha. Moskvin would make a most wonderful Yasha. Nor have I any objection to Leonidov.

(10) The Passer-by—Gromov.

(11) The station-master, who in Act III recites "The Sinner," should be an actor with a bass voice.

Charlotte does not speak broken but pure Russian; only on rare occasions does she use the hard sound instead of the soft, and mix the feminine and masculine adjectives. Pischik is a Russian, smitten with gout, old age, and satiety; corpulent; wears a poddiovka (à la Simov) and top-boots without heels. Lopakhin wears a white waistcoat and brown boots; he swings his arms as he walks, taking wide paces and walking in a line. His hair is not short, and he often throws back his head; when thinking, he fingers his beard, from back to front; that is, from his neck to his mouth. Trofimov seems quite clear. Varya wears a black dress with a broad belt.

For three years I have been intending to write *The Cherry Orchard*, and for three years I have been telling you that you should invite an actress for the part of Liubov Andreyevna. Now, then, get out of the difficulty if you can.

I am now most foolishly placed. Here I sit alone and know not why I am sitting. . . .

Gorki is younger than either you or I; he has his own life. . . . As for the Nijni Theatre, that's a mere detail. Gorki will try it, give a sniff and throw it up. And, by the way, theatres for the people as well as literature for the people is all silliness and candy. Gogol is not to be lowered to the people, but the people raised up to Gogol.

17. TO K. S. ALEKSEYEV (STANISLAVSKY).

Yalta, *November* 5, 1903.

The house in the play is two-storied, a large one. But in the third act does it not speak of a stairway leading down? Nevertheless, this third act worries me. . . . N. has it that the third act takes place in "some kind of hotel;" . . . evidently I made an error in the play. The action does not pass in "some kind of hotel," but in a *drawing-room*. If I mention an hotel in the play, which I cannot now doubt, after VI. Iv.'s* letter, please telegraph me. We must correct it; we cannot issue it thus, with grave errors distorting its meaning.

The house must be large, solid; wooden (like Aksakov's which, I think, S. T. Morozov has seen) or stone, it is all the same. It is very old and imposing; country-residents do not take such houses; such houses are usually wrecked and the material employed for the construction of a country-house. The furniture is ancient, stylish, solid; ruin and debt have not affected the surroundings.

When they buy such a house, they reason thus: it is cheaper and easier to build a new and smaller one than repair this old one.

Your shepherd played well. That was most essential.

18. TO K. S. ALEXEYEV.

Yalta, *November* 10, 1903.

Certainly you can have the same scenery for Acts III and IV [*The Cherry Orchard*]—that is, the hall and staircase. Pray do as you like about the scenery; I leave it to you; usually, I am amazed and sit with my mouth agape at your theatre. There need be no arguing about it; whatever you do will be excellent, a hundred times better than I could invent.

Dunia and Epikhodov stand in Lopakhin's presence; they do not sit. Lopakhin, in fact, maintains his position like a gentleman. He addresses the servants "thou," and they "you" him.

Serguey Savvich has gone to Japan. . . . for the *Russky Listok*? He had better visit the moon to find readers for the *Russky Listok*; there are none on earth. Have you read his plays? He would do better to go to Japan to get material for a book; that would be something to fill all his life. . . .

19. TO THE SAME.

Yalta, *November* 23, 1903.

Haymaking usually takes place about July 20th to 25th, when, I believe, the corncrake has ceased to call; the frogs too have grown silent by then. Only the redbreast continues to sing. There is no cemetery [in

* Nemirovich-Danchenko.

The Cherry Orchard]; it was there once, but very long ago; two or three derelict gravestones lie about, all that is left. The bridge—that's very good. If the train could be shown without any noise, without a single sound, then let's have it. I do not object to the same scenery in Acts III and IV, but it would be convenient in Act IV to have an entrance and exit.

I am anxiously awaiting the day and the hour when my wife at last permits me to come. I begin to suspect my wife is getting up some trick for me.

The weather here is still and warm and wonderful, but when Moscow comes to mind, Moscow and the Sandounovsky baths, all the beauty here becomes a bore and good for nothing.

I sit in my study and gaze all day at the telephone. Telegrams are delivered to me over the telephone, and I expect every moment to be called to Moscow.

20. TO V. F. KOMMISSARZHEVSKAYA.

Moscow, *January* 6, 1904.

I write you this with a light heart, because of my deep conviction that "The Cherry Orchard" is not for you. The central figure in the play is a woman, an old woman, wholly of the past, with nothing in her of the present; the other roles, at least the women, are trivial and uninteresting, not in the least suited for you.

21. TO F. D. BATYUSHKOV.

Moscow, *January* 19, 1904.

I assure you I have not reached my jubilee yet (if you speak about the twenty-five years of my literary activity) nor will it be due soon. I came to Moscow to enter the University in the second half of 1879; my first trifle of about ten or fifteen lines was published in March or April of 1880 in the *Strekosa*—if one be so lenient as to consider that trifle as the beginning. Even so, my jubilee could not be celebrated before 1905....

However, at the first performance of *The Cherry Orchard* on January 17 I was fêted so lavishly, so warmly, and above all so unexpectedly, that I have not yet recovered from it.

It would be nice if you could come in Lent. I should think it will take till Lent for our actors to recover and play *The Cherry Orchard* not so confusedly and with less brilliance than now.* . .

* Two months later when Chekhov had heard from his wife's relatives (who had seen the play in Moscow) that Stanislavsky's performance was bad and that the last act dragged, he wrote to his wife (herself a member of the Moscow Art Theatre): "How awful this is. An act that ought to take no more than twelve minutes lasts forty with you people. I can say one thing: Stanislavsky has ruined my play. But there, bless the man." (Cf. Jacqueline Latham, p. 142, n. 2. I have included the sentence Miss Latham deletes).

PART THREE

DISCUSSIONS OF CHEKHOV
AND *THE CHERRY ORCHARD*

FROM *STANISLAVSKI'S LEGACY**

Konstantin Stanislavski

MESSAGES ABOUT THE CHERRY ORCHARD

Telegram: October 20, 1903

I have just read the play. Deeply moved, scarcely control myself. Am in unheard-of state of enthusiasm. Consider the play the finest of all the fine things you have written. Cordial congratulations to the genius author. I feel, I treasure every word. Thank you for great pleasure already received and also in store.

Letter: same date

Dear Anton Pavlovich:

According to me your *Cherry Orchard* is your best play. I have fallen in love with it even more deeply than with our dear *Seagull*. It is not a comedy, not a farce, as you wrote—it is a tragedy no matter if you do indicate a way out in a better world in the last act. It makes a tremendous impression, and this by means of half tones, tender water-color tints. There is a poetic and lyric quality to it, very theatrical; all the parts, including that of the vagrant, are brilliant. If I were to choose one of the parts to suit my taste, I would be in a quandary, for every one of them is most alluring. I fear this is all too subtle for the public. It will take time for it to understand all the shadings. Alas, how many stupidities we will have to hear about this play! Nevertheless it will have a tremendous success because as a play it holds you. It is so completely a whole one cannot delete a single word from it. It may be that I am prejudiced, yet I cannot find any defect in this play. Oh yes there is one: it requires too great, too subtle actors to bring out all its charms. We shall not be able to do that. When we had our first reading together I was worried by one thing: I was instantly carried away, and my feelings caught up by the play. This was not the case with *The Seagull* or *The Three Sisters*. I am accustomed to a rather vague impression from a

* Konstantin Stanislavski, *Stanislavski's Legacy*, translated and edited by Elizabeth Reynolds Hapgood (New York: Theatre Arts Books, 1958), pp. 123–126. Reprinted by permission of Theatre Arts Books, New York and Max Reinhardt-The Bodley Head, Ltd, London.

first reading of your plays. That is why I was afraid that when I read it for the second time it would not capture me again. Nothing of the sort happened. I wept like a woman, I tried to control myself, but could not. I can hear you say: "But please, this is a farce. . . ." No, for the ordinary person this is a tragedy. I sense an attitude of very special kind of tenderness and affection towards this play. I scarcely heard a word of criticism, yet you know how actors love to be critical. Apparently this time they were all instantly won by it. If someone by chance does utter a word of criticism I merely smile and do not bother to argue. I am only sorry for the critic. Someone said: the fourth is the best act, and the second is least successful. I have only to go over the second act scene by scene and that critic is demolished. The fourth act is good just because the second act is magnificent and vice versa. I proclaim this play *hors concours*, and not subject to criticism. Anyone who does not see that is a fool. That is my sincere conviction. I shall act in it with delight. If I could do so I should love to play all the parts, including that of dear Charlotte. Thank you, dear Anton Pavlovich, for the immense pleasure you have already given and for that which is yet to come. How I wish I could give up everything else, shake off the yoke of playing Brutus, and work on nothing but *The Cherry Orchard* all day. This horrible Brutus weighs on me and draws all the juice out of me. I hate him more than ever after (reading) the sweet *Cherry Orchard*.

My warms regards to you and I beg you not to take me for a neurotic lady admirer.

Your affectionate and devoted,
C. Alexeyev (Stanislavski).

Letter: November 2, 1903

I think I have just found the set for the first act. It is a very difficult set. The windows must be close enough to the front of the stage so that the cherry orchard will be seen from the entire auditorium; there are three doors; one would wish to show a bit of Anya's room, bright and virginal. The room is a passage way, but one must be made to feel that here (in the nursery) it is cozy, warm and light; the room has fallen into disuse, there is a slight sense of vacancy about it. Moreover the set must be comfortable and contain a number of planned acting areas. I think we are now able to encompass all this. Do you remember that last year Simov showed you a model which was made for the Turgenyev play, *Where the Thread Is Thin It Breaks*? At the time we decided, with your approval, to save the set for the last act of your play. I have been looking at the model now and find that, with a few alterations, it is very suitable (for the fourth act). If you recall the model, have you any objections? As I write, the third act of *Uncle Vanya* is beginning. There is an enthusiastic response to it, it's the eighty-ninth performance, and we took in 1400 rubles despite the fact that last night we played *The Three Sisters*. So you have earned one hundred and forty rubles today.

That's not important. But do you know what is important? It's that this year as never before the audience is really understanding you, they listen in absolute silence. Not a cough in the house despite the bad weather.

Letter: November 19, 1903

... I have been busy working on the second act and finally have it in shape. I think it has come out charmingly. Let's hope the scenery will be successful. The little chapel, the ravine, the neglected cemetery in the middle of an oasis of trees in the open steppes. The left side and the centre will not have any wings. You will see only the far horizon. This will be produced by a single semi-circular backdrop with attachments to deepen the perspective. In the distance you see the flash of a stream and the manor house on a slight rise, telegraph poles and a railroad bridge. Do let us have a train go by with a puff of smoke in one of the pauses. That might turn out very well. Before sundown there will be a brief glimpse of the town, and towards the end of the act, a fog: it will be particularly thick above the ditch downstage. The frogs and corn-crakes will strike up at the very end of the act. To the left in the fore-ground a mown field and a small mound of hay, on which the scene is played by the group out walking. This is for the actors, it will help them get into the spirit of their parts. The general tone of the set is like that of a Levitan painting. The landscape is that of the province of Orel not of lower Kursk.

The work is now being carried on as follows: Nemirovich-Dan-chenko rehearsed the first act yesterday and today I wrote (the plan for) the following acts. I haven't rehearsed my own part yet. I am still unde-cided about the sets for acts three and four. The model is made and came out well, it is full of mood and besides it is laid out so that all parts of it are visible to all in the auditorium. Down front there is something like shrubbery. Farther upstage are the stairs and billiard room. The windows are painted on the walls. This set is more convenient for the ball. Still a small voice keeps whispering in my ear that if we have one set, which we change in the fourth act, it would be easier and cozier to play in. The weather, alas, is murderous. Everything is melting again and it rains frequently.

Yours,
C. Alexeyev.

Telegram from St. Petersburg: April 2, 1904

Success of *Cherry Orchard* very great, incomparably greater than in Moscow. After third act there were insistent calls for author. The con-noisseurs are rapturous over play. Newspapers not very understanding. Company in high spirits. I am triumphant. Congratulations.

Alexeyev.

FROM *MY LIFE IN ART**

Konstantin Stanislavski

THE LAST YEAR WITH CHEKHOV

In the autumn of 19— Anton Pavlovich came to Moscow in very ill health. Nevertheless, he was present at almost all the rehearsals of his new play, the name of which he could not yet decide upon. Once of an evening he telephoned me to come to him on business. He was sick and could not leave the house. To visit Anton Pavlovich was a rare happiness. I dropped all my affairs and rushed to see him. He was very high-spirited, notwithstanding his illness. Apparently he did not wish to speak of the business on hand at once, but to leave it for the very end, just as children like to leave sweets for the very end of a meal. Meanwhile we all sat at the tea table and laughed, because it was impossible not to laugh in Chekhov's presence. But tea finished, Anton Pavlovich led me to his study, closed the door, sat down in his traditional corner of the divan, and made me sit before him. But even then he did not begin with the business on hand at once, still keeping it for dessert. Meanwhile he was trying to persuade me that some of the actors did not fit their parts and should be replaced by others.

"But of course, they are wonderful actors," he tried to soften his criticism.

I knew all that was said was only a prelude to what he really wanted to say. Anton Pavlovich was a man of the theatre and knew that parts could not be changed in a play which was trembling on the threshold of its first night. At last we came down to business. Anton Pavlovich made a pause, during which he seemed to chew on what he wanted to tell me. He could not control his lovable smile, which was even triumphant at that moment, notwithstanding the fact that he tried in every way to be serious.

"Listen, I have found a wonderful name for the play. A wonderful name," he declared, looking directly at me.

"What is it?" I was excited.

* Konstantin Stanislavski, *My Life in Art*, translated by J. J. Robbins (London; Geoffrey Bles, 1924), pp. 416–424. Reprinted by permission of Geoffrey Bles, London, and Theatre Arts Books, New York.

"Vishneviy Sad" (The Cherry Orchard), and he rolled with happy laughter.

I confess that I did not thoroughly understand the reason for his gladness, for I found nothing unusual in the name. But I was forced to put on the appearance that his discovery had made an impression on me, and at the same time I wanted to find out from Chekhov what it was that excited him in the new name of the play. But here I stumbled on one of the strange traits of Chekhov. He could not philosophize and explain what he had created. And so he explained the beauty of the name "Vishneviy Sad" by repeating in various ways and with various intonations and color in the voice:

"Vishneviy Sad. Listen, it is a wonderful name. Vishneviy Sad. Vishneviy—"

His intonations made me understand that he was talking of something beautiful, tenderly loved, and this inner meaning of the name was reflected not in the name itself but in the intonation of Anton Pavlovich. I carefully gave him a hint of this. My words saddened him, the gladness and triumph left his face, and our conversation lost life.

Several days, perhaps a week, passed after this meeting. Anton Pavlovich felt better and began to go out. Once, during a performance, he came into my dressing room and with a triumphant smile sat down at my side near the make-up table. He loved to watch actors put on their make-up and costumes. If we looked at him at such moments we could do without a mirror, because the expression of his face told us at once whether we drew a successful or unsuccessful line on our faces.

"Listen, not Vishneviy, but Vishneviy Sad," he stated triumphantly and became all laughter.

At first I did not even understand of what he was speaking, but Chekhov lovingly repeated the word, stressing the tender sound of "e" in the word as though he were trying to caress with its help that former beautiful life which was no longer necessary, which he himself lovingly and with tears was destroying in his play. This time I understood the great and yet delicate difference. Vishneviy Sad is a commercial orchard which brings in profit. Such an orchard is necessary to life even at the present. But Vishneviy Sad brings no profits. It hides in itself and in all of its flowering whiteness the great poetry of the dying life of aristocracy. The Vishneviy Sad grows for the sake of beauty, for the eyes of spoiled aesthetes. It is a pity to destroy it, but it is necessary to do so, for the economics of life demand it.

All remarks, which had to be dragged out of Anton Pavlovich by main force, seemed to be rebuses. He did not like to make them, and he would always hide from the eyes of the stage directors who haunted him. If any one came to a rehearsal and saw Anton Pavlovich modestly sitting somewhere in the back rows, he would never have believed that this was a great poet and the author of the play. No matter how hard we tried to make him sit down at the stage directors' table, so that it might be easier to consult him, our efforts were in vain. We would make him sit down at the table, and he would begin to laugh. It was impossible to understand what made him laugh, whether it was the fact that he had become a stage director and sat at such an important table, or that he was inventing means of deceiving the stage directors and disappearing from their ken.

"I wrote it," he would answer to our questions; "I am not a stage director, I am a doctor," and he would hurry to get away and hide himself in some dark corner.

Comparing the manner in which Chekhov conducted himself at rehearsals with the manner in which other authors conducted themselves, I cannot help but wonder at the extraordinary modesty of the great man and the boundless vanity of the little writers. One of them, for instance, when I suggested that a long-winded and false-sounding monologue in his play be shortened, told me with complete belief and the anger of the insulted in his voice:

"Shorten it, but do not forget that you will be held responsible by history."

But when we dared to suggest to Anton Pavlovich that a whole scene be shortened, the whole end of the second act of "The Cherry Orchard," he became very sad and so pale that we were ourselves frightened at the pain that we had caused him. But after thinking for several minutes, he managed to control himself and said:

"Shorten it."

Never after did he say a single word to us about this incident. And who knows, perhaps he would have been justified in reproaching us, because it may very well be that it was the will of the stage director and not his own which shortened a scene that was excellently written. After the young people left Varya with a great deal of noise, Sharlotta came on the stage with a rifle and lay down in the hay, singing some popular German song. Hardly able to move his feet, there entered Firs, lighting matches, looking in the grass for the fan dropped by his mistress. There takes place a meeting of two lonely people. They have nothing to speak about, but they so want to speak, for a human being must speak to some one. Sharlotta begins to tell Firs of how she worked in her youth in a circus and performed the *salto mortale*, in those very words, which, in our version she says in the beginning of the act when on the stage with Epikhodov, Yasha and the maid. In answer to her story, Firs talks at length and randomly about something that cannot be understood that happened in the days of his youth, when somebody was taken somewhere in a wagon accompanied by sounds of squeaking and crying, and Firs interprets these sounds with the words cling-clang. Sharlotta does not understand anything in his story, but catches up his cue so that the one common moment in the lives of these two lonely people may not be disturbed. They cry "Cling-Clang" to each other and both laugh very sincerely. This was the way Chekhov ended the act.

After the stormy scene with the young people, such a lyric ending lowered the atmosphere of the act and we could not lift it again. I suppose that it was mainly our own fault, but it was the author who paid for our inability. What would a newly baked celebrity have done in the place of Chekhov?

"THE CHERRY ORCHARD"

Is it necessary to describe the production of "The Cherry Orchard"? We have played it so often in Europe and America. But I will say some things about it, not for the sake of following the line of the evolution of the Moscow Art Theatre in it, but in order to tell of the last year in the life of Chekhov and of his death which had a tremendous importance in the life of our Theatre.

The production of "The Cherry Orchard" was accomplished with great hardships. The play is delicate, it has all the tenderness of a flower. Break its stem and the flower dries, its odor vanishes. The play and the rôles live only when the stage director and the artist dig deep enough to reach the secret treasure house of the human spirit in which is hidden the chief nerve of the play. In my great desire to help the actors I tried to create a mood around them, in the hope that it would grip them and call forth creative vision. In those days our inner technique and our ability of reacting on another's creative soul were very primitive. I took all the bypaths I could think of. I invented all sorts of *mises en scène*, the singing of birds, the barking of dogs, and in this enthusiasm for sounds on the stage I went so far that I caused a protest on the part of Chekhov, who loved sounds on the stage himself. The form in which he expressed his disagreement with me was very interesting.

" 'What fine quiet,' the chief person of my play will say," he said to some one so that I could hear him. " 'How wonderful! We hear no birds, no dogs, no cuckoos, no owls, no clocks, no sleigh bells, no crickets.' "

That stone was intended for my garden.

Nemirovich-Danchenko and I did not think that the production would be ripe at its first performance. And meanwhile, until the play was produced, it risked becoming boresome. The success of the play was necessary at all costs, for the health of Anton Pavlovich was in a precarious condition. So we decided to take advantage of the jubilee of Chekhov's literary activity and to stage the first night of the play on that day. Our reckoning was simple. If the actors were not able to put the play over, its failure of great success could be blamed on the unusual conditions of the jubilee evening which would not fail to draw the attention of the spectators away from the actors to the author. But the appointed date was very near and the play was not yet ready. Besides,

I had to think of a present for Anton Pavlovich. This was a hard question to settle. I visited all the antiquaries in Moscow, hoping to find something, but outside of some very fine embroidered cloth I found nothing. As there was nothing better, we decorated the jubilee wreath with this cloth. "At least," I thought, "we will present him with something of artistic value."

But Anton Pavlovich never forgot this gift.

"Listen, this is a wonderful thing, it must be kept in a museum," he upbraided me after the jubilee.

"Tell me, Anton Pavlovich, what should we have given you?" I asked in my confusion.

"A rat trap," he answered seriously, after thinking for some time. "Listen, mice must be destroyed." Here he began laughing himself. "Korovin sent me a beautiful present, a beautiful one!"

"What was it?" I became interested.

"Fishing poles."

None of the other presents he received pleased Chekhov, and some of them angered him with their banality.

"Listen, one shouldn't give a writer a silver pen and an ancient inkwell."

"Well, what should one give?"

"A piece of rubber pipe. Listen, I am a doctor. Or socks. My wife doesn't attend to me as she should. She is an actress. And I walk around in torn socks. 'Listen, little soul,' I say to her, 'the big toe of my right foot is coming out.' 'Wear it on your left foot,' she answers. It can't go on that way—"

And he rolled with happy laughter.

But at the jubilee he was far from happy. It seemed that he foresaw his own end. After the third act he stood deathly pale and thin on the right side of the stage and could not control his coughing while gifts were showered on him and speeches in his honor were being made. Our hearts grew small in us. Some one in the audience cried loudly that he should sit down. But he drew his brows together and stood throughout the duration of the jubilee, over which he laughed so innocently in his works. Even on that evening he could not control his smile. One of the best-known professors in Russia began his speech almost with the same words with which Gaiev greeted the old clothespress in the first act of "The Cherry Orchard."

"Dear and much respected (instead of saying clothespress, the professor used Chekhov's name)—I greet you--"

Anton Pavlovich looked sideways at me (I had played Gaiev) and a villainous smile passed over his lips.

The triumph was a really triumphant occasion, but it smelled of a funeral. Our souls were heavy within us.

The performance itself enjoyed but a mediocre success and we blamed ourselves for not having portrayed much that was in the play.

Chekhov died without ever seeing the real success of his last flower-like play.

The spring of 1904 approached. The health of Anton Pavlovich became worse and worse. There appeared dangerous symptoms in the region of the stomach and there were hints of tuberculosis of the colon. A council of doctors decided to send Chekhov to Badenweiler. He began to prepare to go abroad. All of us tried to see him as often as it was possible. But his health often stood in his way of seeing us. Notwithstanding his illness his love of life did not leave him. He was very interested in the production of Maeterlinck, which was at that time in rehearsal. It was necessary to keep him informed of the course of work, and to show him the models of the scenery and explain the *mise en scène*.

He himself was dreaming of writing a play of a character altogether new to him. Really the theme of his proposed play was not very Chekhov-like. A husband and his friend love the same woman. The common object of their love unites them and their jealousy of each other creates complex interrelationships. The end is that both go on a polar expedition. The scenery of the last act portrays a large ship crushed amid icebergs. The play ends with both friends seeing a white vision slipping over the snow. Apparently this is the shade, soul or symbol of the woman they both love, who has died while they were away. This is all that could be found out from Chekhov about the play he never wrote.

Chekhov was in reality a practical joker and a schoolboy in spirit. During the unrest of pre-revolutionary days Chekhov was riding in an open cab with a large pumpkin in his hands in which there were supposed to be specially prepared pickles. This pumpkin was wrapped in paper and bound with ropes. On the way it became clear that the pickles were not those that Chekhov liked.

"Cabby, stop," Chekhov commanded, as the carriage approached a policeman.

"Take this," he said with decision in his voice to the policeman, giving the latter the heavy, round package.

"You can start, cabby."

The horse moved forward, and Chekhov turned towards the policeman, and pointing to the package, cried, "It is a bomb!"

The policeman remained in an almost petrified pose, holding the pumpkin carefully away from him, while Chekhov and his friends were loudly laughing a good distance away.

During the very middle of spring rehearsals, before the end of the season, Anton Pavlovich invited me and several of the actors from our Theatre, some relatives and friends, to supper. Apparently some ceremony was in preparation. Perhaps he had finished a new play? We were somewhat mystified by the fact that the supper was to take place not in Chekhov's home, but in Vishnevsky's. But we explained this by saying that it was hard for Anton Pavlovich to raise all his household up, especially as he did not feel very well himself.

We met at the appointed hour and waited for Chekhov. An hour passed. The supper was growing cold. We called by telephone, but no one answered from Chekhov's home. We were beginning to become afraid that something out of the way had happened. But here there arrived a telegram from Chekhov and Olga Knipper, asking us to wish them a happy honeymoon. In order to be rid of ceremony, Chekhov had decided to gather all his friends and relatives in one place while he married Olga Knipper at another, and to leave for their honeymoon on the Volga and the Oka without unnecessary farewells.

MEYERHOLD TO CHEKHOV*

May 8, 1904
(Lopatino)

Dear Anton Pavlovich:

. . . Next year my company will play in Tiflis. Come to see us, because we have grown in an artistic sense. We do *The Cherry Orchard* well. After I saw it at the Moscow Art Theatre, I wasn't ashamed of our production. I did not altogether like the performance in Moscow. In general.

I want to say this. When some author with his genius stirs a theatre to life, then he understands the secret of performing his plays, finds the key . . . If the author begins to perfect his technique, gets to the top of his profession, the theatre only loses this key, because it is an association of creators and consequently more cumbersome. The Deutsches Theater in Berlin, for example, has lost the key to performing Hauptmann's plays; the great tragicomedy *Der rote Hahn, Schluck und Jau,* and *Der arme Heinrich* were failures. It seems to me that the Art Theatre was confused when it tackled your *Cherry Orchard.*

Your play is abstract, like a Tchaikovsky symphony. The stage director must above all feel it with his ear. In the third act, against the background of the stupid "stomping"—this "stomping" must be heard—Horror enters unnoticed by anyone.

"The cherry orchard is sold." They dance. "Sold." They dance. And so to the end. When one reads the play, the third act makes the same kind of impression as the ringing in the sick man's ears in your story *Typhus.* Some kind of itch. Gaiety in which sounds of death are heard. In this act there is something Maeterlinck-like, frightful. I only use this comparison because I'm incapable of saying it more precisely. You are incomparable in your great work. When one reads plays by foreign authors you appear particularly original. In drama the West should learn from you.

In the Moscow Art Theatre one did not get such an impression from the third act. The background was not concentrated enough and at the same time not remote enough. In the forefront: the story with the billiard cue and the tricks. Separately. All this did not form a chain of "stomping." And in the meantime all the "dancing" people are unconcerned

* Reprinted from *The Tulane Drama Review,* Fall 1964, by permission of *The Tulane Drama Review.* (Cf. reference to Meyerhold, p. 154).

and do not sense the harm. The tempo of this act was too slow in the Art Theatre. They wanted to convey boredom. That's a mistake. One must picture unconcern. There's a difference. Unconcern is more active: Then the tragedy of the act becomes more concentrated.

Now to particulars: Lopakhin, the Servant, Duniasha, Varia, and Ania were badly acted.

Moskvin and Stanislavski were excellent [as Epikhodov and Gaev].

Firs is not at all like that.

A striking landscape from a decorative standpoint in the second act. . . .

Your warmly loving,
Vs. Meyerhold.
—*Translated by* NORA BEESON

FROM *TCHEKHOV AND THE MOSCOW ART THEATRE**

N. E. Efros

. . . Tchekhov the playwright by no means broke away from the main current of Russian literature, of the Russian drama, i.e. from artistic realism. The author of *The Seagull* and of *Uncle Vanya* is an artistic realist; no other definition can be applied to him. Only he considered that the contents of artistic realism had not been exhausted, that into the sphere of re-creation of life there can and must be brought in such elements of life and of the soul, as used to remain outside the periphery. Tchekhov knew that, apart from distinct and definite feelings, there is a whole gamut of intermediary feelings, half-feelings, and their hardly perceptible nuances. And he knew and deeply and beautifully felt the whole atmosphere of life which is compounded of those half-feelings and half-tones. That atmosphere he above all wished to convey in his plays; for to his creative soul the fascination of such merging psychological contours, of such "misty" emotions was particularly precious; and he was sensitively aware that outside that atmosphere there was no true, genuine presentation of life. At any rate, in his case, in his presentation, to take away those "half-tones", that enveloping fine "mist", meant just to pervert both his creative imagination, as well as the life and the people drawn by him.

And when the old theatre did so—whether it was because the theatre did not yet comprehend Tchekhov and his method, or perhaps because it could not convey those essentially Tchekhovian peculiarities and traits—there appeared not living, complete characters, but very queer, hardly understandable ones. It was not for nothing that people thought that in *The Seagull* all were "mere idiots". And the combination of those characters and the net of their inter-relations lost the greater

* N. E. Efros, "Tchekhov and the Moscow Art Theatre," in *Anton Tchekhov; Literary and Theatrical Reminiscences*, translated by S. S. Kotel: ansky (London: G. Routledge & Sons, 1927, pp. 118–122, 129–133. This article and the following one are reprinted by permission of Routledge & Kegan Paul Ltd., London.

part of their interest and of their agitating influence on the audience. Tchekhov had really seemed "no good for the theatre"; but that was only because the theatre could not be Tchekhovian.

That was the most important difficulty which the Art Theatre was destined to overcome. Otherwise it, too, would have shared the lot of its predecessors in the theatrical realization of Tchekhov's most subtle dramatic creation. To put it concisely, the Theatre had to find the means to communicate "moods". Of course, it was not Tchekhov who created "moods", but Tchekhov introduced them for the first time into dramatic art. They are inherent in every truly poetical work, and one could even find in Ostrovsky, the orthodox playwright of the old theatre, such moments where everything was dependent on the "mood". But Tchekhov gave that element a dominating importance, and he made it the prime condition that the theatre should convey that "mood".

The Art Theatre had in that field no "precedents". It started, in its productions, with an infatuation for Meiningenism, although purified of certain exaggerations, although greatly refined in many aspects. The triumph of that Meiningen method was the first production of the new Theatre, the production of *Tsar Fyodor*. After that the Theatre also applied the Meiningen method to the production of historical and realistic plays, as for instance, to Tolstoy's *Power of Darkness*. But had the Theatre attempted to apply that method to the Tchekhov productions, it would have met with a complete catastrophe. It made certain use here too of the Meiningen method, by ridding itself of superfluous theatrical conventions. But that negative virtue was of no great value. And then began the strenuous, intense work; there began the seeking, guided only by artistic flair and by deep realization of the spirit and of the significance of Tchekhov's creation. Tchekhov was a sort of new realist, and Tchekhov's theatre, too, had to become such a new realist. Tchekhov with one hint suddenly flooded with unexpected light a whole picture— and the Theatre had to learn to avail itself of such scenic hints, to find such details which would make the meaning and mood of whole scenes palpably clear.

There was much noise, much laughter, and many pinpricks directed at the Art Theatre for its shaking window-curtains, crickets, thumping of horses' hooves on the wooden bridge, etc., etc. It was said that the Art Theatre wished to replace the emotions of living characters by such naive devices, wished to amuse by such cheap naturalism and by stage jugglery. But that was sheer misunderstanding. It was not the curtains shaking in the wind, or the crickets singing behind the fire-place, which were needed by the Art Theatre, when it acted Tchekhov's plays and sought how to express them completely and appropriately. These were not things needed *per se*. The Art Theatre did not occupy itself with such puerilities. These were only means. And when those means seemed necessary as when, through the cricket's sounds in the gloomy, empty room of Uncle Vanya and Sonia the mood of the moment was conveyed more fully, more saturatedly—then the Theatre summoned the collabora-tion of the cricket. When the anguish of parting was suddenly conveyed by the sound of the horses' hooves on the wooden bridge—a sound merged in the general tone—then the Theatre joyfully accepted that assistance. People say that on the stage the actor alone has to do every-thing. This sounds perhaps very grand, but it is a great exaggeration: even the old "actor's" theatre was not confined exclusively to the actor's playing. If the old drama then could not do without that, the less so was it possible in the new, Tchekhovian drama.

Certainly those services were only by the way. The centre of grav-ity here, too, was in the actor, in his conveying of emotions, in his manner of living on the stage and of speaking. Words which had "a vague meaning", but which could not be listened to without agitation, demanded also a different manner of uttering them. In the general econ-omy of the performance, silent moments, pauses, intervals in the dia-logues, assumed an increased importance. Again, this was dictated by the very constitution of the Tchekhovian drama. And the Art Theatre fully realized and appreciated all these new resources of scenic art.

And in order to make correct use of them, it was necessary—having rejected the conventional symbols of emotions on the stage—to bring there the *emotions themselves*. All Stanislavsky's hatred for "clichés", from which sprang his theory of acting, his "system" with its "cycle", and so on—may, even unnoticed by himself, have grown out of the Tchekhov productions. That "system", inarticulate, not formulated in words yet, was already living and directing the work of the stage when Tchekhov's plays were being acted. Tchekhov's plays demanded the "return to Schepkin", which eventually became the watchword of the Art Theatre.

And when the Art Theatre, beginning with *The Seagull,* achieved all that—perhaps not fully at first, but always with confidence—the miracle happened that "we all with our programs and opera glasses became the participators of the performance, became the characters of the play". Therein is the great fascination of a Tchekhov performance in the Art Theatre, therein is its charm, its artistic significance. And as at those performances we were called to live with what was particularly dear to us—with what lived, ached, sang in every one of the spectators of that period—those performances have acquired an extraordinary charm and attraction. The public, which had already begun to be indifferent to the theatre, for the theatre had ceased to speak distinctly to its collective soul, the public came back to the theatre and became fused again with it. The gulf was bridged. People said that the success of the Art Theatre was a passing fashion. Surely, a fashion does not last for long years. In the heat of polemics it was perhaps permissible to have talked about fashion, whereas the true and deep causes of the triumph of the Art Theatre in Tchekhov's plays, and the triumph of Tchekhov in the theatre were perfectly clear and obvious. . .

"THE CHERRY ORCHARD"

. . . After the great triumph of *The Three Sisters* there was no longer any need to urge Tchekhov to write for the Art Theatre. His dramatic creation, having secured such an ideal apparatus as the Art Theatre, took on wings. We know now that immediately after he wrote his *Cherry Orchard* Tchekhov was thinking of a new play, the leading figure of which was to be a scientist, disappointed in love, and going to the far North to pursue scientific investigations. . . . In his talks with Stanislavsky and other members of the Art Theatre, soon after the production of *The Three Sisters,* Tchekhov began, as usual, making very vague hints about a new play. There was something said about an open window, looking out on cherry-trees, covered with white blossom; there were mentioned billiard tables; and an old servant, wandering in an old house; a woman. . . . In the soul of the poet there was ripening *The Cherry Orchard*—the sad farewell to the vanishing past, the joyous welcome to the coming future. Jealously did Tchekhov keep the secret of the name of his new play; even to his wife who was laid up then in bed, he did not utter the name aloud. To comfort her, he only whispered to her the title of the play; and to his sister he did not even whisper it; but wrote it down on a scrap of paper and told her to read it to herself. . . . But, finally, he had to part with the secret of the name, and with the manuscript itself. A thick notebook was received by the Art Theatre, and on 17th January, 1904, on Tchekhov's birthday, *The Cherry Orchard* was produced. In *The Cherry Orchard,* Tchekhov's style had become still subtler and more tender, and the play itself was as sweet-smelling as its name.

The soul of the poet is bound up by a thousand ties with his country and through those ties the emotions of his country and of his people reach him. The springtime of life was approaching in Russia, it was felt already in the last frosts. . . . And this found its reflection in *The Cherry Orchard,* however far removed the author may have been from "politics". New notes sounded in that play, they intertwined charmingly with the usual Tchekhovian tone. Tchekhov was always annoyed when people regarded him as a pessimist. In the case of *The Cherry Orchard* he would have been particularly so annoyed. His characters no longer said that "some time we shall see the heaven in diamonds"; they no longer sighed that "life will be beautiful in two or three hundred years". And this gave the stage, which undertook to produce *The Cherry Orchard,* a somewhat different task. For it would not have expressed Tchekhov completely, had it not expressed these new notes as well. If I were asked to point out exactly how those new traits were manifested in the production, I should not be able to do so. They are unseizable; but they were present in the performance, they were adjusted to the general organism. It was a somewhat brighter play than the three preceding plays; there was in it a gladdening freshness as before dawn. And the tears, evoked by Act III— when it was announced that the cherry orchard had been sold—were not the same tears as those evoked by the military march dying away in the distance in *The Three Sisters*; or the tears evoked by "They have gone!" in *Uncle Vanya*; and "Do you remember Kostya? . . . feelings like tender, exquisite flowers," in *The Seagull* . . .

When I try to analyse the beautiful whole of the production of *The Cherry Orchard*, and I recall individual figures—I put in the first place Stanislavsky who acted the part of Gayev. Tchekhov had wished that that actor should act Lopakhin, a character which was particularly dear to the author, and which he considered as the centre of the play. Yet I believe he was not sorry that Stanislavsky had chosen, instead of Lopakhin, the grown-up child Gayev, so perfectly was the character conveyed; so fine was the comicalness of the acting, and so pathetic was that big, funny, naive child. The whole audience loved Gayev as much as Feers did. Mme Knipper found perfect notes for Mme Ranyevsky, she preserved both her shallowness and her lovely nature; lightly, without exaggerating, she conveyed her "light drama", in which "tears mingled with smiles", and "smiles with tears" alternated. The superbly comical part of Yepikhodov remains until now the best creation of Moskvin, and is the model of artistic caricature on our stage. It is said that the actor introduced something of his own in the text itself, and Tchekhov, during the rehearsals adopted a few of his improvizations, so felicitous were they. Through the funny outward appearance of the old student Trofimov, there shone out in Kachalov's acting the whole beauty of that character, his young optimism, and his stiffness combined with tenderness. Perhaps Anya, acted by Mme Lilin, was not so young as the author made her, but her tremendous sincerity and simplicity of feeling redeemed every-thing. Perhaps there was some lack of distinction and an imperfect grasp of character in the part of Varya, as acted by Mme Andreyev, but the moving expression of her face redeemed that.

Perhaps Lopakhin as acted by Leonidov, was different from Tche-khov's conception of that character, but the great power he revealed in the finale of Act III reconciled one to Leonidov's impersonation. I must mention, among the successful players, Artiom, Tchekhov's great favourite, who in the part of Feers acted irreproachably; also Mme Muratov as Charlotte, and Alexandrov as Yakov.

The first performance of *The Cherry Orchard* was also the first meet-ing of the audience with the author. That meeting was made the occasion of a great fête for the author. But that was a festival before a calamity. Only a few months passed, and those who applauded *The Cherry Orchard* and its author, stood before his open grave in the cemetery of the Novodevichiy Monastery. . . .

TCHEKHOV AND THE THEATRE*

Leonid Andreyev

T CHEKHOV'S peculiarity was that he was a most thoroughgoing pan-psychist. If in Tolstoy's works we often find only the human body *animated*, if Dostoevsky is exclusively given to the soul itself—Tchekhov *animated* everything that his eye touched. His landscape is no less psychological than his people; his people are no more psychological than his clouds, stones, chairs, glasses, and houses. All the objects of the visible world come in merely as parts of one great soul. And if his stories are only chapters of one great novel, then his objects are *thoughts* and *sensations* scattered in space, a soul one in action and vision. In a landscape he writes the life of his hero; in clouds he relates his past, in rain he presents his tears, in houses he proves that there is no immortal soul. Such is Tchekhov in his fiction writing— and such he is in his plays.

And to act Tchekhov's plays on the stage there must not be people only—glasses, chairs, crickets, military uniforms and wedding rings must also act. Suddenly Tchekhov introduces in his *Cherry Orchard* the mysterious sound "of a sunken bucket", a sound which is almost impossible to reproduce—but it is necessary, it is a necessary part of the soul of the characters of the play, without that sound they are not they, without it there is no Tchekhov. Hence it becomes clear why all the theatres, in which only human beings act, and objects do not, cannot act Tchekhov's plays, do not like him or understand him. In the provinces they do not produce his plays. And hence it becomes understandable not only why the Moscow Art Theatre can act Tchekhov's plays, but also in what consists the strength, novelty and peculiarity of the Moscow Art Theatre: there not only human beings act, but objects as well. It is a psychological theatre. More than that—it is the theatre of panpsychism, the pure representative of which in literature was Anton Tchekhov.

But not only objects, *time* itself Tchekhov—and the Moscow Art Theatre with him—used, not as a watchmaker, but as a psychologist; time is only the thought and sensation of the characters. And there, where there are no wonderful pause—thoughts, pause-sensations, where

* Leonid Andreyev, "Tchekhov and the Theatre," in *Anton Tchekhov: Literary and Theatrical Reminiscences*, translated S. S. Koteliansky (London: G. Routledge & Sons, 1926), pp. 173–175.

only gifted actors act, and time has not yet learned to act, there is no Tchekhov, nor will there be. Remember how the Germans who knew us, Russians, were moved when, from the stage of the Art Theatre, the *animated* time of Tchekhov's plays began to talk in its international language!

Animated time, animated objects, animated human beings—therein is the secret of the fascination of Tchekhov's plays. Whether the servant plays the *Calalaika* standing at the gate, and wafting on the stage the hardly audible sound of a popular ditty (in *Ivanov*); or whether it is the sound of the cricket (in *Uncle Vanya*); or dogs barking (in *The Cherry Orchard*), or little bells jingling, or voices round a fire; or Natasha walking across the dark rooms, or Epikhodov eating an apple—everything is reduced to panpsyche, everything represents, not objects of actuality, and not real sounds and voices, but the characters' thoughts and sensations scattered across space.

Direct your attention to the dialogue of Tchekhov's plays; it is not plausible; in life people do not speak like that; it is full of unfinished speeches, it is always, as it were, a continuation of something already said; there is not in it that clear-cut beginning with which any other playwright's characters come on the stage; Tchekhov's characters never begin nor end their speech; they always merely continue it. That is why his plays are difficult to read; there is little intrigue and even little action. And in this respect Tolstoy was right when he mercilessly condemned Tchekhov's play, which, I think he could not finish for sheer boredom. But he was wrong in this respect: he did not understand Tchekhov, for he had not seen Tchekhov's *acting* objects and pauses, all that which the Art Theatre had so penetratingly reproduced. Indeed, if Tchekhov's dialogue always does *continue* something, then surely there must be a someone or something that is continued. And that mysterious essence, lacking in the mere reading, consists in the animated objects and animated time. The dialogue, so to speak, never stops; it is transferred from human beings to objects, from objects back to human beings and from human beings to time, to stillness or noise, to the cricket or to voices round a fire. Everything is alive, has a soul and a voice. Oh! how far removed his theatre was from the intolerable naturalism which had been grafted on the stage, and which knows *objects* only. Who wants these?

FROM *ANTON TCHEKHOV: FRAGMENTS OF RECOLLECTIONS**

Maxim Gorki

. . . I think that in Anton Tchekhov's presence every one involuntarily felt in himself a desire to be simpler, more truthful, more oneself; I often saw how people cast off the motley finery of bookish phrases, smart words, and all the other cheap tricks with which a Russian, wishing to figure as a European, adorns himself, like a savage with shells and fish's teeth. Anton Tchekhov disliked fish's teeth and cock's feathers; anything "brilliant" or foreign, assumed by a man to make himself look bigger, disturbed him; I noticed that, whenever he saw any one dressed up in this way, he had a desire to free him from all that oppressive, useless tinsel, and to find underneath the genuine face and living soul of the person. All his life Tchekhov lived on his own soul; he was always himself, inwardly free, and he never troubled about what some people expected and others—coarser people—demanded of Anton Tchekhov. He did not like conversations about deep questions, conversations with which our dear Russians so assiduously comfort themselves, forgetting that it is ridiculous, and not at all amusing, to argue about velvet costumes in the future when in the present one has not even a decent pair of trousers.

Beautifully simple himself, he loved everything simple, genuine, sincere, and he had a peculiar way of making other people simple.

Once, I remember, three luxuriously dressed ladies came to see him; they filled his room with the rustle of silk skirts and the smell of strong scent; they sat down politely opposite their host, pretended that they were interested in politics, and began "putting questions":

"Anton Pavlovitch, what do you think? How will the war end?"

Anton Pavlovitch coughed, thought for a while, and then gently, in a serious and kindly voice, replied:

"Probably in peace."

* Maxim Gorki, "Anton Tchekhov: Fragments of Recollections," in *The Notebooks of Anton Tchekhov, Together with Reminiscences of Tchekhov by Maxim Gorki* (London: The Hogarth Press, 1921), pp. 96–108. Reprinted by permission of Leonard Woolf.

"Well, yes . . . certainly. But who will win? The Greeks or the Turks?"

"It seems to me that those will win who are the stronger."

"And who, do you think, are the stronger?" all the ladies asked together.

"Those who are the better fed and the better educated."

"Ah, how clever," one of them exclaimed.

"And whom do you like best?" another asked.

Anton Pavlovitch looked at her kindly, and answered with a meek smile:

"I love candied fruits . . . don't you?"

"Very much," the lady exclaimed gaily.

"Especially Abrikossov's," the second agreed solidly.

And the third, half closing her eyes, added with relish:

"It smells so good."

And all three began to talk with vivacity, revealing on the subject of candied fruit great erudition and subtle knowledge. It was obvious that they were happy at not having to strain their minds and pretend to be seriously interested in Turks and Greeks, to whom up to that moment they had not given a thought.

When they left, they merrily promised Anton Pavlovitch:

"We will send you some candied fruit."

"You managed that nicely," I observed when they had gone.

Anton Pavlovitch laughed quietly and said:

"Every one should speak his own language."

On another occasion I found at his house a young and prettyish Crown Prosecutor. He was standing in front of Tchekhov, shaking his curly head, and speaking briskly:

"In your story, *The Conspirator,* you, Anton Pavlovitch, put before me a very complex case. If I admit in Denis Grigoriev an evil and conscious intention, then I must, without any reservation, bundle him into prison, in the interests of the community. But he is a savage: he did not realize the criminality of his act. . . . I feel pity for him. But suppose I regard him as a man who acted without understanding, and suppose I yield to my feeling of pity, how can I guarantee the community that Denis will not again unscrew the nut in the sleepers and wreck a train? That's the question. What's to be done?"

He stopped, threw himself back, and fixed an inquiring look on Anton Pavlovitch's face. His uniform was quite new, and the buttons shone as self-confidently and dully on his chest as did the little eyes in the pretty, clean little face of the youthful enthusiast for justice.

"If I were judge," said Anton Pavlovitch gravely, "I would acquit Denis."

"On what grounds?"

"I would say to him, 'You, Denis, have not yet ripened into the type of the deliberate criminal; go—and ripen.' "

The lawyer began to laugh, but instantly again became pompously serious, and said:

"No, sir, the question put by you must be answered only in the interests of the community whose life and property I am called upon to protect. Denis is a savage, but he is also a criminal—that is the truth."

"Do you like gramophones?" suddenly asked Anton Pavlovitch in his soft voice.

"O yes, very much. An amazing invention," the youth answered gaily.

"And I can't stand gramophones," Anton Pavlovitch confessed sadly.

"Why?"

"They speak and sing without feeling. Everything seems like a caricature—dead. Do you like photography?"

It appeared that the lawyer was a passionate lover of photography; he began at once to speak of it with enthusiasm, completely uninterested, as Tchekhov had subtly and truly noticed, in the gramophone, despite his admiration for that "amazing invention." And again I observed how there looked out of that uniform a living and rather amusing little man, whose feelings towards life were still those of a puppy hunting.

When Anton Pavlovitch had seen him out, he said sternly:

"They are like pimples on the seat of justice—disposing of the fate of people."

And after a short silence:

"Crown Prosecutors must be very fond of fishing—especially for little fish."

He had the art of revealing everywhere and driving away banality, an art which is only possible to a man who demands much from life and which comes from a keen desire to see men simple, beautiful, harmonious. Banality always found in him a discerning and merciless judge.

Some one told in his presence how the editor of a popular magazine, who was always talking of the necessity of love and pity, had, for no reason at all, insulted a railway guard, and how he usually acted with extreme rudeness towards his inferiors.

"Well," said Anton Pavlovitch with a gloomy smile, "but isn't he an aristocrat, an educated gentleman? He studied at the seminary. His father wore the best shoes, and he wears patent-leather boots."

And in his tone there was something which at once made the "aristocrat" trivial and ridiculous.

"He's a very gifted man," he said of a certain journalist. "He always writes so nobly, humanely . . . lemonadely. Calls his wife a fool in public . . . the servants' rooms are damp and the maids constantly get rheumatics."

"Don't you like N. N., Anton Pavlovitch?"

"Yes, I do—very much. He's a pleasant fellow," Anton Pavlovitch agrees, coughing. "He knows everything . . . reads a lot . . . he hasn't returned three of my books . . . he's absent-minded. To-day he will tell you that you're a wonderful fellow, and to-morrow he will tell somebody else that you cheat your servants, and you have stolen from your mistress's husband his silk socks—the black ones with the blue stripes."

Some one in his presence complained of the heaviness and tediousness of the "serious" sections in thick monthly magazines.

"But you must not read those articles," said Anton Pavlovitch. "They are friends' literature—written for friends. They are written by Messrs. Red, Black, and White. One writes an article; the other replies to it; and the third reconciles the contradictions of the other two. It is like playing whist with a dummy. Yet none of them asks himself what good it is to the reader."

Once a plump, healthy, handsome, well-dressed lady came to him and began to speak *à la Tchekhov*:—

"Life is so boring, Anton Pavlovitch. Everything is so grey: people, the sea, even the flowers seem to me grey . . . And I have no desires . . . my soul is in pain . . . it is like a disease."

"It is a disease," said Anton Pavlovitch with conviction, "it is a disease; in Latin it is called *morbus fraudulentus*."

Fortunately, the lady did not seem to know Latin, or, perhaps, she pretended not to know it.

"Critics are like horse-flies which prevent the horse from ploughing," he said, smiling his wise smile. "The horse works, all its muscles drawn tight like the strings on a double-bass, and a fly settles on his flanks and tickles and buzzes . . . he has to twitch his skin and swish his tail. And what does the fly buzz about? It scarcely knows itself; simply because it is restless and wants to proclaim: 'Look, I too am living on the earth. See, I can buzz, too, buzz about anything.' For twenty-five years I have read criticisms of my stories, and I don't remember a single remark of any value or one word of valuable advice. Only once Skabitchevsky wrote something which made an impression on me, . . . he said I would die in a ditch, drunk."

Nearly always there was an ironical smile in his grey eyes, but at times they became cold, sharp, hard; at such times a harder tone sounded in his soft, sincere voice, and then it appeared that this modest, gentle man, when he found it necessary, could rouse himself vigorously against a hostile force and would not yield.

But sometimes, I thought, there was in his attitude towards people a feeling of hopelessness, almost of cold, resigned despair.

"A Russian is a strange creature," he said once. "As in a sieve nothing remains in him. In his youth he fills himself greedily with anything which he comes across, and after thirty years nothing remains but a kind of grey rubbish. . . . In order to live well and humanly one must work— work with love and with faith. But we, we can't do it. An architect, having built a couple of decent buildings, sits down to play cards, plays all his life, or else is to be found somewhere behind the scenes of some theatre. A doctor, if he has a practice, ceases to be interested in science, and reads nothing but *The Medical Journal,* and at forty seriously believes that all diseases have their origin in catarrh. I have never met a single civil servant who had any idea of the meaning of his work: usually he sits in the metropolis or the chief town of the province, and writes papers and sends them off to Zmiev or Smorgon for attention. But that those papers will deprive some one in Zmiev or Smorgon of freedom of movement—of that the civil servant thinks as little as an atheist of the tortures of hell. A lawyer who has made a name by a successful defence ceases to care about justice, and defends only the rights of property, gambles on the Turf, eats oysters, figures as a connoisseur of all the arts. An actor, having taken two or three parts tolerably, no longer troubles to learn his parts, puts on a silk hat, and thinks himself a genius. Russia is a land of insatiable and lazy people: they eat enormously of nice things, drink, like to sleep in the daytime, and snore in their sleep. They marry in order to get their house looked after, and keep mistresses in order to get prestige in society. Their psychology is that of a dog; when they are beaten, they whine shrilly and run into their kennels; when petted, they lie on their backs with their paws in the air and wag their tails."

Pain and cold contempt sounded in these words. But, though contemptuous, he felt pity, and, if in his presence you abused any one, Anton Pavlovitch would immediately defend him.

"Why do you say that? He is an old man . . . he's seventy." Or, "But he's still so young . . . it's only stupidity."

And, when he spoke like that, I never saw a sign of aversion in his face.

When a man is young, banality seems only amusing and unimportant, but little by little it possesses a man; it permeates his brain and blood like a poison or asphyxiating fumes; he becomes like an old, rusty signboard: something is painted on it, but what?—You can't make out.

Anton Pavlovitch in his early stories was already able to reveal in the dim sea of banality its tragic humour; one has only to read his "humorous" stories with attention to see what a lot of cruel and disgusting things, behind the humorous words and situations, had been observed by the author with sorrow and were concealed by him.

He was ingenuously shy; he would not say aloud and openly to people, "Now do be more decent;" he hoped in vain that they would themselves see how necessary it was that they should be more decent. He hated everything banal and foul, and he described the abominations of life in the noble language of a poet, with the humorist's gentle smile, and behind the beautiful form of his stories people scarcely noticed the inner meaning, full of bitter reproach.

The dear public, when it reads his *Daughter of Albion,* laughs and hardly realizes how abominable is the well-fed squire's mockery of a person who is lonely and strange to every one and everything. In each of his humorous stories I hear the quiet, deep sigh of a pure and human heart, the hopeless sigh of sympathy for men who do not know how to respect human dignity, who submit without any resistance to mere force, live like fish, believe in nothing but the necessity of swallowing every day as much thick soup as possible, and feel nothing but fear that some one, strong and insolent, will give them a hiding.

No one understood as clearly and finely as Anton Tchekhov, the tragedy of life's trivialities, no one before him showed men with such merciless truth the terrible and shameful picture of their life in the dim chaos of bourgeois everyday existence.

His enemy was banality; he fought it all his life long; he ridiculed it, drawing it with a pointed and unimpassioned pen, finding the mustiness of banality even where at the first glance everything seemed to be arranged very nicely, comfortably, and even brilliantly—and banality revenged itself upon him by a nasty prank, for it saw that his corpse, the corpse of a poet, was put into a railway truck "For the Conveyance of Oysters."

That dirty green railway truck seems to me precisely the great, triumphant laugh of banality over its tired enemy; and all the "Recollections" in the gutter press are hypocritical sorrow, behind which I feel the cold and smelly breath of banality, secretly rejoicing over the death of its enemy.

Reading Anton Tchekhov's stories, one feels oneself in a melancholy day of late autumn, when the air is transparent and the outline of naked trees, narrow houses, greyish people is sharp. Everything is strange, lonely, motionless, helpless. The horizon, blue and empty, melts into the pale sky and its breath is terribly cold upon the earth which is covered with frozen mud. The author's mind, like the autumn sun, shows up in hard outline the monotonous roads, the crooked streets, the little squalid houses in which tiny, miserable people are stifled by boredom and laziness and fill the houses with an unintelligible, drowsy bustle. Here anxiously, like a grey mouse, scurries *The Darling,* the dear, meek woman who loves so slavishly and who can love so much. You can slap her cheek and she won't even dare to utter a sigh aloud, the meek slave. . . . And by her side is Olga of *The Three Sisters:* she too loves much, and submits with resignation to the caprices of the dissolute, banal wife of her good-for-nothing brother; the life of her sisters crumbles before her eyes, she weeps and cannot help any one in anything, and she has not within her a single live, strong word of protest against banality.

And here is the lachrymose Ranevskaya and the other owners of "The Cherry Orchard," egotistical like children, with the flabbiness of senility. They missed the right moment for dying; they whine, seeing nothing of what is going on around them, understanding nothing, parasites without the power of again taking root in life. The wretched little student, Trofimov, speaks eloquently of the necessity of working—and does nothing but amuse himself, out of sheer boredom, with stupid mockery of Varya, who works ceaselessly for the good of idlers.

Vershinin dreams of how pleasant life will be in three hundred years, and lives without perceiving that everything around him is falling into ruin before his eyes; Solyony, from boredom and stupidity, is ready to kill the pitiable Baron Tonsenbach.

There passes before one a long file of men and women, slaves of their love, of their stupidity and idleness, of their greed for the good things of life; there walk the slaves of the dark fear of life; they straggle anxiously along, filling life with incoherent words about the future, feeling that in the present there is no place for them.

At moments out of the grey mass of them one hears the sound of a shot: Ivanov or Triepliev has guessed what he ought to do and has died.

Many of them have nice dreams of how pleasant life will be in two hundred years, but it occurs to none of them to ask themselves who will make life pleasant if we only dream.

In front of that dreary, grey crowd of helpless people there passed a great, wise, and observant man; he looked at all these dreary inhabitants of his country, and, with a sad smile, with a tone of gentle but deep reproach, with anguish in his face and in his heart, in a beautiful and sincere voice, he said to them:

"You live badly, my friends. It is shameful to live like that."

FROM *ANTON CHEHOV**

William Gerhardi

I

. . . " 'Why are thy songs so short?' a bird was once asked. 'Is it because thou art short of breath?'

" 'I have very many songs, and I should like to sing them all.' "

This fragment from Daudet is jotted down in one of Chehov's note-books. And certainly it is all but useless to classify his subject-matter. It encompasses all kinds of Russian life that one can think of; and it is the consummative variety of his works remembered as a whole that fills one with a mingled sense of wonder and of lost opportunities—a sense which springs from the realisation of the vast variety of existence, impossible to experience since life is given but once, and stingily at that. It is in the essence of things that our appetite tends to increase in proportion to our knowledge of the things we miss, must needs go on doing so. But we do not propose to slacken our pace for all that, and readers of Chehov may perhaps console themselves, because, to some extent at all events, literature like his may take the place of actual experience, without the physical exertion, sacrifices, inconvenience, and pain that is inseparable from the business of living; and when they die they may congratulate themselves on having lived a hundred lives—but paid for one!

Progression means a succession of lost opportunities. And this is where Chehov grips us. The element that makes for his disquieting appeal is determined by this phenomenon. But to call him a pessimist is absurd. Nevertheless, this view of him is often held, not only by persons upon whom it is forced by the inevitable inadequacy of translations, but equally by those who read him in his native tongue. Perhaps progression as interpreted above would scarcely appear a cheerful proposition. It is a series of 'farewells,' sad, if you will, but yet inevitable, and beautiful because of their inherent quality of cosmic inevitability. The pessimistic attitude towards such phenomena would be one of whining at the failing

* William Gerhardi, *Anton Chehov* (New York: Duffield, 1923), pp. 11–13, 32–35, 38–41, 166–168, and 194–196. Reprinted by permission of William Gerhardi.

in our common nature—an attitude extreme, crippled, and one-sided.
Because it is unjust to life. For we are not even able to imagine the alternative of a transitory existence. To rebel against it, therefore, would be
unjust. It would, as a practical proposition, be absurd. Chehov, though
the melancholy beauty of his plays and stories is the melancholy of a
transitory world, cannot be called a pessimist, in the face of the ridiculous implication of such an attitude. A pessimistic attitude would mean
that he had no sense of proportion; and it is perhaps the chief determin-
ing cause of his sensibility that he had, if ever a man had, a perfect sense
of proportion. The optimistic attitude, on the other hand, being uncalled
for by the delusive nature of happiness, is not altogether his either. For,
says Colonel Vershinin in the *Three Sisters:*

> "Recently I have been reading the diary of a certain French cabinet
> minister, written while he was in prison. With what rapture, what joy,
> he alludes to the birds he sees through the prison window, which he
> hadn't noticed while he was a minister. Now that he is released, of
> course, as before, he doesn't notice the birds. So you won't notice
> Moscow, when you come to live in it. We have no happiness, and there
> *is* none; we only long for it."

It is better to dream of paradise than to go there. For when you know
you cease to care. Happiness, as we learn in retrospect, is when we
feel we have a heaven in reserve. It was not apathy alone that kept
the three sisters from embarking on the train to Moscow, but a sus-
picion deep down in their hearts that the climax coming at the end
of the crescendo is generally somewhat disappointing. For lack of any
further heaven in reserve. And this needs must be so, since there
seems no existence outside motion. The stationary nature of happiness
is a delusion. Faust wished he could say to a single moment: *"Ver-
weile noch, du bist-so schön!"*

It was an impossible demand; a contradiction in terms; a negation of
life, and with it of beauty. Chehov was neither pessimist nor optimist. To
him life is neither horrible nor happy, but unique, strange, fleeting,
beautiful, and awful.

And all the time, while life is passing, always you can feel in him
that aching isolation of the individual soul. "As I shall lie in the grave
alone so in fact I live alone," is a thought jotted down in his note-book.
His gay, companionable people laugh, but live alone. And mutely, by the
mere fact of their presence upon earth, each seems to put a question. . . .

II

. . . The real cause of his apparent intellectual weariness lies deeper;
it lies in his mistrust of logic. The law of contradiction, by which cruder
minds have laid such store, works so well because it naively overlooks

the fine gradations that lie between its two opposite poles. It must have its Yes *or* No, and is blind to what lies between them. Speculations as to life and death are thrashed out in the same incisive way by the logicians —To be, or not to be—forgetting that it is only necessary to substitute the word *becoming* for that of *being* (since creation does not take place in the twinkling of an eye out of nothing, but is a matter of evolution out of something else) to realise that logic, when it encroaches upon abstract questions, is apt to be rather like a bull in a china-shop. And if the questions that are implied in Chehov's works do not always admit of a logical answer, it is as often as not the fault of logic, which is a mere rule-of-thumb affair—inaccurately precise—when it is confronted by transcendental values. Perhaps in Chehov's mind we may already see an indication of that distant future when the law of contradiction may slowly loose its hold on our mode of thought, as its dams are gradually undermined by the subtler waves of intuitive gradation (if this be in the programme of transcending evolution).

"There is not a single criterion which can serve as the measure of the non-existent, of the non-human," is a thought in his note-book. Thus he rules out non-existence intuitively as effectively as it can be ruled out logically. (The existence of non-existence is a contradiction in terms.) And he leaves us with the anticipation of some middle way, some grada-tion of consciousness in a universe at once static and transitory, one might almost say "static" in its absolute transitoriness, just as living is both transitory in so far as the experience of it is determined by change, and static in so far as the continuity of our consciousness seems inde-pendent of change—as if we were sitting still in a moving vehicle.

All of which logically is nonsense. But the whole point is that possibly the secret of existence is outside logic. It certainly is not inside it. That we know. By the test of logic life makes nonsense. At any rate, we are entitled to suspect that logic is not all, for two good reasons— because logic leaves out a good deal of our spiritual sense of truth, and because logic cannot explain truth even to its own logical satisfaction.

Life would seem to be a sort of self-expression in an infinite variety of ways, which, for want of a "first cause" (which must be ruled out even by the crudely inadequate theory of causation itself), and for want of cosmic choice as to aim, direction, or order of succession, results in chaos: a defiance of continued order, with elusiveness for aim, and so itself a sort of order, fluctuating in the act of cancellation, there being no commanding choice to order its (or an alternative) monopoly the resulting fluctuation being just that impetus of the *perpetuum mobile* called life. In other words, since there is no reason why life be this or otherwise, life is *everywise*: a struggle towards the static and simulta-neous on the part of the transitory and successive, and towards transition and diversity on the part of the static and uniform (since there is no more warrant for one than the other). Otherwise, if life had an attainable goal (for which there is no warrant), life would be committing suicide the moment that this goal was reached, or even earlier—the moment any of its particles conceived it in advance. For which also there would seem no warrant. Therefore life is an equilibrium of transitory values, whereas what is absolute and static is perhaps its equilibrium.

But this is merely an endeavour to approach Chehov's sensibility by way of a metaphysical speculation (my own for choice). Yet while mistrusting the efficacy of logic, particularly in metaphysics, he was deterred by the futility of breaking through those walls. There was, moreover, no earthly reason why logic should not last its time. The value of intuitive gradation was in its gradual realisation: it was nothing if it was not gradual. And thus he felt that there was nothing for him to get excited about either in the matter of religion, or of metaphysics, or of philosophy, or of literature. His contribution was an attitude of discrimination towards life, and he knew that in due course civilisation will have made use of it. His contemplation of Fyodor Dostoevski banging at the walls for all he was worth did not particularly impress him. He writes in a letter that such questions as free-will, predestination, and non-resistance to evil can only be settled in the future. But now and then, when tired of walking round and round in the round cell of reason, Chehov too would stop and gently bang the wall and listen to the hollow sound. Yes, it seemed as though there was something behind the prison wall of reason, after all.

And it seems that in another little while we shall know why we are living, why we are suffering. . . . [Three Sisters.] . . .

IV

. . . I do not presume that I could give the whole of Chehov's outlook in a nutshell. But if pressed to do so, I would rather say that Chehov's outlook in a nutshell was that he thoroughly distrusted nutshells. His intellectual attitude was inconclusive. After he has said his say, there is still the implication that he reserves the right to leave his further thoughts unsaid, even unthought. And this can be understood. It is the cruder writers with undigested things to say who like to end on a conclusive note. Their passion sees them through. Whereas Chehov's passion is a passion for dispassion. It sees him through in his process of digesting life—a process to which, however, there is no proper ending. He ends upon an inconclusive note: indeed, so far as it is his aim to demonstrate that truth is in its very nature inconclusive, he ends on a conclusive note.

"It is time that writers," he says in a letter, "especially those who are artists, recognised that there is no making out anything in this world, as once Socrates recognized it, and Voltaire too."

The mob thinks it knows and understands everything; and the more stupid it is, the wider it imagines its outlook to be. And if a writer whom the mob believes in has the courage to say that he does not understand anything of what he sees, that alone will be something gained in the realm of thought and a great step in advance.

So long as scepticism means (by M. Anatole France's definition) merely a denial of negations, Chehov may be said to be a sceptic in his outlook. (That he feared and hated labels does not in itself exempt him from such labels.) He is very much aware of our mental limitations, and consequently of our hopeless handicap in trying to envisage truth by mental means alone. And he is a sceptic in so far as he suspects philosophers who claim to have captured truth by circumscription of being blind to all the other truth that they have left outside. But "truth," "reason," "God," are confusing terms, and require separate definition on each occasion of their use. Let me, therefore, illustrate exactly what I mean by truth and reason so far as they here concern him. Reason is a sort of a balloon wherein we dwell: you can stretch it at any point you like, but you will have tampered with its natural round shape. Progress in philosophy can be achieved with ease by impairing, as it were, the symmetry of reason at any of its points—by stretching truth. And since Chehov would not recognize as truth any angular conception of it, it would seem that mentally there was nothing left for him but to wander round, like a fly inside a globe, and to discover as it were that truth, for all mental purposes, was a round globe in which he was confined, and, after gaining the conviction of its irrevocable roundness, to tumble to the bright idea that the greater part of truth may be outside the globe of reason. It is only natural that after that his wanderings inside should come to a permanent halt. His case is: Why break your skull over a minor riddle if it is but a portion of a major one, which we can dimly feel but not define? And that he can convey his sense of spiritual truth intuitively into his pages is his one escape from the *impasse* of reason. It is like the calmness which underlies the surface ripples of a restless lake.

But—to have a last go at the image—if reason is comparable to a balloon wherein we dwell, and if the stretching of it at any point would illustrate unreason, so the blowing of it up to an ever larger size would cover such mental progress as is achieved, for instance, by research work. For Chehov had the same belief in ethical and scientific progress as, for example, Mr. Wells. But what he asked himself, and what sometimes he doubted, was whether man at any ultimate stage of his development would be completely able to account for the *raison d'être* of phenomena, and cease to suffer both the anguish of unsatisfied curiosity and the alternative dissatisfaction of *ennui*; whether ever he would get beyond the sense of the *Weltschmerz*. "Not only after two or three hundred, but in a million years, life will still be as it was," replies Baron

Tuzenbach in the *Three Sisters* to Colonel Vershinin, whose thesis is that everything on earth must gradually change, and that some day a new and happy life will begin for mankind; "life does not change, it remains for ever, following its own laws, which do not concern us, or which, at any rate, you will never find out. Migrant birds—cranes, for example— fly and fly, and whatever thoughts, high or low, enter their heads, they will still fly, and not know why or where. They fly, and will continue to fly, whatever philosophers come to life among them; they may philosophise as much as they like, only they will fly. . . ." To this Màsha rejoins: "Still a meaning?" "A meaning . . ." he says. . . .

. . . It is, no doubt, convenient to hang upon a writer of whom one knows little some such label as, for example, that Dostoevski is the exponent of the philosophy of suffering, Tolstoy of that of non-resistance to evil, and Chehov of futility. These remarks are trite, and they have just a grain of truth in them; but if they are concise, they are also negligible. The choice of really ineffectual people is in fact rare in Chehov, and, when it happens, is occasioned by the comic possibilities inherent in them. The old doctor in the *Three Sisters* who had forgotten the little he ever knew of medicine, or the helpless Gaev in the *Cherry Orchard,* are exceptions, and as such can be found in the literature and community of any country. Perhaps, on the whole, Westerners are not inclined to let themselves go quite so easily as some Russians are. Their inhibitions are quite properly allied with their sense of self-preservation. And there is still a fairly prevalent Russian type exponential of its 'broad Russian nature' to which inhibition means nothing more than cowardice. But this gives no ground for generalisation. One need only read Mr. George Moore's *In Single Strictness* to realize that the so-called 'Chehovian' type is not confined to Russia. The only pity is that Mr. Moore has not the gift of humour to portray the subject as it really ought to be portrayed—by blending pathos with humour. All we are given is pathos; and we are left with an unpleasant taste in our mouth, as if we had tasted of an over-seasoned dish, because a necessary ingredient has been omitted. Indubitably the fault of the cook!

Chehov's mind is a search-light cast, not upon the weaklings of society, but upon the average citizen of town and country who, if he saw himself in this clear light, would be astonished and amused at the comitragedy of his self-sufficiency. But people rarely see themselves in this strong light, because their individual visions of themselves are distorted by the perspective of looking to the future with expectancy and hope. They know little of how they look against the background of surrounding life. That withering touch which is so sensible through Chehov's pages comes from seeing life that is at the moment being lived, from the other end as if it had been lived already: for all along we had been made to guess how inevitably it *will* be lived; and in this cold transparent light we see the living hopes as cherished foibles, and the hopes that are to those who hope them sufficient and sustaining blight us by the knowledge of their impending bankruptcy. We are aghast by the spectacle of thwarted life trudging blindly to its near-by grave, terrified by the wonted insufficiency of other people's self-sufficiency. It is the terror of smugness brought to bear on incomprehensible life....

VI

His works are built up as though they were Wagnerian operas—on *Leitmotifs*. These themes are principally determined by the fact that each character in Chehov is, as I have said, an isolated soul that, in essentials, lives alone in a world of its own creation through which it looks upon the life "that is" in a misty, half-uncomprehending way; and the blend, the clash, the incongruity of it is what moves us: there is beauty in that blend of comicality and pathos. There is Madame Ranevskaya, the owner of the Cherry Orchard, who has a world of her own—one can feel it plainly throughout the play—and only every now and then she comes down to earth to face reality, but not for long. And there is Anya, her daughter of seventeen, who also has her world and her "new life"; and there is the poor "eternal student," who lives mostly outside the present. And what each thinks about he lets out inadvertently between relevant sentences in the colloquial way, and—strangely—it so happens that what matters to him most is to appear irrelevant to the company in which he lives. In the *Sea-Gull* the young teacher always broods over his poverty and the fact that he has to keep a family on twenty-three roubles a month, while the estate-agent is always lost in reminiscence of theatrical news of the past generation. Thus, when the estate-agent relates how a famous bass, Silva, once took the low C, and a church cantor in the gallery consternated every one by booming out "Bravo, Silva!" a whole octave lower, the teacher only asks: "And what is the pay of a church cantor?"

The thematic construction is nowhere more apparent than in his plays. There is the young doctor's theme in *Uncle Vanya*,

"Those who will live one or two hundred years after us."

This is how he puts it in the course of a narration in the first act when he relates how a patient died before him under chloroform:

"I sat down, closed my eyes—like that, and thought: those who will live one or two hundred years after us, and for whom we are now treading the path, will they remember us gratefully?"

He takes up the theme again in the fourth act, thus:

"Those who will live one or two hundred years after us, and who will despise us for having lived our lives so stupidly and so tastelessly—they may perhaps find the means to be happy, but we.... You and I have but one hope. The hope that when we shall sleep in our graves, we shall see visions, perhaps even pleasant ones."

And at the conclusion of the play Sonia takes up a theme which may, in part, be said to flow out of the theme I have quoted:

". . . and there, beyond the grave, we shall say that we had suffered, that we had cried, that our lot had been bitter, and God will take pity on us, and both of us, uncle, dear uncle, shall see a life lofty and tender and beautiful, we shall know gladness and look on our present predicaments, with affection, a smile—and we shall rest."

It runs on:

"We shall rest! We shall hear angels, we shall see heaven all diamonds, we shall see how all evil drowns in the mercy that shall engulf the whole world, and our life will be peaceful and tender and sweet, like a caress. . . ."

This passage is strikingly beautiful in the original. And it is interesting to note here that the particular element which lends it (and the final passages in the *Three Sisters*) its peculiar, disturbing beauty is perhaps the inadequacy, almost falseness, of the consolation. In the final passages of the *Three Sisters* that particular emotional effect is even more crushing because, whereas Sonia, in *Uncle Vanya*, for the moment is really fervent about the things which are to make up for her thwarted life, (the three sisters are not so sure of their consolations: hence the more disquieting effect of Olga's final speech in the *Three Sisters*)—to which, however, I shall presently return. But there is, of course, an alternative (or even a simultaneous) interpretation of the final passage from *Uncle Vanya*, since Chehov never disclaimed the possibility of immortality for the individual soul, if only as part of the "world soul," or something of that sort, something necessarily vague, of course. Chehov's attitude was that he did not know one way or the other, but that he suspected that there may be a way which, by our present standards of logic, was neither one way nor the other, but somehow utterly another. Was it Ibsen who said that one can believe and doubt at the same time? At worst, extinction itself was a sort of bliss.

FROM *CHEKHOV AND HIS RUSSIA**

W. H. Bruford

CHAPTER IV. THE LANDOWNER

Russian society was still divided at the end of the nineteenth century, like France before the Revolution, into orders or estates with unequal legal rights. 81.6% were classified as peasants, but they would include a considerable number of urban proletariate of peasant origin at one extreme, and of prosperous farmers at the other. 9.3% were merchants and lesser townsfolk, 6.1% military, 0.9% clergy, and 1.3% gentry. Apart from the military, these were at least in theory hereditary classes, so that sons of village priests who did not enter the church or merchants' sons who did not trade had to be classified for passport purposes as miscellaneous 'raznochintsy' ('of no particular class'). They were no longer water-tight compartments in fact, and if one became a civil servant, there was by now a regular hierarchy, a ladder of fourteen rungs which could be climbed, though until 1906 not beyond a certain point by peasants. The 'estates' ('sostoyaniya', imitated from the German 'Stände') had developed since the time of Peter the Great out of the primary distinction, which still left clear traces, especially on peasant thought, between 'masters' (gospoda) and 'people' (narod), the bearded and the cleanshaven—the gentry had of course been compelled by Peter to shave their chins.

Among the smooth-faced there were wide variations. We may note first the distinction, something like that made in Germany between high and lesser nobility, between the old aristocracy, claiming descent from Rurik, or Lithuanian or Tartar rulers, and the 'pomeshchiki' or country squires. The former, to whose number only fourteen families had been added by the Emperor since 1700, bore the title 'knyaz'. There were also about 70 counts and ten barons (these mostly foreign bankers) dating from Peter's time, and the Baltic aristocracy of German origin. The 'pomeshchiki' were descended from 'men of service' who had received grants of land from the Emperor for military or other state service, par-

* W. H. Bruford, *Chekhov and His Russia* (New York: Oxford Univ. Press, 1948), pp. 76–85. Reprinted by permission of Routledge & Kegan Paul Ltd., London.

ticularly in the period following the great expansion and tightening-up of the central power in the reign of Ivan the Great (just before 1500). When trade and a money economy were little developed this was the only convenient means of payment a ruler had. It was in exactly the same way that 'ministeriales' in Germany had been rewarded three or four centuries earlier, and as with them, the estates granted at first temporarily, during the tenure of office, became hereditary, and gave rise to a landed class similar in many ways to the old aristocracy.

But the gentry of Russia had in other respects a very different history behind them from that of their counterparts in Germany, or in France and England. In all three countries the aristocracy had a much stronger esprit de corps, born of the struggle to defend their privileges against the monarchy and the rising middle class. In Russia they had to toe the line with the rest of the Czar's subjects from an early date, under a despotism influenced by oriental traditions. They had derived their rights from the monarch alone, and Peter the Great had insisted on service to the state from all in return for these rights, which he readily conferred on others, of whatever origin they might be, who served him well. Thus rank in the official hierarchy came to confer higher social distinction than did hereditary rank. 'We find plenty of Russians who are proud of their wealth, of their culture, or of their official position,' says Mackenzie Wallace, 'but we rarely find a Russian who is proud of his birth.' Even the court nobility had none of the characteristics of a closed caste, he says, found for instance in Germany, and titles in general did not mean as much as in the West. Nor was the Russian nobility rooted in its native soil in the same way as in the West. They did not call themselves after their native seats, there was nothing in their titles corresponding to the French 'de' or the German 'von'. There were in fact no family seats of the baronial type at all. 'Nature herself in Russia,' says Leroy-Beaulieu, 'seems to discourage these domestic fortresses, it refused, so to speak, both site and materials for them, steep rocks on which to build them and stone for their walls. The wooden house, so often burnt down, so quickly decayed, so easy to move and to rebuild, is a true symbol of Russian life. The very type of their homes is an indication of the uncertain fortunes of the aristocracy.' Some authorities contend that there was in consequence less class feeling in Russia than in the West, but whatever the truth may be about that, there was at the least mutual aloofness between gentlemen and peasantry, which rapidly increased after the Emancipation as old ideas of a social hierarchy broke down.[1]

The ideal age of the gentry had been the reign of Catherine II, for she had confirmed their privileges, and also the abolition decreed by her husband Peter III in 1762, just before she usurped the throne, of

[1] Maynard, *Russia in Flux*, III ff.

that obligation to serve which alone justified their privileged position. They had succeeded in following in this the example of the German and French aristocracy, and Catherine, like the petty princes of her native country, did everything she could to make her court brilliant and impressive on the model of Versailles, while attracting the gentry to the public service by social and material rewards, instead of driving them by sheer compulsion. It was the beginning of the westernising movement in Russian culture, built on the foundation of Peter the Great's state as power. As in Germany, the cultivated courtier had to speak French, the language of civilisation, and his country cousin followed his example as best he could, but this was only a necessary step to the creation of that great national literature in the European tradition, of which Pushkin, in the next generation, was the first outstanding figure.

In the century between 1762 and 1861 the land-owning class, enjoying a life of sheltered ease based on serf labour, were the undisputed leaders in Russian literature and thought, and by far the most influential section of the reading public, which was of course small. There was a popular literature, addressed to the lower middle and tradesman class of the towns, but it was quite separate from literature in the European tradition, and consisted at first of chapbook romances and lives of saints. The literature of what Prince Mirsky calls the 'Golden age of Russian poetry' has an eighteenth-century, 'Augustan' flavour, although contemporary with the European Romantic movement, principally because of 'its distinct social colouring. It was a movement inside the gentry, a movement of *gentlemen*. Hence, in its early stages, the prevalence of light, society verse, of convivial and anacreontic subjects; the cult of friendship, of good company, and of wine. Socially the age of Pushkin marks the high-water mark of the literary hegemony of the gentry. Higher literature is completely monopolized by men of that class.' [2] After the Decembrist Revolt (1825) and the repression of liberal opinion among the gentry which followed it, lower class journalists came to the fore, leading up to Belinsky, the son of an army doctor, 'the father of the intelligentsia'. 'Socially he marks the end of the rule of the gentry and the advent of the non-class intelligentsia of raznochintsy to cultural leadership' (Mirsky). Yet the great age of the realistic novel which followed would be poor indeed without the names of Aksakov, Goncharov, Turgeniev, Tolstoy and Shchedrin, following Gogol in the preceding period, all sprung from the land-owning class.

Besides the small number of country gentlemen with literary or scientific leanings there were of course a great many who were primarily officials, serving in some town, and leaving the management of their estates entirely to their bailiff, and probably a still larger number who were backwoodsmen of the type described by Aksakov in his charming

[2] Mirsky, *History of Russian Literature to 1881*, 96.

Family chronicle, or Goncharov in Oblomov's dream, or Mackenzie Wallace in his picture of landed proprietors of the old school. The latter's Ivan Ivanovitch, who is extraordinarily like the elder Oblomov, gave the impression of living entirely outside the struggle for existence. He had been educated at home, and never made to work hard lest it should injure his health. Having no natural inclination for any kind of activity he gladly accepted a nominal office post which allowed him to live on his estate and steadily rise in rank. His marriage with the only daughter of a neighbour was arranged by his parents and turned out happily, for his wife found contentment in satisfying his simple material wants, and monotony did not trouble either of them. Every day in summer he would sit by an open window, sometimes questioning a passing servant and giving him an order. After an ample midday meal, the whole household slept for a couple of hours; even the servants could be heard snoring in the corridors. Then came tea, a drive in the fields, some talk with the peasants and long discussions of plans for the next day with the steward. Occasionally there was a visitor, but their chief link with the outside world was through their two sons in the army, though to write a letter to one of them was a serious bit of work that was not embarked on lightly. They read little and did not even play cards, the chief resource of bored officials in country retirement. It was enough just to live and meditate.

Chekhov introduces us to a number of country squires who are made in the same mould as Ivan Ivanovitch, but have had the bottom knocked out of their world by the collapse of the serf system. They find themselves no longer in a self-contained little world where with the minimum of effort and thought they find their simple needs supplied.

For many of them, who could carry on, somehow, in the old traditional ways, but possessed neither the capital nor the knowledge and initiative necessary to reorganize their farming on new lines, the Emancipation spelt ruin. Indeed, the qualifications now required of a large farmer were very different from those of the old-fashioned Russian country squire. In the case of the latter, one of the principal items of costs did not count, since the necessary labour was supplied by the serfs, who were paid for it not in money, but in land—a commodity still plentiful and possessing in itself, apart from the peasants' labour, very little value. The cost of equipment was also reduced to a minimum, the cultivation of the fields and the cartage of produce being done by the peasants with their own stock. . . . The commercial problems of farming were easily solved, even when, in the second quarter of the last century, the excessive concentration on the production of cereals brought their prices down to a very low level. Since the Emancipation everything changed completely, and the problems of labour and of capital assumed an enormous importance, especially in those localities in which the population was relatively sparse, the peasants' holdings more or less sufficient or easily supplemented by leases, or where other sources of earnings diverted the peasants from employment on the land. Moreover, the peasants had still to get used to

employment as hired labour, while the land owners had to learn to
handle free labour over which they did not possess the disciplinary
powers which made the management of serf labour relatively easy. . . .
The extreme shortage of capital was another difficulty, only partly
mitigated by the issue to the land owners of redemption bonds in payment for the land allocated to their former serfs.

Small or thriftless land owners were therefore almost always heavily
in debt, living from hand to mouth in houses with perhaps signs of
former glories but badly in need of repair, surrounded by neglected
woods and fields. Their attitude to life was marked by lack of initiative
and energy, combined with a certain Micawber-like fatalism, the product
of a long tradition of easy living. One of the old school is seen in Vera's
grandfather in *At home*, who sat in the same place day in, day out, playing patience or dozing, ate enormous meals in spite of his age, and glared
at the servants. In the old days it had been twenty-five strokes of the
birch for the slightest offence, but now only the steward occasionally
beat them. Everything on the estate was neglected, 'in fact there was no
systematic farming. They ploughed and sowed simply from habit' and
little work was done, although the bustle in the house began at five in
the morning. In summer the old man would sometimes drive out to look
at the oats and hay. When quarter day drew near they began to look
depressed, and aunt Dasha asked Vera to help them with the interest on
the mortgage, from the money she had inherited from her engineer father.
A younger man, equally feckless, is the prince in *A trivial incident*, 'a
man of no great gifts, with something oriental about him. He was straightforward and honest, not a bully, a fop or a rake, and therefore in the eyes
of the general run of people rather a colourless nonentity'. He was
known in the district as 'His Excellency the Dunce', but the narrator
liked him and sympathized with him in the endless series of misfortunes
and failures that marked his life. In the first place, he was poor. He had
somehow contrived to get through the thirty to forty thousand roubles
left to him by his father, though he did not play cards, or speculate, or
spend money on women. His stewards, agents and even lackeys ran away
with a lot, for lack of supervision, and he was carelessly generous in
loans and gifts to all comers, not so much from kindness of heart or
over-trustfulness as from the desire to appear the perfect gentleman.
There was hardly a squire in the district who was not in his debt, and
he was now hopelessly insolvent himself. Some days he would go without lunch and carry an empty cigar case, but he was always well-
groomed, fashionably dressed and scented with ilang-ilang. Secondly
he was terribly lonely. He was unmarried, and had neither relatives nor
friends. He did not easily become intimate with people because of his
silent reserve and the exaggerated correctness with which he masked
his poverty. He saw little of women and could not be bothered with

[1] Pavlovsky, *op. cit.*, 99f.

romances. A certain sincerity and delicacy of feeling, or what he called his abnormal timidity, prevented him from marrying a rich neighbour who was in love with him or, even when his estate was about to be sold up, from taking an official post for which he felt he had no qualifications, though he saw many around him drawing salaries for nothing.

In *Ariadne* there is another decayed gentleman, a bankrupt squire, who had pine-apples and wonderful peaches growing on his estate, and a fountain in the middle of the courtyard, but not a penny in his pocket. He did nothing, knew nothing, was as spineless as if made out of a boiled turnip, and occupied himself with homoeopathy and spiritualism. His sister, a beautiful clever girl, was utterly reckless with family property. If she needed a riding-horse and had no money, she would have a portion of the iron roof torn off and sold for scrap, or sell farm horses for a song in the middle of the harvest. The story of her love affair with an idealistic young neighbour is a study in cold sensuality and love of power.

There is hardly a single land owner in the stories and plays who is not in debt. In *Neighbours* the proprietor of the neighbouring estate, who has such an inexplicable attraction for Ivashin's sister, is paying 12% on a second mortgage, and to raise the interest is reduced to asking all his friends for loans. He is so improvident that when short of fuel he will burn a length of trellis or a cold frame from the garden, after selling all his winter store of fire-wood for five roubles. In politics he is a wholly-minded liberal, who makes any idea that he talks about sound dull and commonplace. He married à la Dostoyevsky, from pity, a girl seduced by a fellow-officer, only to find that he had caught a Tartar, and even at forty-one he is still on the look-out for prodigies of moral valour to perform. He is the kind of fool whose eyes are in the ends of the earth, who will never be able to lay to heart, though he needs it more than most, Goethe's advice to regard as his duty 'what the day requires of him'.

The fullest study of this ineffective quixotism, which Chekhov considered to be so common in his time, is in the first serious play, *Ivanov*. When it was about to be produced in St. Petersburg the company misunderstood it so badly that Chekhov wrote a long letter explaining the characters. 'Ivanov is a gentleman, a university man, and not remarkable in any way. He is excitable, hot-headed, easily carried away, honest and straightforward like most people of his class. He has lived on his estate and served on the zemstvo. What he has been doing and how he has behaved, what he has been interested in and enthusiastic over, can be seen from the following words of his, addressed to the doctor (Act I, scene 5): "Don't marry Jewesses or neurotic women or blue-stockings . . . don't fight with thousands single-handed, don't wage war on windmills, don't batter your head against the wall. . . . God preserve you from scientific farming, wonderful schools, enthusiastic speeches . . ." This is what he has in his past. . . . His past is beautiful, as is generally the case with educated Russians. There is not, or there hardly is, a single Russian gentleman or university man who does not boast of his past. Why? Because Russian excitability has one specific characteristic: it is quickly followed by exhaustion. A man has scarcely left the classroom before he rushes to take up a burden beyond his strength; he tackles at once the schools, the peasants, scientific farming, and the *Vyestnik Evropi*, he makes speeches, writes to the minister, combats evil, applauds good, falls in love, not in an ordinary, simple way, but selects either a blue-stocking or a neurotic or a Jewess, or even a prostitute whom he tries to save, and so on, and so on. But by the time he is thirty he begins to feel tired and board. . . . He is ready to reject the zemstvo and scientific farming, and science and love. . . . He looks for the causes outside himself and fails to find them; he begins to look for them inside and finds only an indefinite feeling of guilt. It is a Russian feeling. . . . To exhaustion, boredom, and the feeling of guilt add one more enemy: loneliness. Were Ivanov an official, an actor, a priest, a professor, he would have grown used to his position. But he lives on his estate. He is in the country. His neighbours are either drunkards or fond of cards, or are of the same type as the doctor. . . . But life makes its legitimate demands on him, he must settle problems. . . . Men like Ivanov do not solve difficulties but collapse under their weight.'[1] It is interesting to note that Leroy-Beaulieu in the early 'eighties made a very similar observation about the Russian character, in discussing the rapid cooling-off of the ideals of the 'sixties: 'Dans l'âme russe le découragement semble toujours sur les pas de l'enthousiasme, l'abattement suit de près l'èxaltation.'

In his last and finest play, *The cherry orchard*, Chekhov returns to the theme of the land-owning class and its problems, but he presents their failure now not so much as a matter of personal or national character as of changing conditions of life. The play symbolises, poetically, yet without ever losing touch with reality, the transition from a purely agrarian to a more and more industrial Russia. It brings home to us the perplexity of the older generation of the aristocracy as the ground slips from under their feet, their attachment to the home and the way of life of their youth, with the sentiments of carefree ease and beauty associated with them in their minds, and their inability to master either their economic or their personal problems by resolutely facing facts. The central characters are the mondaine Liubov Andreyevna, the owner, with her brother Gaev, of an estate with a fine old cherry orchard, and Lopakhin, the merchant son of the village shopkeeper. We have come across him already as a representative of the peasant who has risen out of his class, in the new age of money, through his energy and business ability. Though he stands for another world, he is not hostile to Liubov. On the contrary, he remembers with gratitude her kindness to him as a boy. But the aristocrats, almost in spite of themselves, tend to look down on him, and

[1] *Letters*, tr. Garnett, III ff.

his proposal for saving their estate, by letting the ground where the cherry orchard stands for building sites, fills them with horror. It is simply unthinkable, yet they see no other way out of their predicament. They watch their doom approaching with paralysed will, still vaguely hoping that somehow they will escape, and bringing their ruin nearer all the time by the reckless extravagance to which they are accustomed.

Gaev, the brother, and his friend Simeonov-Pishchik, are merely background figures, not drawn in the round, but they suggest two types of decadent squire, the one seeking refuge from reality in fine words and sentiments, or solacing himself with billiards and lollypops, and the other, cruder, living on his friends, until minerals are found on his land by English prospectors. The Chekhov who wrote to Suvorin in 1891: 'Alas, I shall never be a Tolstoyan. In women I love beauty above all things; and in the history of mankind, culture, expressed in carpets, carriages with springs, and keenness of wit'—was drawn emotionally, one feels, to his aristocrats, as Goethe had been to his poet Tasso. But just as Goethe's wisdom had seen something right too in the prosaic Antonio, because even poets must have some regard for the society around them, so Chekhov would have the Russians realise that Lopakhin is a good fellow, and that what he represents is something to which Russia has to reconcile herself. For post-revolutionary critics he is even too kind to this bourgeois. He tries to marry him off with Varya, Liubov's adopted daughter, but there is always a hitch, perhaps because their classes are not quite ripe for fusion. And he holds out hope for the future in his picture of Liubov's young daughter, Anya, and the former tutor, Trofimov. Trofimov, the 'eternal student', the raisonneur of the piece, is given lines which express Chekhov's own thought as we know it from his letters, that men have little till now to be proud of; they should cease to be so pleased with themselves and simply work, as at present few do in Russia. Anya, under his influence, is ready to part from her dear cherry orchard. There will be still better places in the world that is yet to be. 'All Russia is our garden', Trofimov tells her, and the garden they are leaving is spoilt for them by the odour of selfdom which still clings to it. But this young man himself, who has not succeeded at thirty in taking a degree, is not a very promising leader towards the better world. As a representative of revolutionary youth he is not really convincing, and that not merely because of the caution imposed on any author by the censorship, say post-revolutionary critics. It may be, as they assume, because Chekhov was here drawing a type he did not know sufficiently well. Or it may be that he saw a good deal of the Ivanov even in Trofimov, and could not help treating him with a certain irony. . .

FROM *THE IDEA OF A THEATRE**

Francis Fergusson

THE PLOT OF *THE CHERRY ORCHARD*

The Cherry Orchard is often accused of having no plot whatever, and it
is true that the story gives little indication of the play's content or meaning; nothing happens, as the Broadway reviewers so often point out.
Nor does it have a thesis, though many attempts have been made to
attribute a thesis to it, to make it into a Marxian tract, or into a nostalgic
defense of the old regime. The play does not have much of a plot in
either of these accepted meanings of the word, for it is not addressed to
the rationalizing mind but to the poetic and histrionic sensibility. It is
an imitation of an action in the strictest sense, and it is plotted according
to the first meaning of this word which I have distinguished in other
contexts: the incidents are selected and arranged to define an action
in a certain mode; a complete action, with a beginning, middle, and end
in time. Its freedom from the mechanical order of the thesis or the
intrigue is the sign of the perfection of Chekhov's realistic art. And its
apparently casual incidents are actually composed with most elaborate
and conscious skill to reveal the underlying life, and the natural, objective form of the play as a whole.

In *Ghosts*, as I showed, the action is distorted by the stereotyped
requirements of the thesis and the intrigue. That is partly a matter of the
mode of action which Ibsen was trying to show; a quest "of ethical
motivation" which requires some sort of intellectual framework, and yet
can have no final meaning in the purely literal terms of Ibsen's theater.
The Cherry Orchard, on the other hand, is a drama "of pathetic motivation," a theater-poem of the suffering of change; and this mode of action
and awareness is much closer to the skeptical basis of modern realism,
and to the histrionic basis of all realism. Direct perception before predi-
cation is always true, says Aristotle; and the extraordinary feat of
Chekhov is to predicate nothing. This he achieves by means of his plot:
he selects only those incidents, those moments in his characters' lives,

* Francis Fergusson, *The Idea of a Theatre* (Princeton, N.J.: Princeton
Univ. Press, 1949), pp. 161–172. Reprinted by permission of Princeton University Press.

between their rationalized efforts, when they sense their situation and destiny most directly. So he contrives to show the action of the play as a whole—the unsuccessful attempt to cling to the Cherry Orchard—in many diverse reflectors and without propounding any thesis about it.

The slight narrative thread which ties these incidents and characters together for the inquiring mind, is quickly recounted. The family that owns the old estate named after its famous orchard—Lyubov, her brother Gaev, and her daughters Varya and Anya—is all but bankrupt, and the question is how to prevent the bailiffs from selling the estate to pay their debts. Lopahin, whose family were formerly serfs on the estate, is now rapidly growing rich as a businessman, and he offers a very sensible plan: chop down the orchard, divide the property into small lots, and sell them off to make a residential suburb for the growing industrial town nearby. Thus the cash value of the estate could be not only preserved, but increased. But this would not save what Lyubov and her brother find valuable in the old estate; they cannot consent to the destruction of the orchard. But they cannot find, or earn, or borrow the money to pay their debts either; and in due course the estate is sold at auction to Lopahin himself, who will make a very good thing of it. His workmen are hacking at the old trees before the family is out of the house.

The play may be briefly described as a realistic ensemble pathos: the characters all suffer the passing of the estate in different ways, thus adumbrating this change at a deeper and more generally significant level than that of any individual's experience. The action which they all share by analogy, and which informs the suffering of the destined change of the Cherry Orchard, is "to save the Cherry Orchard": that is, each character sees some value in it—economic, sentimental, social, cultural— which he wishes to keep. By means of his plot, Chekhov always focuses attention on the general action: his crowded stage, full of the characters I have mentioned as well as half a dozen hangers-on, is like an implicit discussion of the fatality which concerns them all; but Chekhov does not believe in their ideas, and the interplay he shows among his *dramatis personae* is not so much the play of thought as the alternation of his characters' perceptions of their situation, as the moods shift and the time for decision comes and goes.

Though the action which Chekhov chooses to show on-stage is "pathetic," i.e., suffering and perception, it is complete: the Cherry Orchard is constituted before our eyes, and then dissolved. The first act is a prologue: it is the occasion of Lyubov's return from Paris to try to resume her old life. Through her eyes and those of her daughter Anya, as well as from the complementary perspectives of Lopahin and Trofimov, we see the estate as it were in the round, in its many possible meanings. The second act corresponds to the agon; it is in this act that we become aware of the conflicting values of all the characters, and of the efforts they make (off-stage) to save each one *his* Orchard. The third act corresponds to the pathos and peripety of the traditional tragic form. The occasion is a rather hysterical party which Lyubov gives while her estate is being sold at auction in the nearby town; it ends with Lopahin's announcement, in pride and the bitterness of guilt, that he was the purchaser. The last act is the epiphany: we see the action, now completed, in a new and ironic light. The occasion is the departure of the family: the windows are boarded up, the furniture piled in the corners, and the bags packed. All the characters feel, and the audience sees in a thousand ways, that the wish to save the Orchard has amounted in fact to destroying it; the gathering of its denizens to separation; the homecoming to departure. What this "means" we are not told. But the action is completed, and the poem of the suffering of change concludes in a new and final perception, and a rich chord of feeling.

The structure of each act is based upon a more or less ceremonious social occasion. In his use of the social ceremony—arrivals, departures, anniversaries, parties—Chekhov is akin to James. His purpose is the same: to focus attention on an action which all share by analogy, instead of upon the reasoned purpose of any individual, as Ibsen does in his drama of ethical motivation. Chekhov uses the social occasion also to reveal the individual at moments when he is least enclosed in his private rationalization and most open to disinterested insights. The Chekhovian ensembles may appear superficially to be mere pointless stalemates— too like family gatherings and arbitrary meetings which we know off-stage. So they are. But in his miraculous arrangement the very discomfort of many presences is made to reveal fundamental aspects of the human situation.

That Chekhov's art of plotting is extremely conscious and deliberate is clear the moment one considers the distinction between the stories of his characters as we learn about them, and the moments of their lives which he chose to show directly onstage. Lopahin, for example, is a man of action like one of the new capitalists in Gorki's plays. Chekhov knew all about him, and could have shown us an exciting episode from his career if he had not chosen to see him only when he was forced to pause and pathetically sense his own motives in a wider context which qualifies their importance. Lyubov has been dragged about Europe for years by her ne'er-do-well lover, and her life might have yielded several sure-fire erotic intrigues like those of the commercial theater. But Chekhov, like all the great artists of modern times, rejected these standard motivations as both stale and false. The actress Arkadina, in *The Seagull*, remarks, as she closes a novel of Maupassant's, "Well, among the French that may be, but here with us there's nothing of the kind, we've no set program." In the context the irony of her remark is deep: she is herself a purest product of the commercial theater, and at that very time she is engaged in a love affair of the kind she objects to in Maupassant. But Chekhov, with his subtle art of plotting, has caught her in a situation, and at a brief moment of clarity and pause, when the falsity of her career is clear to all, even herself.

Thus Chekhov, by his art of plot-making, defines an action in the opposite mode to that of *Ghosts*. Ibsen defines a desperate quest for reasons and for ultimate, intelligible moral values. This action falls naturally into the form of the agon, and at the end of the play Ibsen is at a loss to develop the final pathos, or bring it to an end with an accepted perception. But the pathetic is the very mode of action and awareness which seems to Chekhov closest to the reality of the human situation, and by means of his plot he shows, even in characters who are not in themselves unusually passive, the suffering and the perception of change. The "moment" of human experience which *The Cherry Orchard* presents thus corresponds to that of the Sophoclean chorus, and of the evenings in the *Purgatorio*. *Ghosts* is a fighting play, armed for its sharp encounter with the rationalizing mind, its poetry concealed by its reasons. Chekhov's poetry, like Ibsen's, is behind the naturalistic surfaces; but the form of the play as a whole is "nothing but" poetry in the widest sense: the coherence of the concrete elements of the composition. Hence the curious vulnerability of Chekhov on the contemporary stage: he does not argue, he merely presents; and though his audiences even on Broadway are touched by the time they reach the last act, they are at a loss to say what it is all about.

It is this reticent objectivity of Chekhov also which makes him so difficult to analyze in words: he appeals exclusively to the histrionic sensibility where the little poetry of modern realism is to be found. Nevertheless, the effort of analysis must be made if one is to understand this art at all; and if the reader will bear with me, he is asked to consider one element, that of the scene, in the composition of the second act.

ACT II: THE SCENE AS A BASIC ELEMENT IN THE COMPOSITION

M. Cocteau writes, in his preface to *Les Mariés de la Tour Eiffel*: "The action of my play is in images (*imagée*) while the text is not: I attempt to substitute a 'poetry of the theater' for 'poetry in the theater.' Poetry in the theater is a piece of lace which it is impossible to see at a distance. Poetry of the theater would be coarse lace; a lace of ropes, a ship at sea. *Les Maries* should have the frightening look of a drop of poetry under the microscope. The *scenes* are integrated like the *words* of a poem."

This description applies very exactly to *The Cherry Orchard*: the larger elements of the composition—the scenes or episodes, the setting and the developing story—are composed in such a way as to make a poetry of the theater; but the "text" as we read it literally, is not. Chekhov's method, as Mr. Stark Young puts it in the preface to his translation of *The Seagull*, "is to take actual material such as we find in life and manage it in such a way that the inner meanings are made to appear. On the surface the life in his plays is natural, possible, and at times in effect even casual."

Mr. Young's translations of Chekhov's plays, together with his beautifully accurate notes, explanations, and interpretations, have made the text of Chekhov at last available for the English-speaking stage, and for any reader who will bring to his reading a little patience and imagination.* Mr. Young shows us what Chekhov means in detail: by the particular words his characters use; by their rhythms of speech; by their gestures, pauses, and bits of stage business. In short, he makes the text transparent, enabling us to see through it to the music of action, the underlying poetry of the composition as a whole—and this is as much as to say that any study of Chekhov (lacking as we do adequate and available productions) must be based upon Mr. Young's work. At this point I propose to take this work for granted; to assume the translucent text; and to consider the role of the setting in the poetic or musical order of Act II.

The second act, as I have said, corresponds to the agon of the traditional plot scheme: it is here that we see most clearly the divisive purposes of the characters, the contrasts between their views of the Cherry Orchard itself. But the center of interest is not in these individual conflicts, nor in the contrasting visions for their own sake, but in the common fatality which they reveal: the passing of the old estate. The setting, as we come to know it behind the casual surfaces of the text, is one of the chief elements in this poem of change: if Act II were a lyric, instead of an act of a play, the setting would be a crucial word appearing in a succession of rich contexts which endow it with a developing meaning.

Chekhov describes the setting in the following realistic terms. "A field. An old chapel, long abandoned, with crooked walls, near it a well, big stones that apparently were once tombstones, and an old bench. A road to the estate of Gaev can be seen. On one side poplars rise, casting their shadows, the cherry orchard begins there. In the distance a row of telegraph poles; and far, far away, faintly traced on the horizon, is a large town, visible only in the clearest weather. The sun will soon be down."

To make this set out of a cyclorama, flats, cut-out silhouettes, and lighting-effects, would be difficult, without producing that unbelievable but literally intended—and in any case indigestible—scene which modern realism demands; and here Chekhov is uncomfortably bound by the convention of his time. The best strategy in production is that adopted by Robert Edmund Jones in his setting for *The Seagull*: to pay

* The quotations from *The Cherry Orchard* are taken from the translation by Stark Young (New York: Samuel French). Copyright, 1947, by Stark Young. All rights reserved. Reprinted by permission of the author and Samuel French.

lip service only to the convention of photographic realism, and make the trees, the chapel and all the other elements as simple as possible. The less closely the setting is defined by the carpenter, the freer it is to play the role Chekhov wrote for it: a role which changes and develops in relation to the story. Shakespeare did not have this problem; he could present his setting in different ways at different moments in a few lines of verse:

> Alack! the night comes on, and the bleak winds
> Do sorely ruffle; for many miles about
> There's scarce a bush.

Chekhov, as we shall see, gives his setting life and flexibility in spite of the visible elements on-stage, not by means of the poetry of words but by means of his characters' changing sense of it.

When the curtain rises we see the setting simply as the country at the sentimental hour of sunset. Epihodov is playing his guitar and other hangers-on of the estate are loafing, as is their habit, before supper. The dialogue which starts after a brief pause focuses attention upon individuals in the group: Charlotta, the governess, boasting of her culture and complaining that no one understands her; the silly maid Dunyasha, who is infatuated with Yasha, Lyubov's valet. The scene, as reflected by these characters, is a satirical period-piece like the "Stag at eve" or "The Maiden's Prayer"; and when the group falls silent and begins to drift away (having heard Lyubov, Gaev, and Lopahin approaching along the path) Chekhov expects us to smile at the sentimental clichés which the place and the hour have produced.

But Lyubov's party brings with it a very different atmosphere: of irritation, frustration, and fear. It is here we learn that Lopahin cannot persuade Lyubov and Gaev to put their affairs in order; that Gaev has been making futile gestures toward getting a job and borrowing money; that Lyubov is worried about the estate, about her daughters, and about her lover, who has now fallen ill in Paris. Lopahin, in a huff, offers to leave; but Lyubov will not let him go—"It's more cheerful with you here," she says; and this group in its turn falls silent. In the distance we hear the music of the Jewish orchestra—when Chekhov wishes us to raise our eyes from the people in the foreground to their wider setting, he often uses music as a signal and an inducement. This time the musical entrance of the setting into our consciousness is more urgent and sinister than it was before: we see not so much the peace of evening as the silhouette of the dynamic industrial town on the horizon, and the approach of darkness. After a little more desultory conversation, there is another pause, this time without music, and the foreboding aspect of the scene in silence is more intense.

In this silence Firs, the ancient servant, hurries on with Gaev's coat, to protect him from the evening chill, and we briefly see the scene through Fir's eyes. He remembers the estate before the emancipation of the serfs, when it was the scene of a way of life which made sense to him; and now we become aware of the frail relics of this life: the old gravestones and the chapel "fallen out of the perpendicular."

In sharpest contrast with this vision come the young voices of Anya, Varya, and Trofimov who are approaching along the path. The middle-aged and the old in the foreground are pathetically grateful for this note of youth, of strength, and of hope; and presently they are listening happily (though without agreement or belief) to Trofimov's aspirations, his creed of social progress, and his conviction that their generation is no longer important to the life of Russia. When the group falls silent again, they are all disposed to contentment with the moment; and when Epihodov's guitar is heard, and we look up, we feel the country and the evening under the aspect of hope—as offering freedom from the responsibilities and conflicts of the estate itself:

> (*Epihodov passes by at the back, playing his guitar.*)
> Lyubov. (*Lost in thought.*) Epihodov is coming—
> Anya. (*Lost in thought.*) Epihodov is coming.
> Gaev. The sun has set, ladies and gentlemen.
> Trofimov. Yes.
> Gaev. (*Not loud and as if he were declaiming.*) Oh, Nature, wonderful, you gleam with eternal radiance, beautiful and indifferent, you, whom we call Mother, combine in yourself both life and death, you give life and take it away.
> Varya. (*Beseechingly.*) Uncle!

Gaev's false, rhetorical note ends the harmony, brings us back to the present and to the awareness of change on the horizon, and produces a sort of empty stalemate—a silent pause with worry and fear in it.

> (*All sit absorbed in their thoughts. There is only the silence. Firs is heard muttering to himself softly. Suddenly a distant sound is heard, as if from the sky, like the sound of a snapped string, dying away, mournful.*)

This mysterious sound is used like Epihodov's strumming to remind us of the wider scene, but (though distant) it is sharp, almost a warning signal, and all the characters listen and peer toward the dim edges of the horizon. In their attitudes and guesses Chekhov reflects, in rapid succession, the contradictory aspects of the scene which have been developed at more length before us:

> Lyubov. What's that?
> Lopahin. I don't know. Somewhere far off in a mine shaft a bucket fell. But somewhere very far off.
> Gaev. And it may be some bird—like a heron.
> Trofimov. Or an owl—
> Lyubov. (*Shivering.*) It's unpleasant, somehow. (*A pause.*)
> Firs. Before the disaster it was like that. The owl hooted and the samovar hummed without stopping, both.
> Gaev. Before what disaster?
> Firs. Before the emancipation.
> (*A pause.*)
> Lyubov. You know, my friends, let's go. . . .

Lyubov feels the need to retreat, but the retreat is turned into flight when "the wayfarer" suddenly appears on the path asking for money. Lyubov in her bewilderment, her sympathy, and her bad conscience, gives him gold. The party breaks up, each in his own way thwarted and demoralized.

Anya and Trofimov are left on-stage; and, to conclude his theatrical poem of the suffering of change, Chekhov reflects the setting in them:

> *Anya.* (*A pause.*) It's wonderful here today!
> *Trofimov.* Yes, the weather is marvelous.
> *Anya.* What have you done to me, Petya, why don't I love the cherry orchard any longer the way I used to? I loved it too tenderly; it seemed to me there was not a better place on earth than our orchard.
> *Trofimov.* All Russia is our garden. The earth is immense and beautiful. . . .

The sun has set, the moon is rising with its chill and its ancient animal excitement, and the estate is dissolved in the darkness as Nineveh is dissolved in a pile of rubble with vegetation creeping over it. Chekhov wishes to show the Cherry Orchard as "gone"; but for this purpose he employs not only the literal time-scheme (sunset to moonrise) but, as reflectors, Anya and Trofimov, for whom the present in any form is already gone and only the bodiless future is real. Anya's young love for Trofimov's intellectual enthusiasm (like Juliet's "all as boundless as the sea") has freed her from her actual childhood home, made her feel "at home in the world" anywhere. Trofimov's abstract aspirations give him a chillier and more artificial, but equally complete, detachment not only from the estate itself (he disapproves of it on theoretical grounds) but from Anya (he thinks it would be vulgar to be in love with her). We hear the worried Varya calling for Anya in the distance; Anya and Trofimov run down to the river to discuss the socialistic *Paradiso Terrestre;* and with these complementary images of the human scene, and this subtle chord of feeling, Chekhov ends the act.

The "scene" is only one element in the composition of Act II, but it illustrates the nature of Chekhov's poetry of the theater. It is very clear, I think, that Chekhov is not trying to present us with a rationalization of social change à la Marx, or even with a subtler rationalization à la Shaw. On the other hand, he is not seeking, like Wagner, to seduce us into one passion. He shows us a moment of change in society, and he shows us a "pathos"; but the elements of his composition are always taken as objectively real. He offers us various rationalizations, various images and various feelings, which cannot be reduced either to one emotion or to one idea: they indicate an action and a scene which is "there" before the rational formulations. or the emotionally charged attitudes, of any of the characters.

The surrounding scene of *The Cherry Orchard* corresponds to the significant stage of human life which Sophocles' choruses reveal, and to the empty wilderness beyond Ibsen's little parlor. We miss, in Chekhov's scene, any fixed points of human significance, and that is why, compared with Sophocles, he seems limited and partial—a bit too pathetic even for our bewildered times. But, precisely because he subtly and elaborately develops the moments of pathos with their sad insights, he sees much more in the little scene of modern realism than Ibsen does. Ibsen's snowpeaks strike us as rather hysterical; but the "stage of Europe" which we divine behind the Cherry Orchard is confirmed by a thousand impressions derived from other sources. We may recognize its main elements in a cocktail party in Connecticut or Westchester: someone's lawn full of voluble people; a dry white clapboard church (instead of an Orthodox chapel) just visible across a field; time passing, and the muffled roar of a four-lane highway under the hill—or we may be reminded of it in the final section of *The Wasteland*, with its twittering voices, its old gravestones and deserted chapel, and its dim crowd on the horizon foreboding change. It is because Chekhov says so little that he reveals so much, providing a concrete basis for many conflicting rationalizations of contemporary social change: by accepting the immediacy and unintelligibility of modern realism so completely, he in some ways transcends its limitations, and prepares the way for subsequent developments in the modern theater. . .

FROM *CHEKHOV THE DRAMATIST**

David Magarshack

In declaring that there was not a single pistol shot in *The Cherry Orchard,* Chekhov overlooked another remarkable feature which distinguishes his last play from all his other plays, namely that there is not a single love triangle in it, either. Indeed, Chekhov seems to have been so anxious that nothing should obscure the essentially comic character of the play that he eliminated everything from it that might introduce any deeper emotional undercurrents. The play, it is true, has plenty of emotional undercurrents, but they are all of a "comic" nature, that is to say, the ludicrous element is never missing from them. *The Cherry Orchard,* in fact, conforms entirely to Aristotle's definition of comedy as "an imitation of characters of a lower type who are not bad in themselves but whose faults possess something ludicrous in them". What—to take one instance—can be more ludicrous, nay, grotesque, than a typical patrician like Gayev, whose main characteristics, according to Chekhov, were "suavity and elegance," turning to his sister and demanding that she should choose between him and some absurd fool of a footman like Yasha? And is not the fact that Gayev became "a bank official" ludicrous, particularly as it is quite clear that he would not be able to hold down his job even for a month? And is not his sister's love affair ludicrous from beginning to end? (Chekhov was very anxious to make it absolutely clear that he regarded it as an unwarranted distortion of Lyubov Ranevsky's character to represent her on the stage as "subdued by suffering." In a letter to his wife he pointed out that "nothing but death could subdue a woman like that." He saw her as "tastefully but not gorgeously dressed; intelligent, very good-natured, absentminded; friendly and gracious to everyone, always a smile on her face." These are all the outward expressions of a woman who, as Charlotte says at the end of the first version of Act II, "has lost her life," or in other words has thrown it away on trifles, and it is this that forms the ludicrous or comic essence of her character.) Or—to take another instance—are not the circumstances leading up to the sale of the cherry

* David Magarshack, *Chekhov the Dramatist* (London: John Lehmann Ltd., 1952), pp. 272–287. Reprinted by permission of David Magarshack.

orchard and the Gayev estate ludicrous in the extreme? And is not the attitude of Gayev and his sister to this incident of the play ludicrous? At first the sale of the country seat, which has belonged to their family for generations, is regarded by them as a great tragedy, but does their attitude after the sale justify all the heartbreak which it has aroused? According to Chekhov's stage directions, Gayev in the last act says *gaily*: "Really, everything is all right now. Before the cherry orchard was sold we were all worried and upset, but afterwards when the question was finally and irrevocably settled we all calmed down and even felt cheerful. I am a bank official now—a financier—cannon off the red—and say what you like, Lyuba, you certainly look much better than you used to." To which his sister replies: "Yes, my nerves are much better, that's true. I'm sleeping well." That is hardly the way people in a tragedy would react to an event which forms the dramatic core of the play.

The misinterpretation of *The Cherry Orchard* as a tragedy (Stanislavsky, in the first flush of excitement after reading Chekhov's last play, rushed off a letter to Chekhov in which he vowed that it was a tragedy and not, as Chekhov insisted, a comedy) is mainly due to a misunderstanding of the nature of a comic character. A "comic" character is generally supposed to keep an audience in fits of laughter, but that is not always so. No one would deny that Falstaff is essentially a comic character, but his fall from favour is one of the most moving incidents in *Henry IV*. Don Quixote, too, is essentially a comic character, but what has made him immortal is his creator's ability to arouse the compassion and the sympathy of the reader for him. The same is true of the chief characters of *The Cherry Orchard*: the sympathy and compassion they arouse in the spectator should not be allowed to blind him to the fact that they are essentially comic characters. It should be the producer's aim to bring out their comic traits and not, as is all too often done, to sentimentalise them. All the characters in the play, in fact, with perhaps the single exception of the seventeen-year-old Anya, possess this unmistakably ludicrous streak in their natures which makes them into comic characters.

The main theme of the play is generally taken to be the passing of the old order, symbolised by the sale of the cherry orchard. But that theme was stale by the time Chekhov wrote his play. Alexander Ostrovsky had practically exhausted it, and so had many other Russian novelists and playwrights before Chekhov, who himself had already used it in *Platonov*. What is new about this theme is the comic twist Chekhov gave it. Stanislavsky, who was himself a member of the old order, could not help regarding the passing of the Gayev estate into the hands of a successful business man who had once been a peasant on it as a tragedy. But Chekhov belonged to "the lower orders" himself and he could therefore take a completely detached view of it. Not being personally involved, he saw the comedy of it all and gave it an artistic form of a play full of comic characters. Nothing indeed was further from Chekhov's thoughts than that his characters should spread a feeling of gloom among his audience. In reply to a telegram from Nemirovich-Danchenko who complained that there were too many "weeping characters" in the play, Chekhov wrote: "Where are they? There is only one such character —Varya, but that is because she is a crybaby by nature and her tears ought not to arouse any feelings of gloom in the audience. I often put down 'through tears' in my stage directions, but that shows only the mood of the characters and not tears."

The symbolism of the cherry orchard, then, has nothing to do with its sale. All it expresses is one of the recurrent themes in Chekhov's plays: the destruction of beauty by those who are utterly blind to it. "All Russia is our garden," Trofimov says to Anya at the end of Act II, and he adds: "The earth is great and beautiful and there are many wonderful places in it." And his words are meant not only as a consolation to Anya, but as a warning against the Lopakhins of this world, a warning that can be understood everywhere, since the menace of the speculative builder has been felt not only in Russia. The cherry orchard indeed is a purely aesthetic symbol which its owners with the traditions of an old culture behind them fully understand; to Firs it merely means the cartloads of dried cherries sent off to town in the good old days, and to Lopakhin it is only an excellent site for "development."

That the sale of the cherry orchard does not form the main theme of the play can also be deduced from the fact that the peripetia element has very little, if anything, to do with it. Indeed, the moment its owners appear on the stage, it ought to become clear to the discerning playgoer that they are certainly not going to save it. The whole dramatic interest of the play is therefore centred on Lopakhin, the future owner of the cherry orchard. "When I was writing Lopakhin's part," Chekhov wrote to Stanislavsky, "I could not help thinking of it as yours. It is true, Lopakhin is a merchant, but he is a decent fellow in every respect; he must behave with the utmost courtesy and decorum, without any vulgarity or silly jokes, and that is why it seemed to me that you would have handled this part, *the central one in the play*,[1] brilliantly. . . . In choosing an actor for this part," Chekhov added, "it must be borne in mind that such a serious and religious girl as Varya was in love with Lopakhin; she would never have fallen in love with some cheap moneymaker." And in a letter to Nemirovich-Danchenko Chekhov gave this further characterisation of Lopakhin: "Lopakhin—a white waistcoat and brown shoes, walks about waving his hands and taking large steps; he is always deep in thought—he walks along one straight line."

In this description Chekhov put his finger on the most essential point of Lopakhin's character. Lopakhin, Chekhov pointed out, "is not a

* My italics.

merchant in the vulgar sense of the word—that must be clearly understood. He must not be played as a loud and noisy man. There is no
need for him to be the typical merchant. He is a tender-hearted man."
Lopakhin, however, waves his hands about, that is, he is full of himself
as a successful business man and a self-made man, too, but he does not
realise that his success has killed the finest traits of his character: it has
killed the artist in him. He has, Trofimov remarks, the delicate fingers
and the sensitive soul of an artist. He makes a profit of forty thousand
roubles from his poppy seeds, but what really moves him is the fine
sight of his fields of poppies in flower. He walks through life like a blind
man, keeping to the one straight line which he believes has already led
him to success and which he hopes will lead him to even greater success.
Nothing in the world will convince him that it really leads him to failure,
the failure of a man who is deeply sensitive to beauty, but whose obses-
sion with worldly success makes him into a destroyer of beauty. It is
the absence of a conflict between the artist and the money-maker in
Lopakhin that makes him into a typically comic figure.

Lopakhin can well afford to buy the estate on which his father has
been a serf, but it never occurs to him to do so. At first he is absolutely
genuine in trying to save the estate for its owners, but in the end it is he
who becomes the owner of the estate—a complete reversal of the situation. It is the inner conflict between the son of the former serf and the
rich business man round which the peripetia element in the play revolves. At the very beginning of the play Chekhov makes use of a
device of the chorus element which gives the audience a vague hint
of what the development of the plot is going to be while leaving the
characters themselves completely in the dark. In *The Three Sisters* this
device is associated with Protopopov and the two lines about the bear
from Krylov's fable. In *The Cherry Orchard* it is more openly comic in
character. It occurs at the very beginning of Act I in the scene between
Varya and Anya:

> *Anya.* Well, what's happening? Have you paid the interest on the
> mortgage?
> *Varya.* Good heavens no.
> *Anya.* Oh dear, oh dear. . . .
> *Varya.* In August the estate will be sold.
> *Anya.* Oh dear—
> *Lopakhin (peeps through the door and bleats).* Bah-h-h! *(Goes out.)*

This is the first time the impending sale of the cherry orchard is
mentioned in the play and at once we get this comic intrusion of its
future owner: the peripetia element compressed in a few lines. Lopakhin's mocking bleat epitomises both the hopelessness of the position of
the hereditary owners of the estate and his own powerful position as the
heir of all the thousands of serfs whose sweat and toil went to the up-
keep of the old country mansion. ("The house," Chekhov was careful

to explain in a letter to his wife on October 14th, 1903, "is an old country mansion: at one time people lived in great style there and this ought to be felt in the staging. Wealthy and comfortable.") The symbolic meaning of this brief scene is much cruder than of the scene at the beginning of Act I of *The Three Sisters,* but this is so because *The Cherry Orchard* is a comedy while *The Three Sisters* is a "drama." On the realistic plane, it is true, Lopakhin's intrusion can be interpreted as merely showing his goodnatured contempt for Varya, whom Chekhov characterised in his correspondence as "a perfect fool," "a goodnatured fool," "a nun, a foolish creature," and, finally, as "crude and rather stupid, but very good-natured." She is the only "crybaby" in the play, a deeply religious girl who is in love with Lopakhin. It is both in his relations to Varya and in his attitude towards the owners of the Gayev estate that another side of the "comic" element in Lopakin's character is revealed. It is the serf in him he cannot get rid of. The long years of serfdom and humiliation have left an indelible mark on his soul. He does not cringe, it is true. He speaks to his former masters not as his superiors but as their equal. But deep down inside him the serf is still lurking. In the fine drawing room of the Gayev country house he can't help feeling that he is just a country yokel. He has plenty of money, but at heart he is still a common peasant.

This dualism in Lopakhin's nature is brought out at once in the opening scene of the play. That is why in spite of his "white waistcoat and brown shoes" the idea that he might become the owner of the Gayev estate never occurs to him. And that is why his marriage to a gentle-woman like Varya seems unreal to him, though when pressed by Mrs. Ranevsky in Act II, he declares that he is quite ready to marry her, and in Act IV when Mrs. Ranevsky again expresses her surprise at the way he and Varya are avoiding each other, he replies: "I must say I don't understand it myself. The whole thing is sort of queer. If there's still time, I'm quite ready even now to—Let's settle it once and for all, and let's get it done with. But," he adds significantly, "without you I feel I shall never propose to her." And that of course is quite true. Face to face with Varya he is so conscious of her social superiority that he can-not bring himself to propose to her, while Varya ("the perfect fool") is quite incapable of disregarding the conventions which demand that the lady has to wait for the gentleman to propose to her. It is to conceal this typically peasant feeling of awe for the gentry that is so deeply embed-ded in his character which makes Lopakhin treat Varya with such good-humoured contempt. When in Act II Varya, in reply to Mrs. Ranevsky's congratulations on the satisfactory result of her attempt to arrange a match between her and Lopakhin, exclaims *through tears,* "You mustn't joke about that, mother!" Lopakhin cannot but interpret this exclamation as an expression of Varya's reluctance to marry beneath her, and that is why he immediately hurls the two quotations from *Hamlet* at her. Lopakhin's contempt is expressed in his deliberate distortion of

Ophelia's name into its vulgarised Russian equivalent of "Okhmelia." And while it is quite possible that Lopakhin would use the first quotation without distorting it, namely "Okhmelia, get thee to a nunnery," he would never use the second quotation in its original form of "O nymph, in thy orisons be all my sins remember'd." Lopakhin, as he himself confesses, is an uneducated man. "My father," he tells Mrs. Ranevsky in Act II, "was a peasant, an idiot. He knew nothing and taught me nothing. Only beat me when he was drunk, and always with a stick. And I too am really the same stupid idiot. I haven't learnt anything and my handwriting is just awful—makes me feel ashamed before people." And a little earlier in the same act Chekhov gives us a hint of the sort of plays Lopakhin went to see in the snatch of a song from a a popular musical play he hums. "What a wonderful play I saw last night," he says. "It was very funny." It is quite clear that Lopakhin would never have seen *Hamlet* performed, and he most certainly never read it. He must have just heard people quoting from it and he could not possibly be expected to quote the second line from *Hamlet* correctly. Indeed, Chekhov himself makes him misquote the line. What Lopakhin says is: "Okhmelia, O nymph, remember me in your prayers!" To make Lopakhin use the exact quotation of this line on the English stage is to distort his character and give the audience quite a wrong impression of his background. (In *Platonov* Voynitsev quotes the same line correctly at the end of Act II.)

It is in Act II that the peasant in Lopakhin breaks through his "white waistcoat and brown shoes" and for once asserts himself. Why did Lopakhin buy the estate after all? He bought it because his chief opponent at the auction was not Gayev (he would never have bid against him) but another rich merchant like himself. Already in Act II Lopakhin sounds the alarm:

> *Lopakhin.* The rich merchant Deriganov is thinking of buying your estate. I'm told he's coming to the auction himself.
> *Mrs. Ranevsky.* Where did you hear that?
> *Lopakhin.* That's what they say in town.
> *Gayev.* Our Yaroslavl aunt has promised to send us money, but when and how much we don't know.
> *Lopakhin.* How much will she send? A hundred thousand? Two hundred?
> *Mrs. Ranevsky.* Well, I hardly think so. Ten or fifteen thousand at most, and we must be thankful for that.
> *Lopakhin.* I'm sorry, but such improvident people as you—such queer, unbusiness-like people—I've never met in my life. You're told in plain language that your estate is going to be sold and you don't seem to understand.
> *Mrs. Ranevsky.* But what are we to do? Please, tell us.
> *Lopakhin.* I tell you every day. Every day I say the same thing over and over again. You must let the cherry orchard and the land under buildings leases for summer cottages, and you must do it now, as

quickly as possible, or the auction will be on top of you! Try to understand! The moment you decide to let your land for summer cottages, you will be able to raise as much money as you like and you'll be saved.

Mrs. Ranevsky. Summer cottages and holiday-makers—excuse me, but it is so vulgar.

Gayev. I'm entirely of your opinion.

Lopakhin. I'll burst into tears or scream or have a fit. I can't stand it. You're driving me mad. (To Gayev.) You're an old woman!

Gayev. I beg your pardon?

Lopakhin. An old woman! (Gets up to go.)

Mrs. Ranevsky (in dismay). No, don't go. Please, stay. I beg you. Perhaps we'll think of something.

Lopakhin. What's there to think of?

Mrs. Ranevsky. Please, don't go. I feel so much more cheerful with you here. (Pause.) I keep expecting something to happen, as though the house were going to collapse on top of us.

As for Gayev, he does not seem to care whether the house collapses on top of him or not. He is *deep in thought,* wondering how to retrieve an imaginary billiard shot.

Even the intervention of another rich merchant, then, does not change the situation as far as Lopakhin is concerned. He still tries to save the estate for the two comic characters who even in the hour of their greatest peril are entirely ignorant of what is happening around them. It is only at the auction itself after Deriganov's first bid of "thirty thousand over and above the arrears," as Lopakhin, still apologetic in the hour of his greatest triumph, tells them at the ball, that he enters the fray himself. Nothing now stands in the way of his becoming the owner of the estate where "his father and grandfather were slaves and where they were not even admitted to the kitchen." But back at the country house he is once more overwhelmed by his old qualms of conscience: the serf re-awakens in him. When Mrs. Ranevsky presses him to tell her what happened at the auction, he is embarrassed, *afraid of betraying his joy,* as Chekhov puts it in his stage direction. His return as the owner of the Gayev estate, by the way, is accompanied by another comic interlude. As he enters, Varya hits him over the head with a stick. It is as if Varya, who had intended the blow for Yepikhodov, wanted to remind the new "squire" of his childhood beatings. (The stick is the symbol of the serf in Lopakhin.)

Lopakhin. Thank you very much.

Varya (angrily and ironically). I'm so sorry!

Lopakhin. It's all right, ma'am. I'm greatly obliged to you for the kind reception, I'm sure.

Varya. Don't mention it. (Walks away, then looks round and inquires gently.) I haven't hurt you, have I?

Lopakhin. Oh no, not at all. But there's going to be an enormous bump on my head for all that.

Even his triumphant entry into his new possessions (Lopakhin is so intoxicated with his transformation into a landed gentleman that he behaves like a man drunk), Chekhov marks by a comic incident:

Lopakhin. . . . (Ironically.) Here comes the new squire, the owner of the cherry orchard. (He tips over a little table accidentally, nearly upsetting the candelabra.)

But at first Lopakhin refuses to speak, and it is only after Gayev has rushed out of the room in tears, having handed to Firs the anchovies and the Kerch herrings he had not forgotten to bring from town in spite of the disaster of the auction, that he cannot hold out any longer.

Pishchik. Well, what happened at the auction? Come on, tell!
Mrs. Ranevsky. Has the cherry orchard been sold?
Lopakhin. It has.
Mrs. Ranevsky. Who bought it?
Lopakhin. I bought it. (Pause.)

It is a perfect climax brought about by only three short words, perhaps the most perfect climax in any of Chekhov's plays. The reversal of the situation is not only complete, it is not only underlined by the absurd ball arranged at that "inopportune moment," as Mrs. Ranevsky remarks earlier, humming a tune (did she really hope in spite of everything that the estate would somehow or other remain her property?), but it also contains a double surprise: "the most beautiful estate in the world" has passed out of the hands of its aristocratic owners and into the hands of the son of one of their former serfs. It is the last circumstance that in one blinding flash opens up the great social gulf that divides Lopakhin from the Gayevs. That is why Lopakhin is so terrifically excited. That is why Mrs. Ranevsky is so crushed by the news that *she would collapse if she were not standing near a table and a chair,* as the stage direction states. And would Varya have flung her keys with such contempt at Lopakhin's feet and stormed out of the room if she, too, had not become aware of the social implications of the sale of the cherry orchard? Lopakhin's remark as he picks up the bunch of keys that Varya "wanted to show that she was no longer mistress here" has a much wider implication than would appear at first sight. This indeed emerges from Lopakhin's words to Mrs. Ranevsky:

Lopakhin (reproachfully). Why, why did you not listen to me? You poor darling, you will never get it back now. (With tears.) Oh, if only all this could be over soon, if only our unhappy and disjointed life could somehow be changed soon!

The social implications of the play emerge more clearly in the character of Peter Trofimov. Here again Chekhov was faced with the dilemma of either having his play banned or getting it past the censorship by avoiding all purely controversial issues of a political nature. Writing to his wife on October 19th, 1903, he expressed his fear of "a certain incompleteness" in the characterisation of Trofimov. "You see," he wrote, "Trofimov has been exiled many times for his political views, he is being continually sent down from the university, and how is one to show all these things?" But even Trofimov, the only idealist in the play, is essentially a comic character. His exterior itself is comic. "A motheaten gentleman," a shrewd country woman called him, and Mrs. Ranevsky half cries and half laughs when she looks at his beard. But his outward appearance is merely a pointer to the deep-seated comic streak in his nature. He is "an eternal student" in more senses than one. He is the eternal adolescent because reason means everything to him and experience nothing. He belongs to those men who never really grow up because they can never see the distinction between what is reasonable and what is wise. Trofimov sees through everybody except himself. "For once in your life," he tells Mrs. Ranevsky in Act III, "you must looks truth straight in the face." But when it comes to himself, all he does is to utter cliches. "We are higher than love," he tells Mrs. Ranevsky apropos of himself and Anya. And when Mrs. Ranevsky exposes the silliness of such a remark by telling him that it is absurd for a man of his age not to have a mistress, all he can do is to deliver himself of another cliche: "All is finished between us!" and rush out of the room.

Chekhov underlines this comic streak in Trofimov's nature by involving him immediately in a comic incident.

> Mrs. Ranevsky (shouts after him). Peter, wait! You funny man, I was only joking.
> (Someone can be heard running quickly downstairs and suddenly falling down with a crash. Anya and Varya utter a scream, which is at once followed by laughter.)
> Mrs. Ranevsky. What's happened?
> (Anya runs in.)
> Anya (laughing). Peter fell down the stairs.
> Mrs. Ranevsky. What a queer fellow that Peter is!

And that is true: Peter is a queer fellow, but being queer does not prevent a man from having a great aim in life. Trofimov, besides, is the kind of idealist who not only dreams, but also works for the fulfilment of his dream. It is in that that he differs from Vershinin, whom he resembles in many other respects. It is through Trofimov's mouth that the theme of hard work as the key to future happiness is expressed in The Cherry Orchard. And it is to the seventeen-year-old Anya, who personifies this brighter future, that Trofimov turns for the realisation of his ideal of a better life. He sees it coming. "Already," he tells Anya at the end of Act II, "I can hear its footsteps. And," he adds, "if we never see it, if we never know it, what does it matter? Others will see it!"

Anya, who, according to Chekhov, "is first and foremost a child, lighthearted all through, and not crying once, except in Act II, and then she only has tears in her eyes," does not join in her mother's and uncle's lamentations over the sale of the cherry orchard. She is glad to bid fare-well to the past. "Goodbye, my home!" she exclaims gaily at the end of Act IV. "Goodbye, my old life!" And Trofimov echoes her confidently and ecstatically: "Welcome, new life!"

Chekhov endowed the minor characters of his last play with many purely farcical features without, however, sacrificing their essential humanity. Simeonov-Pishchik is such a broad comic figure, as his double-barrelled name implies. The first half of it is impressively aristocratic and the second farcical (its English equivalent would be Squeaker). Yepikhodov, too, is a broadly comic characterisation of a conceited half-wit who imagines himself a highly educated person because he possesses the bovine patience to wade through "learned" books he has not the brains to understand. The only love triangle in the play is that in which he figures—Yepikhodov-Dunya-Yasha—and it is entirely farcical. Chek-hov drew him partly from a well-known circus clown. Charlotte, another broadly comic character, was also partly drawn from life. While staying at Stanislavsky's country house during his wife's convalescence in 1902, he became friendly with the family of Stanislavsky's cousin Smirnov and it was at his house that he met an English governess ("A very plain girl, neither man nor woman," Stanislavsky's daughter described her), who seems to have been a very jolly person to whom Chekhov took a great liking. It was she he used for his model of Charlotte.

The two servants, Dunya and Yasha, are also broad comic figures. In *Platonov* Dr. Triletsky (Act II, Sc. 1) tells the two drunken footmen that they are "awfully like their masters," and that is also true of Dunya and Yasha. They are caricatures of their masters. The relations between them and their masters are not what one would expect the relations between servants and masters to be. Yasha openly makes fun of Gayev and treats his mistress almost like an equal. "If you go back to Paris," he says to her in Act III, "will you please take me with you. Do me a favour. It is absolutely impossible for me to stay here. You can see for yourself how uncivilised this country is. The people have no morals, it's so dull here, the food in the kitchen is horrible, and there's that Firs walking about the place and muttering all sorts of objectionable words. Take me with you, please!"

The "objectionable word" which Firs uses all through the play and which Yasha dislikes so much because it describes him so neatly, has been variously translated as "ne'er-do-well," "good for nothing," and even by one translator, who was obviously expressing his own views of Chekhov's characters, as "a job lot." Actually, the word Firs is so fond of happens to have been a word Chekhov himself often used during the last years of his life—*nedotyopa,* a very colloquial word which could perhaps be best translated by "duffer," which the Oxford English Dic-tionary defines as "a person without practical ability or capacity, or, generally, a stupid or foolish person." In his notebook Chekhov gave Varya, "the perfect fool," the family name of Nedotyopina. Another reference to the same word which occurs in Chekhov's note-book is: "*nedotyopa*—on the cross (in a graveyard) someone has written: Here lies a *nedotyopa*." Gayev, Trofimov, Mrs. Ranevsky and Yasha are all people "without practical ability or capacity," they are all "duffers" by nature. And, of course, so is Firs himself, whose loyalty to his masters is perhaps the most farcical, though also the most touching, thing in the whole play. "My life has slipped by as though I hadn't lived," he mutters at the end of the play, and those words could be used as his own epitaph. "Oh, you—duffer!" are his last words, addressed to himself.

In their attempts to wring the last drop of pathos out of the final scene of *The Cherry Orchard*, many producers tend to sentimentalise even Firs by leading their audiences to believe that he has been left to die by his lackadaisical masters. But there is nothing in the play to indicate that Chekhov's stage direction: "lies motionless" means "dies." If Chekhov had meant Firs to die, he would have said so. But in fact nothing could have been further from Chekhov's thoughts than to end his play with the death of an abandoned old servant. That would have introduced a completely alien note in a play which Chekhov never meant to be anything but a comedy.

The dying, melancholy sound of a broken string of a musical instrument (the Russian word does not specify the particular nature of the instrument, it might have been a balalaika), which first occurs in Act II and with which the play ends, is all Chekhov needed to convey his own attitude to the "dreary" lives of his characters. It was a sound Chekhov remembered from his own boyhood days when he used to spend his summer months at a little hamlet in the Don basin. It was there that he first heard the mysterious sound, which seemed to be coming from the sky, but which was caused by the fall of a bucket in some distant coalmine. With the years this sound acquired a nostalgic ring, and it is this sad, nostalgic feeling Chekhov wanted to convey by it. It is a sort of requiem for the "unhappy and disjointed" lives of his characters.

So many unnecessary tears have been shed in this play both on the stage and in the auditorium that it would seem almost hopeless to re-establish it as a comedy. It is much easier to misrepresent it as a tragedy than to present it for what it really is, namely "a comedy, and in places almost a farce." But unless it is treated as such, it will never be Chekhov's play.

It has been the purpose of this Essay to provide an analysis of the development of Chekhov's art as a dramatist and, particularly, of the "architecture" of his great plays. For without a thorough understanding of the problems which faced Chekhov when he embarked on the writing of indirect-action plays and the way he solved them, no proper answer can be given either to the perennial question of what it is all about or to the more fundamental question of whether or not these highly original plays contain "a suggestion of a desirable life," or, in other words, whether or not they show us not only life as it is, but also life at is should be. The contention, so frequently repeated and so firmly held, that Chekhov's favourite theme was disillusionment and that, moreover, he was, as Mr. MacCarthy expressed it, "the poet and apologist of ineffectualness," appears in the light of the foregoing argument to be wholly untenable. Nothing, indeed, could be further from the truth than the opinion expressed by Bernard Shaw in his Preface to *Heartbreak House* in a reference to *The Cherry Orchard*, an opinion, incidentally, that has probably shaped the attitude to Chekhov in England more than any other critical appraisal of his plays. "Chekhov," Shaw wrote, "more of a fatalist than Tolstoy, had no faith in these charming people extricating themselves. They would, he thought, be sold up and sent adrift by the bailiffs; therefore, he had no scruple in exploiting and flattering their charm." Now, Chekhov was certainly not a fatalist, nor did he dream of exploiting and flattering the charm of his characters; that is done by the producers and actors who find themselves entirely at sea in face of a drama that seems to defy every canon of stagecraft and yet contains such wonderful stage material; therefore, they fall back on the more obvious and dramatically insignificant details, the mere bricks and mortar of a Chekhov play which, without its steel frame, is more of a picturesque ruin than an enduring monument to a great creative artist.

SOME ASPECTS OF CHEKOV'S DRAMATURGY*

Robert W. Corrigan

I

Chekov's importance in the drama is due to the fact that he carried the realistic tradition of drama to its completion. If we take Ibsen as the pivotal figure of naturalism in the drama, we can go in one of two directions: toward the expressionism of Strindberg's later plays or toward the indirect realism of Chekhov's mature work. In Ibsen we find the realistic view centered in the struggles of a hero. This is not photographic naturalism; Ibsen tried to show that the greatest realities of human existence could be represented artistically by focusing them in the relationships of a strong central hero to himself, to those around him, and to society in general. Strindberg felt that the only reality was that of the dream, or at best of the secret inner workings of the mind. His last plays sharply point out the unreality of externals. Everything is fraudulent; people are not what they pretend to be and the only way to know them is to explore the shady recesses of their subconscious minds as manifested in their dreams.

Chekov went in the other direction. He viewed life in such a way that the greatest reality of existence was, in fact, the pretense that people wear like a mask through life. We must not, however, confuse this "mask" concept with the way it is used by Pirandello or Yeats. Like them, Chekov did believe that people do put on the appropriate mask to meet each situation in life; furthermore he believed that the mask stays on even when a person is alone. But, and here is the important difference, Chekov did not feel that the mask *is* the person. For Pirandello the appearance is the reality; Chekov saw the appearance as an apparent reality which hides the true nature of the individual. For example, in an often quoted passage written by Chekov while he was working on *The Wood Demon*, an early play which was later reworked to become *Uncle Vanya*, Chekov formulated an attitude toward the drama which has often been badly misinterpreted. He wrote:

* Robert W. Corrigan, "Some Aspects of Chekhov's Dramaturgy," *The Educational Theatre Journal*, VII (May 1955), 107–114. This article and the two following ones are reprinted by permission of the The Educational Theatre Association, Inc., Robert J. Schneidemann, Executive Secretary and Treasurer.

> The demand is made that the hero and the heroine (of a play) should be dramatically effective. But in life people do not shoot themselves, or hang themselves, or fall in love, or deliver themselves of clever sayings every minute. They spend most of their time eating, drinking, running after women or men, or talking nonsense. It is therefore necessary that this should be shown on the stage. A play ought to be written in which the people should come and go, dine, talk of the weather, or play cards, not because the author wants it but because that is what happens in real life. Life on the stage should be as it really is and the people, too, should be as they are and not stilted.[1]

The crucial sentences in the passage are: "But in life people do not shoot themselves, or hang themselves, or fall in love, or deliver themselves of clever sayings every minute. They spend most of their time eating, drinking, running after women or men, or talking nonsense. It is therefore necessary that this should be shown on the stage." In spite of these remarks, the fact remains that in Chekov's last four plays we do find occurring just those things which he said do not happen in life. Konstantin Treplev does kill himself in *The Sea Gull*. Solyony does shoot Tusenback in a duel in *The Three Sisters*; Vanya does try to shoot Serebryakov in *Uncle Vanya*. Uncle Vanya does say, "What a fine day to hang oneself!" Furthermore, Chekov's characters are always quoting and trying to be clever. And ironically we see that the people in his plays are always falling in love. Very seldom do we find Chekov's characters "running after women or men" in any active sense; they are rather inactively "falling in love" with one another. In fact, in those cases where "falling in love" becomes more than talk and is in any sense realized, it only more sharply points at the constant proclamations of love which never materialize.

Let us briefly look at one of his later plays. In *The Sea Gull* we discover seven occurrences of "falling in love." Konstantin with Nina, Nina with Trigorin, Masha with Konstantin, Polina with Dorn, Madame Arkadin with Trigorin, Medvedenko with Masha, and the unconscious and almost incestuous ambivalence of Konstantin for his mother, Madame Arkadin. In *The Sea Gull* half of these relationships are realized; Nina has an affair with Trigorin, Polina is married to Shamraev, Masha finally marries Medvedenko, and the affairs of Madame Arkadin and Trigorin goes on throughout the play. These relationships are normal, dull, and quite true to life; they are "what happen in real life." Nina's affair is brief and fruitless; Polina is dully but inextricably married to Shamraev; Masha marries Medvedenko out of frustration and proceeds to make life miserable for him; and Madame Arkadin and Trigorin stick together not only out of weakness, but because of their common need for a mutual admiration society. But here is my point: the chief function

[1] As quoted in David Magarshack, *Chekov as Dramatist* (London, 1952), p. 84.

of these realized relationships is to focus our attention on those relationships which never are and never can be realized. Chekov is thus able to present a truer picture of life "as it is" and to represent that inner world of emotion which exists under the mask of outward appearance.

His drama is an attempt to show what the nature of man's existence is in reality—an attempt to show life as it is. He achieves this by heightening the apparent reality to such a point that it becomes ludicrous; in this way we come to recognize the meaning of the all-important inner world of emotion which exists beneath the surface. This results in a dramaturgy which is much more complex than that required by either Ibsen's or Strindberg's art. Rather than doing away with appearances, he works indirectly through them in order to present reality. Thus his mature plays, aptly called dramas of indirection, neither concentrate the experience of reality into a hero, nor do they reduce experience to the subconscious reality of the dream. Since Chekov works indirectly through appearance to reality, his dramaturgy is at once oblique and inferential in its nature. What does this mean in terms of his dramaturgy? What effect will it have on the structure of his plays?

II

The first factor to be considered is that Chekov always presents what he sees to be the truth of reality in an exaggerated way. He cannot show both appearance and reality simultaneously unless he disguises the reality in exaggeration. Thus we find in all of Chekov's plays characters making brilliantly incisive remarks about the nature of things and yet they are said in such a way and are put in such an incongruous and ludicrous context that we do not stop to take them seriously when we hear them. The force of these statements is driven home cumulatively; we are suddenly aware as the act of the play ends that the characters have done just the opposite in their actions to what they have expounded they should do in their dialogue. These flashes of self-revelation have been more than static, isolated, and disconnected statements of opinion; despite all their apparent ludicrousness, they have become ironically true. Thus, Yelena in *Uncle Vanya* says to Sonya in the second act:

> You must not look at people that way. It isn't right. You must trust and believe in people, *(pause)* or life becomes impossible.

Even at this point in the play we know that this is just what Yelena does not do. We tend to laugh at the incongruity of the situation; but as we leave the theatre, our stomachs begin to squirm as the truth of her statement begins to sink in. Look at Yelena and you can see in dramatic terms just how impossible life can really become. But Chekov has achieved his effect indirectly.

In order to work in this manner Chekov is required to change the generally accepted view of presenting character in his plays. He must ask himself the question: "How can I make this exposition of truths both plausible and ludicrous?" He achieves it by making all his characters dramatize themselves. They all become, as does Astrov, introspective and consumed with critical self-analysis. This is not done in order that they may know themselves, but rather to heighten themselves in their own opinion: such is Konstantin's discussion of his art in *The Sea Gull* or Kuligin's gift of his book to Vershinin in *Three Sisters*. They look inward and see all their problems—real or imaginary—and then they build them up with great enjoyment. They either wallow sentimentally in themselves, or they project their own inadequacies and failures on to others.

The young Chekov showed remarkable insight into human nature when, in his early "That Worthless Fellow Platonov," he has Triletsky point out to Platonov that Marya is not a fool, but merely a victim of his dissatisfaction with his own life. "There are moments, my friend," he tells Platonov, "when one wants to hate someone, to take it out of someone, to make someone suffer for something one is ashamed of. So why not try it on with her? She's just the person for it. She is weak, timid, and quite stupidly trustful, so far as you are concerned." Chekov presented this idea dramatically in Act II of *Uncle Vanya* in the bitter opening scene where Serebryakov almost destroys Yelena (if she could be destroyed) in his attempts to justify a life which he knows has been a failure.

This self-dramatization makes it necessary for each of Chekov's characters to build and then operate in his own little world. To be completely self-centered makes social responsibility of any kind nearly impossible. Each character has his own thoughts and problems with which he is usually morbidly consumed. As a result the people in Chekov's plays never seem to hear or notice one another. Each has room only for himself and each acts in a social vacuum. The world of *The Cherry Orchard* or of *Uncle Vanya* is one world, but its unity is that of similarity. Each of the characters is an individual world and this is the common, unifying element of the play's world.

And yet it is not always easy to keep the walls of these private worlds from breaking down. We notice that Chekov generally sets his characters in restricted areas. The interiors are always closely confined rooms; the exteriors are usually attached to the house or are near by; and always the settings in their confinement symbolically mirror the play's action. This is most brilliantly seen in *Three Sisters* where there is a progression of settings parallel to Natasha's victory over Andrey and his three sisters. The first act opens with the three sisters in the drawing room dominating the action, and the act ends with the visit of Natasha. The second act opens with Natasha, now married to Andrey, carrying her sinister candle and in control of the drawing room; she soon suggests that Irina move. into Olga's room so that the baby may have a warm nursery. The third act finds the two sisters together in one room; Andrey is allowed only in his study, and Natasha, still with candle, is suggesting that her child by Protopopov be put in the study. The fourth act opens with all the sisters out of doors and about to leave the Prozorov mansion; Andrey is outside wheeling his child in a buggy, while Natasha and Protopopov are inside with their child playing "The Maiden's Prayer" on the piano. Chekov symbolically brings the eviction to an end by having Andrey follow Tchebutykin's advice "to take your stick and walk off" —to accept the role of the wandering "mendicant."

Chekov's characters are always in contact with one another and it is sometimes difficult to maintain a complete self-centeredness. As a result all of the characters must have a protective escape to which they can resort if too much is demanded of them. *The Cherry Orchard* is filled with escapes from reality. Notice the constant reference to stimulants: coffee, tea, vodka, brandy, and kvass for the peasants. For some, like Sonya in *Uncle Vanya,* unknowing religious belief is an escape; for others, such as Vanya, it is sleep; for Astrov it is beauty; for Gaev it is billiards and gum drops; for Andrey it is his violin and his book; and for the rest (and especially Vanya, Sonya, and Irina) it is work. No matter what the nature of the escape may be, they are all means by which Chekov's characters can return to their own little personal world when outside demands become too great.

III

This fact also explains another element of Chekov's drama. We are continually told that Chekov is funny; in fact, Chekov calls most of his plays comedies. Yet we know that the lines themselves are very seldom humorous. I do not believe that Chekov's plays are comic in the sense that Magarshack suggests in his valuable book *Chekov as Dramatist.* Magarshack states that Chekov's plays conform more or less to "Aristotle's definition of comedy as 'an imitation of characters of a lower type who are not bad in themselves but whose faults possess something ludicrous in them.' " [2] Chekov is imitating an action larger than this, and Aristotle's definition (when applied to Chekov's plays) is not only limiting, but it excludes those elements of isolation, defeat, and futility in the plays which Magarshack, I believe, unsuccessfully tries to reinterpret.

Essentially, the comedy lies in the incongruous order of the dialogue. The incongruous substitution of what is for what ought to be is funny. All comedy is one kind of exemplification of the proposition that nothing actual is wholly logical. As a result one character in Chekov's plays says something that makes sense and is important in terms of his own little world. The person with whom he is talking is in his own little

[2] Ibid., p. 272.

world; and if he is listening at all, it is within an entirely different context. This results in a reply which makes very little sense. The comedy
is further heightened when the first character continues as if the second
had made a logical reply. Chekov achieves a comic effect as well as an
ironic comment on the action by this chaotic presentation of conflicting
actions and speeches. We recall a passage from Act II of *Three Sisters*
which illustrates this chaos:

> *Masha:* Gogol says: It is boring to live in this world, gentlemen.
> *Tusenbach:* And I say: It is difficult to argue with you, gentlemen! Why
> you completely . . .
> *Tchebutykin:* (*Reading a newspaper.*) Balzac was married in Ber-
> ditcheff . . .
> *Irina:* (*As she lays out cards for patience, musing*) Balzac was married
> in Berditcheff.
> *Tusenbach:* The die is cast. You know, Maria Sergeyevna, I have
> tendered my resignation.

Such dialogue not only provides the essence of Chekov's humor, but as
Henry Popkin pointed out:

> Such dialogue gives us an ironic insight into the unimportance of
> self-importance. As the loose talk spills out in all directions, a few
> persistent souls endeavor to interpret their precious individualities and
> encounter obstacles—the precious individualities of others. Trying
> to communicate out of their solitude, they are able to convey only to
> the audience in the theatre. The superficial chaos, it turns out, con-
> ceals a perfectly constructed ironic mechanism for the display of
> human frailty.[3]

Finally, let us take one example from *Uncle Vanya*. In the first act
Vanya has been arguing with his mother and he concludes by saying, "It
is a fine day to hang oneself!" This line is immediately followed by the
old maid coming in to look for the chickens. "Here chick, chick, chick,"
she says. In her world of doing her job this is a perfectly logical line; but
coming after Vanya's ironic self-dramatizing, it is not only immensely
funny, but it acts as a commentary on Vanya's line. The result is a kind
of grotesque humor which makes us laugh with a lump in our throat. It is
funny until we realize the total implications of our laughter.

IV

This brings us back to the matter of masks. Chekov is too much of an
artist and a realist to portray such characters in a unilateral way. Realistically he knows that such people cover their main psychic abnormal-
ities and shortcomings with those masks which they think will best hide
their real selves, thus ironically exposing themselves more clearly than

---

[3] Henry Popkin, "Chekov, the Ironic Spectator," *Theatre Arts,* XXXVI
(March, 1952), 17.

ever. For example, in *Uncle Vanya*, Yelena's distant dallying with love only more sharply shows us her complete inability to love and incapacity to be loved. This accounts for another aspect of Chekov's dramaturgy. Artistically Chekov knew that no audience would ever be able to stand the raw emotions of such people in a clinical case-history manner. There must be some kind of aesthetic distance provided so that the audience does not empathize and identify itself too strongly with the characters on the stage. We are meant to identify ourselves sympathetically with each of the play's characters and yet Chekov wishes us to view them objectively.

The mask serves the all-important function of breaking down our sympathy after Chekov has allowed it to grow. When Gaev makes his pathetic speech to the bookcase, we feel extreme pity that he could be so deluded. Our sympathy mounts, and suddenly Gaev himself, cannoning off the red with his billiard cue, admits the rhetorical ludicrousness of the speech; and our sympathy is shattered. We once again view Gaev with a kind of detached objectivity. We have already noted that this creates much of the comic element in Chekov's plays; it further requires something more of him as a dramatist. He must include in his plays these pin-points of reality. Gaev must see his ludicrousness; Lyubov must be aware of her childishness; Yelena see that she is incapable of loving; Vanya realize his failure without rhapsodizing; in short, each character must know his own reality. For the dramatist to achieve this he cannot depend on certain moments of clarity. No audience could accept them; he therefore gives his plays a base which is set in preciseness of fact and detail. Note how in the first scene of *The Cherry Orchard* Epihodov says, "It is chilly this morning, three degrees of frost, though the cherries are still in flower." As the play is drawing to a close—it is now autumn—Lopakhin remarks:

> This time last year we had snow already, if you remember; but now it's so fine and sunny. Though it's cold, to be sure—three degrees of frost.

The play begins and ends with that kind of specific detail which gives it a foundation in reality. Another example: we know that the debt is due on the 22nd of August. In short, the whole action is tied up and encased in this realistic preciseness of fact.

Finally, we come to the last point related to this idea of masks. Chekov makes no mortal judgments about his characters; nor does he demand that we make them. In his plays there are neither heroes nor villains, only people. In a letter to his brother, Alexander, written October 13, 1887, he writes:

> Our modern playwrights stuff their plays exclusively with angels, villains and buffoons—go and find these elements in the whole of Russia! . . . I wanted to be original: there is not a single villain or

angel in my play (though I could not resist the temptation of putting in a few buffoons). I have not found anyone guilty, nor have I acquitted anyone.[4]

And again in a letter written to Suvorin on May 30, 1888, he says:

The creative artist must not set himself up as a judge of his characters or of their opinions, but must be an impartial witness. If I happen to hear a rather confused discussion about pessimism which does not solve anything, I have to report this conversation in the form in which I heard it, and it is for the members of the jury, i.e. for my readers, to express an opinion about it. My business consists in being talented, that is, in being able to distinguish the important depositions from the unimportant ones and in being able to throw light on my characters and to speak their language. . . .[5]

Three Sisters seems to be the exception to this statement. Natasha, Protopopov, and Solyony are destructive forces of evil; and Andrey and his sisters are destroyed. Even here, however, we never sense that Chekov as playwright or as man is standing over his creations in judgment. Chekov wants us to identify ourselves sympathetically with each of the play's characters, and yet he knows that we must view them objectively. The result: tragicomic pity; the wisdom of objectification which comedy affords and the pity of subjectification which tragedy demands. Structurally Chekov achieves this by constantly having his characters deflate us. The fact that they all live in their own little private worlds precludes our entering them for long, and as we begin to enter in we are thrust out by the character's self-revelation. We note also that the characters do not make such judgments about one another. Gaev knows about his sister's behavior in France, but he can never condemn her for it, nor does he praise her. It is rather a kind of neutral acceptance of both good and bad. This tone is achieved by the many contrasts that run throughout his plays. Everything from the main thematic material to the smallest detail is juxtaposed in such a way that we can never identify with a character long enough to make any moral judgments about him.

V

All of these facts lead to the final element of Chekovian dramaturgy on which I wish to focus in this essay: the aestheticizing of life. All of the people in Chekov's plays are seen to be either consciously or uncon-

[4] The Life and Letters of Anton Chekov, eds. S. S. Koteliansky and Philip Tomlinson (London, 1925), p. 93.

[5] Ibid., p. 110.

sciously realizing their own inadequacies as people. They realize that in one way or another they have failed as human beings, and they therefore attempt to make their lives like works of art. Consider Astrov's remarks about Yelena in the second act of *Uncle Vanya:*

> Everything ought to be beautiful in a human being; face, and dress, and soul, and ideas. She is beautiful, there is no denying that, but. . . . You know she does nothing but eat, sleep, walk about, fascinate us all by her beauty—nothing more. She has no duties, other people work for her. . . .

> I have grown old, I have worked too hard, I have grown vulgar, all my feelings are blunted, and I believe I am not capable of being fond of anyone. I don't love anyone . . . and I don't believe I ever shall. What still affects me is beauty. That does stir me. I fancy if Yelena Andre-yevna, for example, wanted to, she could turn my head in one day. . . .

Finally, he forces the affair with Yelena; his outburst is not one of physical passion but a reaction to her beauty which culminates in his asking her to keep a tryst in a beautiful forest arbor. We are reminded of Hedda Gabler's request that Lövborg kill himself beautifully through the head. Thus the man who has failed, who is incapable of loving anyone, attempts to substitute an erotic picture of idyllic love for a mature and demanding relationship.

This is also seen in the way Chekov's characters are extremely conscious of how they say things rather than what they say. In the third act of *The Cherry Orchard* Epihodov says to Varya: "I beg you to express yourself with delicacy." He does not care what is said as long as it is said beautifully. This also is one explanation for the numerous quotations from the works of other authors in Chekov's plays. In many ways there is a direct parallel between *The Sea Gull* and *Hamlet*. In *The Cherry Orchard* there are many quotations from *Hamlet, Macbeth,* Tolstoy's *Magdalene,* and the works of Ostrovsky. In *Uncle Vanya* there are literary allusions to Ostrovsky, Gogol, Batuskov, Turgenev, and Shakespeare. The people in Chekov's plays are always quoting, talking, talking; in short, finding comfort in words. They are giving meaning to their otherwise empty lives through words by giving their words artistic form.

This trait is further developed when we notice the great concern for outward beauty. Trofimov is partially rejected because he has grown ugly; Anya has become so beautiful that she becomes untouchable. It is much like the Astrov-Yelena relationship in *Uncle Vanya*. There is the fear that if the beauty is ever touched that it will wilt like the "Autumn Roses."

Trofimov is that character in which this aestheticization of life has been carried to its furthest limits. Like Astrov, he has become a walking vegetable, an emotional turnip. He loves life and the beauties of nature, but he hates anything animal or physical. Thus his whole relationship with Anya is vegetative. He wants to look at her, but even the slightest trace of physical desire is repulsive. He cannot accept the responsibility of human-animal existence and must escape in this ideal life which is bloodless but extremely beautiful.

When one reads the plays of Chekov, and through an increased understanding of his complex dramaturgy comes to know Chekov's characters, he is soon faced with two unsolvable problems. First, Chekov's art seems to be beyond total comprehension; and second, critical analysis, no matter how penetrating, seems to devitalize his plays to the point that it is almost possible to forget Chekov's warm humanity. Such analysis could almost make one expect a production of Chekov to bring us a stage full of maladjusted and physically distorted figures who would tend to torture us as they destroyed each other during the play. Chekov, however, was neither a clinical psychologist nor a naturalistic photographer. He knew, as we have already described, that there must be some kind of aesthetic distance provided so that the audience does not empathize and identify itself too fully with the characters on the stage. Chekov wanted the audience to realize the entire scope of the situation. The result is a group of plays dealing with as frightening themes as can be found in dramatic literature encased in a kind of brittle and translucent comedy. We tend to laugh throughout the plays and yet between the acts and as the curtain is finally drawn we are aware of the terror of the situation and are deeply and finally moved.

Thus Chekov the artist, the realist, and the poet has constructed a group of plays in which horror and humor—the most essential of many contrasts—are juxtaposed in such a way that the audience, by seeing life artistically imitated within the limitations of the stage medium, can leave the theatre taking with it additional insights into the problems of reality.

SPEECH AS ACTION IN CHEKHOV'S
*THE CHERRY ORCHARD**

Irving Deer

Both directors and actors are confronted with many perplexing problems when they deal with Chekhov's full length plays. Perhaps the most perplexing are those which they meet in the attempt to discover and express the dramatic significance of Chekhov's dialogue. The difficulty is not that Chekhov's dialogue requires any unusual acting techniques, but rather that it had no obvious form. It seems to be rambling, disconnected, and irrelevant. Take for example a brief scene from the first act of *The Three Sisters*. Olga has been grading papers and thinking aloud about her father's funeral, the drudgery of her job, and her long held hope of going to Moscow. Irina picks up the Moscow refrain and then Olga again goes into one of her "catch-all" speeches:

> You look radiant today, lovelier than ever. And Masha is lovely, too. Andrey would be good looking if he hadn't got so heavy, it's not becoming to him. And I've grown older, a lot thinner; it must be because I get cross with the girls. Now that I'm free today and am here at home and my head's not aching. I feel younger than yesterday. I'm only twenty-eight. . . . It's all good, all God's will, but it seems to me if I had married and stayed at home all day long, it would have been better. (A pause) I'd have loved my husband.[1]

When one realizes how much of this kind of associative talk goes on in Chekhov, it is not too difficult to understand why some critics (Walter Kerr and William Archer, for example) see in Chekhov's plays only a formless mass without conflict or progession.

The apparent formlessness of Chekhov's dialogue is even more clear when we compare Olga's speech with a more conventional speech in modern drama, say a speech by Lady Utterword in Shaw's "Chekhovian"

---

* Irving Deer, "Speech as Action in The Cherry Orchard," *The Educational Theatre Journal*, X (March 1958), 30–34. Reprinted by permission of *The Educational Theatre Journal*.

[1] Anton Chekhov, *The Three Sisters*, Stark Young, trans. (New York, 1941), p. 5.

play, *Heartbreak House*. Lady Utterword is home after an absence of twenty-three years and she finds everything as chaotic as ever. Her father and the nurse are disrespectful. She cannot even get a cup of tea. "Sitting down with a flounce on the sofa," she says to Ellie Dunn, who also has not been received properly:

> I know what you must feel. Oh, this house, this house! I come back to it after twenty-three years; and it is just the same: nobody at home to receive anybody, no regular meals, nobody ever hungry because they're always gnawing bread and butter or munching apples, and what is worse the same disorder in ideas, in talk, in feeling. When I was a child I was used to it: I had never known anything better, though I was unhappy, and longed all the time—Oh, how I longed! to be respectable, to be a lady, to live as others did, not to have to think of everything for myself. . . . And now the state of the house! the way I'm received! the casual impudence of that woman Guinness. . . . You must excuse my going on in this way; but I am really very much hurt and annoyed and disillusioned: . . .[2]

Like Olga, Lady Utterword is also "thinking aloud" about her home, her past and her family. She also is distressed. But unlike Olga, her speech is obviously prompted by events around her. She feels herself horribly insulted and everything she says represents her reaction against those who affront her sense of conventional decency. She sticks to the point; her ideas are clearly connected. The speech is obviously dramatic.

Even when the ideas in a Chekhov speech are clearly and logically connected, the speech is often confusing for another reason. Conventionally, speech in drama is a device for simultaneous two way communication: the characters talk directly with each other and at the same time they talk indirectly to the audience. But in Chekhov, these two functions of dialogue seem often separated. The characters seem to be talking to themselves in a daze primarily for the purpose of giving the audience direct exposition. Chekhov appears to have done Scribe one better. Scribe had to have two servants dusting while they gave the audience background information. Chekhov can get by with only one character, who need not even be dusting.

Consider, for example, the opening conversation between Lopahin and Dunyasha in *The Cherry Orchard*. Lopahin, the merchant, and Dunyasha, the maid, have been anxiously awaiting the train which will bring Madame Ranevskaya and her entourage. Dunyasha tells Lopahin that the train has arrived. He answers: ". . . thank God . . . But how late was the train? Two hours at least. (Yawning and stretching.) I'm a fine one, I am, look what a fool thing I did!—You could have waked me up."

---

[2] George Bernard Shaw, *Selected Plays of George Bernard Shaw*, Vol. I (New York, 1948), p. 495.

Dunyasha then replies: "I thought you had gone. (Listening) Listen, I think they are coming now." Lopahin listens and then says:

> No—no, there's the luggage and one thing and another. (A pause) Lyuboff Andreyevna has been living abroad five years. I don't know what she is like now—She is a good woman. An easy-going simple woman. I remember when I was a boy about fifteen, my father, who is at rest—in those days he ran a shop here in the village—hit me in the face with his fist, my nose was bleeding—we'd come to the yard together for something or other, and he was a little drunk. Lyuboff Andreyevna, I can see her now, still so young, so slim, led me to the wash-basin here in this very room, in the nursery. "Don't cry," she says, "little peasant, it will be well in time for your wedding"— (a pause) Yes, little peasant—My father was a peasant truly, and here I am in a white waistcoat and yellow shoes. Like a pig rooting in a pastry shop—I've got this rich, lots of money, but if you really stop and think of it, I'm just a peasant—(turning the pages of a book) Here I was reading a book and didn't get a thing out of it. Reading and went to sleep. (A pause)[3]

As if she had not heard a word, Dunyasha replies: "And all night long the dogs were not asleep, they know their masters are coming."

As we can see, Lopahin and Dunyasha communicate with each other only occasionally. Although they both share the stage, they seem to be talking more to themselves than to each other. Lopahin's long monologue seems to be there merely to get background information across to the audience. Dunyasha does not engage in any conflict with Lopahin which would force him to talk at such length. She either knows most of what he says or she is not interested in it at the moment. It does not affect her in any way. There seems to be no dramatic relationship between the characters or between them and the situation in which they find themselves.

When a Shakespearean character speaks to himself, he is obviously engaging in a struggle which is an expression of the central conflict of the play and which leads to new action. Take Macbeth's "If it were done when 't is done" speech for example. Everything Macbeth says there expresses his struggle to overcome his qualms of conscience or his fear of retribution. This speech is part of the process by which he whips himself up to the point of murdering Duncan. Like Shakespeare's soliloquies, most modern soliloquies are obviously relevant to the central conflict and plot of the play. When Peer Gynt, for example, expostulates to himself on the beauty of Anitra the slave girl,[4] we are not at a loss for one moment. We have seen his daydreaming tendencies before. The contrast between his idealized version of the girl and her dirty

[3] Chekhov, *The Cherry Orchard*, Stark Young, trans. (New York, 1947), pp. 3–4.

[4] Henrik Ibsen, *Peer Gynt* (London, 1950), p. 138–39.

legs and selfish actions shows us immediately not only what kind of a man Peer is, but also points ahead to his financial ruin at her hands.

Even if we suppose that Lopahin is in a semi-conscious state, and therefore cannot be expected to talk with as much point as Macbeth or Peer Gynt, the speech still seems mere verbiage. Arthur Miller's salesman, Willy Loman, is a dazed and broken character who often talks to himself. But although he may be dazed and prone to "lose himself in reminiscences," Miller always makes obvious the meaning of Willy's speeches to himself. As the flashbacks which usually attend Willy's "thinking aloud" sessions indicate, he is either trying to relive an idealized dream of the past, or he is punishing himself for having committed some wrong. On the other hand, nothing Lopahin says seem to express his feelings or desires. It is no wonder then that directors and actors have difficulty understanding how Chekhov's speech reveals character or expresses the conflicts within the play.

But a close examination of the dialogue reveals that Lopahin's rambling remarks are, in fact, actually expressive of internal conflict which is an integral part of the central conflict of the play. Lopahin has only partially accomplished his purpose of greeting the Ranevskayas by going to the Cherry Orchard. Once there, instead of going to the station to meet the returning party, he goes to sleep. Upon awakening, he chides himself for not completing his purpose. He both starts and ends his musings on this chiding note. He seems to be scolding some impulse or desire within himself which has prevented his conscious will from achieving its aim.

Lopahin is torn by guilt for deeper causes, however, than mere oversleeping. He questions his right even to be at the Cherry Orchard. "My father was a peasant truly, . . . I'm just a peasant [too] . . ." As a peasant by birth and upbringing, he feels that he is subservient to the Ranevskayas. He still remembers the time when the honor of being in the nursery could compensate for his father's beatings. Yet, as a freed serf, he has the money and the desire to be an aristocrat. He scolds himself for desiring to rise above his class, "like a pig rooting in a pastry shop," and yet he wants to do just that. Thus, when he meditates upon the incongruity of the peasant in white waistcoat, he is struggling to reconcile the conflicting desires within himself.

He is so torn by conflicting desires that even his attempt to "talk himself awake" becomes a form of day dreaming. For at the very moment that he is trying to "wake up" so that he can greet the Ranevskayas, he goes into a kind of reverie about what the orchard has meant to him in the past: "I remember when I was a boy about fifteen . . . ." His reverie begins as an attempt to define his problem, but it becomes a means of escaping from it. By concentrating on what appears to him an insoluble conflict, he loses the will to act. Instead he ends by merely scolding himself because he really does not properly use his aristocratic skill of reading. He substitutes recognition of his problem for solution of the problem.

Lopahin's apparently non-functional speech is really functional in several ways. In the first place, it is a means by which he chides himself for shirking his responsibilities toward the Ranevskayas. Second, it helps to build up in his own mind the importance of those responsibilities and to define them more clearly so that he will try harder to accomplish them. And third, it allows him to talk and thus escape the reality of his problems by letting him concentrate on merely recognizing the problem instead of on trying to solve it. Since the third of these functions is opposed to the other two, Lopahin's speech works like his dream-seeking action: it sets up a tension which keeps him acting in the attempt to reconcile the contradictions within himself.

All of the major characters in the play face problems similar to Lopahin's: like him, they are torn by contradictory impulses and desires. Madame Ranevskaya and Gayeff can passionately desire to save the Orchard at any cost, and yet refrain completely from doing anything to save it because they desire to keep the Orchard intact as a symbol of past bliss. Anna and Trofimoff can love each other deeply and yet refrain from marriage because of their dedication to abstract ideals.

Since the characters' attempts to achieve any of their important aims are thwarted by their opposing desires, like Lopahin they indulge in daydreams. But again like Lopahin, they do even this for two opposing reasons: one, to reaffirm their aims, and two, to escape from the difficulties they have in achieving those aims. Madame Ranevskaya and Gayeff grow angry when faced with reality of their problems, and like Lopahin, they escape into the past. Madame Ranevskaya rhapsodizes about what the nursery has meant to her;[5] Gayeff makes a speech to the desk about how it has served the family.[6] But rhapsodizing about the nursery and eulogizing the desk serve finally to again remind Madame Ranevskaya and Gayeff of their present problems. Like Lopahin, they become more determined to solve the problems; and also like Lopahin, they use recognition of a problem as a comfortable escape from attempting any real solution to it.

Like the daydreams of Lopahin, Madame Ranevskaya, and Gayeff, those of the other important characters usually take the form of sentimental talk about the Cherry Orchard. Nearly everyone envisages it as a Utopia where he can achieve the purposeful, unified life he so desperately wants. It becomes for everyone a symbol of the ideal for which he is striving. By thinking and talking about the ideal world they envision, Chekhov's characters gain a feeling of purpose. They delude themselves

[5] The Cherry Orchard, p. 21.
[6] The Cherry Orchard, p. 18.

into believing that they are actually bringing unity and purpose into their lives.

But occasionally they discover that their escape into sentimental daydreams is actually preventing them from solving any of the problems. As Trofimoff says, "Apparently, with us, all the fine talk is only to divert the attention of ourselves and of others."[7] Varya, too, realizes that talk will not make Lopahin propose. As she says, "It's two years now; everyone has been talking to me about him, everyone talks, and he either remains silent or jokes."[8] It is this partial awareness of the discrepancy between their aims and their achievements which keeps them struggling to achieve their aims. Lopahin tries again and again to persuade Madame Ranevskaya that she must divide the Orchard into commercial lots if she is to save it. Gayeff tries to face his problems despite his tendency to lapse into daydreams or sentimental talk. Madame Ranevskaya struggles to keep her mind on her present problems, and not on her past bliss. But always the characters allow the dream of unity and purpose to substitute for actions which will achieve their purpose. And since they allow their thoughts and words to take the place of any direct action which might help them achieve what they want, they must fall. As Lopahin says to Madame Ranevskaya after he has bought the orchard, "Why, then, didn't you listen to me? My poor dear, it can't be undone now. Oh, if this could all be over soon if somehow our awkward, unhappy life would be changed!"[9]

Chekhov's dialogue then is functional because of its rambling, formless quality, not in spite of it. With such dialogue Chekhov has hit upon a perfect means of making objective the constant struggle his characters have between their desire to act realistically in order to solve their problems and their desire to daydream in one form or another in order to avoid their problems. But because talk gives them both a way of struggling and a way of avoiding struggle, they allow it to divert them from saving the Orchard. Thus, far from being irrelevant, Chekhov's dialogue is actually the essential expression of the central conflict in *The Cherry Orchard*.

[7] *The Cherry Orchard*, p. 43.
[8] *The Cherry Orchard*, p. 58.
[9] *The Cherry Orchard*, p. 70.

THE CHERRY ORCHARD AS COMEDY*

Jacqueline E. M. Latham

Chekhov suffered during his lifetime from bad productions of his plays. Even Stanislavsky, the founder of the Moscow Art Theatre, misunderstood the nature of his comedies, *The Seagull* and *The Cherry Orchard*, and after the production of the latter Chekhov wrote to his wife: "How awful it is! An act that ought to take twelve minutes at most lasts forty minutes. There is only one thing I can say: Stanislavsky has ruined my play for me." [1] Stanislavsky and his fellow-director Nemirovich-Danchenko believed that Chekhov was wrong in thinking that he had written comedies; when Stanislavsky had read *The Cherry Orchard* he wrote to Chekhov informing him that it was, in fact, a tragedy. These Moscow productions, which were, of course, in many ways very fine, displeased Chekhov who was too ill to protest forcibly about them, and so they became the first of the line of melancholy productions which today we accept almost without question in England and the United States. Indeed, the pattern is so well established that it was brilliantly and easily parodied in Peter Ustinov's *The Love of Four Colonels*. Desmond MacCarthy (as did Shaw and many others) fully accepted Chekhov's plays as tragedies of frustration and in 1937, in *The New Statesman and Nation*, he reviewed a production of *Uncle Vanya* sharply criticizing the humor and comedy in the performance. However, his criticisms elicited a letter from Dorothy Sayers (whose first acquaintance with Chekhov this was) in defense of the production, saying "But the whole tragedy of futility is that it never succeeds in achieving tragedy. In its blackest moments it is inevitably doomed to the comic gesture." [2] This, the central point of Chekhov's comedy, is what so many critics have missed. In the United

---

* Jacqueline Latham, "The Cherry Orchard as Comedy," *The Educational Theatre Journal*, X (March 1958), 21–29. Reprinted by permission of *The Educational Theatre Journal*.

[1] March 29, 1904. *The Letters of Anton Pavlovitch Tchehov to Olga Leonardovna Knipper*, trans. Constance Garnett (New York, n.d.), p. 374. The last sentence is omitted here. It is given in full by David Magarshack, in *Chekhov a Life* (London, 1952), footnote on p. 383.

[2] Dorothy Sayers, *The New Statesman and Nation*, Feb. 27, 1937, p. 324.

States, too, Edmund Wilson writing in *The New Yorker*[3] admits that in rereading Chekhov's plays he can find a broader humour than he remembers in stage productions. Indeed, the tradition is established and Chekhov has been accepted as a writer of gloomy tragedies of frustration; I doubt whether he can be reinstated as he would wish.

The Cherry Orchard,[4] Chekhov's last play, was written slowly and painfully in 1903. It was produced in January, 1904, by Stanislavsky at the Moscow Art Theatre only six months before the author's death. The subject of the play is the impoverishment of an aristocratic family who sell their house and orchard to one of their ex-serfs who wishes to build summer cottages. The passing of an era is a favourite subject for sentimentalists and it would have been easy for Chekhov to have shown aristocratic nobility and integrity at the mercy of an unscrupulous bourgeois. But he did not write that play, although many producers have wished that he had. He wrote instead a comedy. "The play has turned out not a drama, but a comedy, in parts even a farce." [5] He did not see the passing of the old order as tragic, and, in emphasizing the social uselessness of the aristocratic family, he treats the subject from a comic viewpoint. He sees in them no love, no sense of responsibility; their deepest emotion is only sentiment.

Chekhov's father was of peasant stock, for the grandfather had purchased their freedom, although he was, said Chekhov, "a most rabid upholder of serfdom." [6] Chekhov's love for humanity was universal; he neither idealized the serfs from whom he sprang nor did he fawn upon the rich who were now his friends. Lydia Avilov, in her memoir, *Chekhov in my Life,* quotes Chekhov as saying, "I will describe life to you truthfully, that is artistically, and you will see in it what you have not seen before, what you never noticed before: its divergence from the norms, its contradictions." [7] It is exactly this that Chekhov achieves in *The Cherry Orchard* (although it was not, of course, of this play that he was speaking). All classes of men were for Chekhov possible subjects of comedy; his plays are about human nature and his sympathies did not lie exclusively with one class, nor did he wish to satirize the other. It is because he shows "divergence from the norms" that *The Cherry Orchard* is a comedy, and these anormalities he sees in the wealthy as well as in their servants. The play has, cer-

[3] Edmund Wilson, "Seeing Chekhov Plain," *The New Yorker*, Nov. 22, 1952, p. 180–194.

[4] The text used is the translation by Stark Young in *Best Plays by Chekhov* (New York, 1956). All names will be given in his spelling.

[5] Letter to Madame Stanislavsky, Sept. 15, 1903. *The Life and Letters of Anton Tchekhov,* ed. and trans. S. S. Koteliansky & Philip Tomlinson (New York, n.d.), p. 290.

[6] Quoted in *Chekhov a Life*, p. 18.

[7] *Chekhov in my Life*, trans. David Magarshack (London, 1950), p. 32.

trainly, tragic overtones, as has Molière's Le Misanthrope, but the point of view of the author is definitely comic, and as if he wishes to emphasize this he introduces certain farcical incidents: squeaking boots, clumsiness, conjuring tricks, a governess dressed as a man jumping about in a ball-room, and an accidental blow with a stick struck by Varya on the man she loves.

Chekhov's purpose in writing The Cherry Orchard was to give a criticism of life by showing characters who deviate from the norm. The cherry orchard itself is not a constant symbol of beauty wantonly destroyed, but, as the centre of the play, it has a different significance for each character. There are twelve people who make up the comèdie humaine, all individuals, all more or less comic, some contributing to a central pattern of meaning, others merely performing peripherally their own comic dance and only occasionally impinging on the central pattern.

Although Chekhov considered the merchant Lopahin the central figure in the play,[8] it is best for us to consider first the brother and sister, Gayeff and Madame Ranevskaya. They are middle-aged children. For Gayeff life is a game, no more serious than the game of billiards which cheers him when his estate is sold and which he plays in imagination (though with words and gestures) whenever the problems of the material world seem too much for him. He leaves his estate for a life as a bank official saying "I am a financier now—yellow ball into the side pocket."[9] Even his tardily acquired career as a financier—for which his own financial failure has ill-prepared him—seems to be only a continuation of his life at the billiard table: trying to make a big break before he finally loses.

Gayeff's ridiculousness is accentuated by his continual eating of candies. "They say I've eaten my fortune up in hard candies" (II) he says laughing, but we know he doesn't believe it. This candy eating is a symbol of his childishness, of his unfitness for the adult world. Even old Fiers, the butler, treats him like a child, worrying whether he is dressed properly when he goes out and bringing him his coat when it is cold. His sister, too, has never matured. When her husband had died and her son had been drowned shortly afterwards, she left Russia with her lover, leaving her two daughters behind. Her lover has been unfaithful and has spent all her money, yet at the end of the play she returns to him. She has spent her life avoiding real sorrow, for she has not the depth of character to accept it and to be purified by it. She is a creature of moods and in Act I appears like a child in her unconscious selfconsciousness: "Is it really me sitting here? (Laughing) I'd like to jump around and wave my arms. (Covering

[8] Letter to Stanislavsky, Oct. 30, 1903. Life and Letters, p. 291.
[9] Act IV. Subsequent quotations will be identified by act number in parentheses.

her face with her hands) But I may be dreaming." Soon she is tearful, then kissing Fiers and the bookcase too.[10] For the brother and sister the orchard is a symbol of their youth, the youth they have never left. As Madame Ranevskaya looks out at it from their childhood nursery, she imagines that one of the trees in blossom is their mother, dressed in white, walking through the orchard. "I slept in this nursery," she exclaims, "and looked out on the orchard from here, every morning happiness awoke with me, it was just as it is now, then, nothing has changed." (I) This is, of course, Chekhov's point. The brother and sister have not changed, yet the world has. They are children in an adult world, and for the most part they are unaware of reality; even in their rare moments of self-knowledge they lack the power of coming to grips with reality.

Madame Ranevskaya's embrace of the bookcase is matched by her brother's even more ludicrous piece of self-dramatization, also in Act I, when he salutes the bookcase (tearfully) as "sustaining through the generations of our family our courage and our faith in a better future and nurturing in us ideals of goodness and of a social consciousness." This comic gesture not only helps us to see Gayeff's essential ridiculousness, but serves as an ironic commentary on his sister's character. The generosity shown when Madame Ranevskaya gives the drunken stranger a gold piece despite their extreme poverty is ludicrous, not admirable, for it is not based upon altruism or love but is an automatic gesture paralleled by her extravagance at restaurants where they cannot pay the bills. There is no longer any ideal of "goodness and of a social consciousness" in the family; had there been, the play might have been a tragedy. Rather, there is continual self-deception, punctuated by mawkish moments of self-awareness, as when at the end of Act I Gayeff says "And today I made a speech to the bookcase—so silly! And it was only when I finished it that I could see it was silly," only to add shortly after "On my honour I'll swear, by anything you like, that the estate shall not be sold! By my happiness, I swear! Here's my hand, call me a worthless, dishonourable man, if I allow it to come up for auction! With all my soul I swear it!" Chekhov's stage directions indicate that before he says this he puts a candy in his mouth.

This brings us to the central dramatic action—whether the estate should be sold to raise the necessary money or whether Gayeff and his sister should be prepared to raise money by letting part or all of it for building summer cottages. This is their dilemma and this is the issue they steadfastly refuse to face. When Lopahin suggests that they let the land, they refuse to. Gayeff promises that the estate will not be auctioned, deceiving himself into confidence in uninterested generals and a parsimonious rich aunt. The estate, of course, is auctioned and

[10] It is in character that the only books she mentions are fairy tales.

while Gayeff bids 15,000 roubles (provided by the rich aunt and eventually spent in Paris by Madame Ranevskaya with her lover), his sister is giving a ball to which the station-master and post-office clerk are invited. With magnificent understatement she says "We planned the ball at an unfortunate moment—well, it doesn't matter." (III) Their essential indifference to the fate of their estate is shown in the absence of practical measures to preserve it. They dramatize, pose, and make unreal gestures but they have protested too much; in the end they have forfeited their claim to our sympathy.

Lopahin, the ex-serf who has succeeded in life, is presented far more sympathetically by Chekhov. It is he who has the plan which will enable Gayeff and his sister to keep the estate, and even when eventually he buys it Chekhov is careful to point out that he bid for it only against an outsider and after Gayeff had withdrawn for the auction. In a letter to Stanislavsky, Chekhov writes:

> Lopahin is a merchant, but he is a decent man in every sense; he has to behave with perfect manners, like an educated man . . . Varya, a serious and religious girl, loved Lopahin; she would not have fallen in love with a money grubber.[11]

and later:

> Dunya and Epihodoff stand in Lopahin's presence; they do not sit. Lopahin, in fact, maintains his position like a gentleman. He addresses the servants "thou" and they "you" him.[12]

Lopahin, then, is not a Dogberry, neither is he a Monsieur Jourdain. In his efforts to save their estate he is practical, though perhaps a little unfeeling, but Chekhov does not ask us to laugh at him for this. Indeed he embodies in many ways Chekhov's hopes for the future as expressed in Act II by the perennial student Trofimoff: the past can only be atoned for "through uncommon, incessant labor." Lopahin, though, is comic in another way; he who is successful in business matters is unsuccessful in his private life. Despite the fact that he is loved and respected by the family he is incapable of proposing marriage to Varya of of whom he is fond and who loves him. As he has said in Act I to Dunyasha the maid, "You must know your place." He knows his too well, or rather, he is caught in his childhood sense of inferiority. He idealizes Madame Ranevskaya and is unable to marry her adopted daughter. She had said to him, when he had been hit by his father as a child, " 'Don't cry . . . little peasant,' " (I) and he still sees himself as a peasant and still worships Madame Ranevskaya. The stick, as David Magarshack noted,[13] is a symbol of his servitude ("My father . . . just beat me in his drunken fits and always with a stick" (II) and it is ironical that when in Act I he mocks Anya and Varya, who are

[11] Oct. 30, 1903. *Life and Letters*, p. 291.
[12] Nov. 10, 1903. *Life and Letters*, p. 293.
[13] *Chekhov the Dramatist* (London, 1952), p. 281.

perturbed about the debts incurred by the family, Varya threatens "I'd land him one like that (*shaking her fist*.)" In fact she does, accidentally, hit him with a stick when he returns from the auction to tell them that he has bought the estate; he may be master of the house, but he is not the master in his private life. For all his success as a business-man, for all his kindness and integrity, he yet remains the slave, un-able to master his own happiness in his relationship with the family.

As if to emphasize this gulf between practical success and success in personal relationships, Chekhov has associated a second symbol with Lopahin: his watch. At the very beginning of the play Lopahin, who has come especially to meet Madame Ranevskaya at the station, wakes up to find that the train is in and that he has overslept. He never seems to overcome this initial setback; though he can be de-cisive about the remedy the family should take to save their estate, yet he cannot meet the people around him on equal terms. He seems to need the moral support of his watch—which is associated with the well-regulated business world of which he is master—when he is with Gayeff and his family. When he tries to tell them his idea for saving the estate and to take his departure, he four times refers to his watch as if for support. Finally, in Act IV, during his last talk with Varya, when he has already told Madame Ranevskaya that he will ask Varya to marry him, he is unable to broach the subject at all to her. When she enters, he is looking at his watch and the conversation ends when he calls to someone off-stage "The minute." The stick and watch are symbols of Lopahin's divided personality. He is still in subjection spiri-tually and he is unable to conquer time and circumstances in his private life and to impose his will upon them. We know from Chekhov's letters that he wished us to admire Lopahin, for in many ways he is the embodiment of Chekhov's ideal for society, practical hard work. Yet in his inability to bring his personal desires and relationships into his control in the same way that he has dominated the commercial world, he is anormal. It is thus that he is a comic figure, though he is far more sympathetically portrayed than Gayeff and his sister.

The action of the play revolves around the debts incurred by the family and the way they can raise money on the estate. The solu-tion that Gayeff and his sister are forced to accept—in spite of their illusory belief that they deserve to be saved from their predicament—is not an ideal one. Neither is Lopahin's suggestion of letting the orchard for commercial building wholly satisfactory to us. However, Chekhov does imply a different course of action, though it is now too late to implement it. It is Fiers, the deaf butler to whom no-one listens, who in Act I indicates a positive solution:

Fiers: There was a time forty-fifty years ago when the cherries were dried, soaked, pickled, cooked into jam and it used to be—
Gayeff: Keep quiet, Fiers.
Fiers: And it used to be that the dried cherries were shipped by the

wagon-load to Moscow and to Kharkov. And the money there was!
And the dried cherries were soft then, juicy, sweet, fragrant—They had
a way of treating them then—
Madame Ranevskaya: And where is that way now?
Fiers: They have forgotten it. Nobody remembers now.

Chekhov's criticism of this aristocratic family, then goes deeper:
they have not only lived in an imaginary world, avoiding responsibility
like children, but they have lost the means by which a life like this
can be made possible; they have lost the secret and they do not even
realize what they have done.

Only Fiers realizes what has been lost and only he of the servants
knows what it is to serve, to work, and to maintain order. Significantly
enough, like Chekhov's grandfather, he refers to the emancipation of
serfs as the "disaster" and says that he did not take his freedom but
stayed instead with his master. Although his aim in life is to serve, the
irony of his situation lies in the fact that those whom he serves are
unworthy of this dedication. Madame Ranevskaya's affection for Fiers
is merely sentimental. He is part of the world that is slipping from
her; he does not exist as a human being worthy of love or of gratitude.
His life-long devotion is not even rewarded by a warm farewell when
she thinks he is going to the hospital. Instead she relies upon another
servant to make certain that he is taken and cared for. His end, left
behind in the doomed house, is the one discordant note in the comedy.
His rejection is, of course, symbolic. The days of which he is a legacy
are over, the days when, as he says, "there were generals, barons,
admirals dancing at our parties," (III) and a new era has begun. Gayeff
and his sister cannot even command respect from their other servants,
and when at the end they lock the house with Fiers inside, it is their
final gesture of irresponsibility; it is symbolically very effective. However, on the literal level it introduces an alien note into the play, though
as David Magarshack points out[14] there is no reason to suppose that
Fiers dies, for Chekhov states clearly that Epihodoff, the clerk, is to
remain behind. There is fine irony in Fiers' last speech in which he
worries lest Gayeff may not have worn his topcoat and then, as if in
final recognition, he applies to himself the epithet he has been applying
to others, "good-for-nothing." He seems at this moment to realize that
his life has passed in a cause which was not worthy of him. This, I believe, is Chekhov's only wholly tragic note. It becomes tragic because,
although Fiers is self-deceived as the other characters are, we can
admire him for his devotion and integrity.

Of Madame Ranevskaya's two daughters, Chekov told Nemirovich-
Danchenko:

[14] *Chekhov the Dramatist*, p. 285–6.

Anya can be acted by anyone, even by a quite unknown actress, provided she is young and looks like a girl, and speaks in a young ringing
voice. This is not one of the important parts . . . Varya's is a more
serious part . . . she is a figure in a black dress, nun-like, a silly, a cry-
baby etc. etc.[15]

Varya is a complementary character to Lopahin. She is unable to secure
happiness because of her indecision yet in her management of the
household she imposes a severe discipline. She loves Lopahin but "is
quite incapable of disregarding the conventions which demand that
the lady has to wait for the gentleman to propose to her." [16] Varya,
as Chekhov wrote to his wife, is "a foolish creature" [17] and it is in her
lack of purpose, her frequent weeping, and above all her inability to
show any affection to the man she loves, that she is a comic character.
Anya, too, is a feeble person but she resembles her mother, as Gayeff
notices. She is as easily reassured as her mother is, and Gayeff's
promises that the estate will be saved make at once confident. Her
joy in the cherry orchard is, like her mother's, a child's joy and she
wishes to run out into the orchard in the early morning. For Varya,
her proposed marriage is "like a dream" (I) and for Anya, too, reality
hardly exists. When at the end of the play her mother leaves again
for Paris and her lover, Anya promises her that she will work and
pass examinations: "Then I'll work, I will help you. We'll read all
sorts of books together. Mama isn't that so? We'll read in the autumn
evenings, read lots of books and a new, wonderful world will open
up before us."

In Anya's love affair with Trofimoff one can see another theme with
which Chekhov is preoccupied. Trofimoff is a young intellectual—a
student who has been sent down from his university for political reasons—and he becomes in some measure a spokesman for Chekhov and
hence in this respect a normative character. He sees physical work as
the key to social progress: "One must work and must help with all
one's might those who see the truth. With us in Russia so far only a
few work." (II)[18] But, ironically he is not one of these few. He is as
ineffectual as Gayeff and his sister, but whereas they will not act
because they cannot see reality, he does not act although he can
see the future plainly. He perceives the truth but does not act on it
and he is in this a comic figure. His appearance reinforces his ineffectualness and he says that a peasant woman called him "a mangy-
looking gentleman" (I) But it is in his affection for Anya that he is

[15] Nov. 2, 1903. *Life and Letters*, p. 292.
[16] *Chekhov the Dramatist*, p. 278.
[17] Nov. 1, 1903. *Letters to Olga Knipper*, p. 336.
[18] The orchard is for Trofimoff a symbol of tyranny. He says in Act II
"All Russia is our orchard."

really made to look ludicrous. He believes that they are "above love."
(II) It is Madame Ranevskaya who points out the absurdity of this pose
saying that he is a "ridiculous crank, a freak." (III) However, Madame
Ranevskaya, who has abandoned herself to an unworthy lover and
whose love for her daughters is so sentimental, is not the norm but
another extreme. The norm we must see to lie between these paths,
yet not in the timidity of Varya and Lopahin. Different attitudes to
love, one of Chekhov's main comic themes, are handled here far more
simply than in The Seagull.

Madame Ranevskaya, Gayeff, Lopahin, Varya, Anya, Trofimoff,
and Fiers are the central characters in The Cherry Orchard and in
their divergence from the norms they illustrate most seriously and
effectively Chekhov's main comic themes. However, around them are
grouped less important characters who are perhaps more obviously
comic in themselves though they have less bearing on the main comic
purpose. David Magarshack points out that Semyonoff-Pischtchik's
name is itself comic. "The first half of it is impressively aristocratic and
the second farcical (its English equivalent would be Squeaker)." [19] He
is the lucky fool, the third son of the fairy tales, the man who deserves
nothing—he even asks Gayeff for money—yet who wins everything.
He misses jokes and laughs in the wrong place; he is so absent minded
that he even forgets that the house has been sold and promises to drop
in on Thursday when they are just departing. Finally, with a reversal
which Chekhov so loved, he gives back to Gayeff and his sister the
money he owes them, for, extraordinarily, white clay has been found
on his land. He is magnificently vague and inconsequential, talking
about his daughter Dashenka who is of interest to no one in the self-
centered family.

Charlotta, the governess, is another broadly comic character. She
says very little but enlivens the untimely ball by a conjuring and
ventriloquist display. She is completely alone in the world; she does
not even know how old she is. In her loneliness she gains for herself
a group of admirers by her conjuring. She, unlike Madame Ranevskaya,
Varya, and Anya who love although they are not able to achieve happiness in their love, loves no one. She seems to thirst for affection and
pathetically in her ventriloquist act she converses with herself thus:
" 'You are so nice, you're my ideal.' The Voice: 'Madame, you too
please me greatly.' " (III) Charlotta might easily have been a tragic
figure except that Chekhov has not explored her character deeply. In
a letter to his wife he insists that the actress "must be funny in
Charlotta, that's the chief thing," [20] and later he adds that her dog "must

---

[19] Chekhov the Dramatist, p. 284.
[20] Nov. 8, 1903. Letters to Olga Knipper, p. 341.

be long-haired, small with no life in it, with sour eyes." [21] A well-cast Charlotta and a well-cast dog would make an amusing pair.

Finally, there are the younger servants. Epihodoff—or twenty-two misfortunes as he is called—is a man in squeaky boots who drops flowers on the floor, falls over the chair, and puts a suitcase on top of a hat-box crushing it just as the family are about to leave with their luggage. He even welcomes misfortunes which help to justify the nickname which he thinks has been given to him in affection. He is pedantic and priggish, congratulating himself on his culture and yet uncertain whether to live or to shoot himself. His lack of control, which manifests itself in his clumsiness, is a reflection of his master's lack of self-discipline, and in his self-conscious (and stupid) pedantry we can see something of Gayeff's eloquent dramatization. He is a microcosm of the family, the most ludicrous traits of which are brought together in him. He loves the foolish maid Dunyasha and sings sad songs celebrating his happiness, yet he has no sense of his position in the house as a clerk. Dunyasha, in her indecision over whether to marry the pompous Epihodoff or the good-for-nothing Yasha, both of whom consider themselves superior to her, reveals her essential triviality. One of the most telling indictments of the family is their inability to handle their insolent servants or to appreciate the devotion of Fiers. In Act II Yasha insults Gayeff with impunity, and Gayeff even turns to his sister saying "Either I or he—." Dunyasha, in her abandoned love for the pretentious Yasha, echoes Madame Ranevskaya's passion for her lover and this preserves the balance of morality between servants and masters.

The purpose of this article has been to show in what ways *The Cherry Orchard* is a comedy. It cannot be denied that there are occasional overtones of pathos and tragedy but these contribute to the depth and complexity of the comedy and provide the "contradictions" which, Chekhov said, "you never noticed before." As Dorothy Sayers says, the "tragedy of futility is that . . . it is inevitably doomed to the comic gesture," and if one wishes to see *The Cherry Orchard* as a tragedy of futility, one must grant that it is revealed in comedy. In his revelation of the ludicrous in human nature Chekhov successfully achieves a very rare blend of sympathetic and judicial comedy; although the audience are aware of the triviality and inadequacies of the comic characters yet they cannot completely dissociate themselves from them, to assume a superior position. The picture is complex: Chekhov criticizes his characters both in their relation to the material world and in their relation to each other; they are self-deceived, complacent, self-indulgent, ill-adjusted to the outside world, ill-adjusted to themselves,

[21] Nov. 27, 1903. *Letters to Olga Knipper*, p. 349.

and often merely foolish. The pattern of this criticism is most easily discerned in the main characters, yet the minor characters perform small steps to the same tune, while retaining their sharp individuality. Chekhov wrote of a story "I have let the subject filter through my memory, so that only what is important or typical is left, as in a filter"; [22] this is his method, too, in his very complex plays.

[22] Letter to F. D. Batyushkov, Dec. 15, 1897. *Life and Letters,* p. 252.

FROM *INTONATION AND RHYTHM IN CHEKHOV'S PLAYS**

Nils Ake Nilsson

. . . But on the other hand, the modern drama—as Chekhov himself often points out—shifts the interest more and more from the main action to the inner man, from the outward intrigue to the psychological conflict. How to combine scenic realism with "the drama of souls"? How is the realistic playwright to reproduce feeling, the innermost thoughts of man on the stage? How much can words express? How far can he use every day words without their losing their dramatic tension and—on the other hand—how far can he "dramatise" words without their ceasing to appear natural?

"No, not that. It was not that I wanted to say" (*ne to, ne to*) Chekhov's characters are often forced to say. They cannot find the right words for their thoughts and feelings, noticing suddenly that the words they are using do not express what they are really thinking. In the third act of "Uncle Vanja," Sonja tries to explain to her father how difficult a time she and uncle Vanja have had, but the words do not suffice: "That was not what I wanted to say (*ja govorju ne to, ne to ja govorju*), but you must understand us, Papa." "I am a gull. No, not that," Nina reiterates in conversation with Trigorin in the final scene of "The Seagull." In the third act of "Uncle Vanja," Elena Andreevna thinks of Sonja and her love for Astrov: "He is not in love with her—that is clear, but why should he not be able to marry her? She is not beautiful, but for a country practitioner, of his age, she would make an excellent wife. She is intelligent, so good and pure. . . No, it is not that, not that" (*Net, eto ne to, ne to*). Her words do not express her inner thoughts: she is herself interested in Astrov. "Why am I saying these words?", Masa exclaims in despair in the first act of "Three Sisters," abstractedly repeating a line from a poem by Puskin.

Like Tolstoj, Chekhov had to find other means of expressing feelings and thoughts outside of the words. The most important of these were

In this article and the following one the spelling of some proper names has been anglicized, e.g. Chekhov for Cechov, Vershinin for Veršinin.

* Nils Nilsson, "Intonation and Rhythm in Chekhov's Plays," *Anton Chekhov 1860–1960, Some Essays,* edited by T. Eekman (Leiden: E. J. Brill, 1960), pp. 171–179. Reprinted by permission of E. J. Brill, Leiden.

to be: first of all the voice, then different sounds (from the night-
watchman's hammering, from guitar playing to the snapping string in
"The Cherry Orchard"), associatively charged objects (from the symbolic gull to Natasha's belt in "Three Sisters"), the pauses, used very
frequently and with great variation, silent scenes (the last scene in
"Uncle Vanja" where Marija Vasilevna sits writing and Marina knits
stockings; the last scene in "Three Sisters," where Kulygin and Andrej
appear in the background during the three sisters' monologue as a
reminder of commonplace life), and lastly the language itself, the
structure of the sentences.

These devices are not used only to create a background atmosphere
on the stage. The aim is also to communicate to the audience things
which concern the characters or the setting or the action, things which
the realistic drama according to Chekhov neither could nor should express in words.

Research in Chekhov's dramatic technique ought to tackle this
system of devices as a whole and study it in its opposition towards
or cooperation with the dramatic diction. No other dramatic writer,
I think, is so interesting from this special point of view as Chekhov.
Lack of space will not allow of it here; I shall only attempt to give
some remarks on a component of this system which as far as I know
has received rather little attention: the intonation and its rhythm.

For Chekhov intonation was one of the realistic playwright's most
important aids. In a letter to Ol'ga Knipper dated 2nd January 1900
he wrote: "I have written to Mejerchol'd and recommended him not
to be so exaggerated when representing a nervous person. The greater
majority of people are nervous, the majority suffer, only a very few
feel a sharp pain, but where, outdoors or indoors, do you see people
running about, hopping and holding their heads in their hands? Suffering must be shown as it is shown in life, i.e. not with feet and hands
but with tone of voice, and eyes, not with gesticulation but with
grace. The subtler emotions characteristic of cultured people must
also be given subtle outward expression. Conditions on the stage do
not allow of this, you will say, but no conditions justify a lie"
(XVIII 292).

This was advice given to an actor as to how he should express
emotions on the stage. Yet it was also advice to the playwright. If an
actor's voice was going to be of such great importance, then it was
essential for the author to intimate carefully how the lines were to
be spoken. And it is in fact so that no playwright before Chekhov,
hardly anyone after him either, lays such great importance on directions for intonation. His four great plays overflow with them, cul-
minating in his last play "The Cherry Orchard." In this play one can
find about 175 directions as to how the lines are to be spoken. And
here it is important to note that these directions are by no means
stereotyped or trivial. On the contrary, they are notable for an abun-

dance of variation, in actual fact each rarely occurs more than once. It is thus possible to find some 80 different directions for speaking. They are often complicated, sometimes being composed of wholly opposing parts, for instance: "cheerfully, in tears" (*radostno, skvoz' slezy*), "happily, disturbed" (*veselo, vozbuzhdenno*), "angrily and mockingly" (*serdito i nasmeshlivo*), "impatiently, with tears" (*neterpelivo, so slezami*).

It is also possible to see that certain characters or scenes in Chekhov's plays are acoustically thought out, that a certain tone of voice or certain sounds are a dominating and characteristic element of them. When "Uncle Vanja" was to be performed at the Moscow Art Theatre, Chekhov wrote to Stanislavskij about the last scene: "He [Astrov] whistles, you know. . . Whistles. Uncle Vanja is crying but Astrov whistles."[9] Stanislavskij understood what Chekhov wanted to say with this laconic note. Here he found something characteristic of the doctor Astrov, fighting with his own despair, who is outwardly trying to appear unmoved. He thus included this detail in the first act as well. As soon as Astrov shows himself he starts whistling, it becomes a sort of signature-tune which characterises an important part of him much more clearly than any words.

Chekhov wrote to Ol'ga Knipper about Ranevskaja in "The Cherry Orchard": "It is not difficult to play Ranevskaja, only one has to find the right key from the very beginning; one has to find a smile and way of laughing, one must be able to dress" [XX 164]. Just as whistling is something characteristic for Astrov so is the laugh something important for the picture of Ranevskaja. With his words Chekhov wanted to point out her limitations, an emotionally static person who lives through the sale of the property and the cherry orchard without being affected. Her unchanged laugh and smile tell her story more clearly than any words.

Against this background of the careful directions for intonation one understands better why Chekhov sometimes so energetically maintained that it was necessary to follow the author's directions on the stage, that the author really ought to have more to say on the stage even than the producer. On one occasion he was thus able to say that "I really do believe that no play can be set up by even the most talented producer without the author's personal guidance and directions. . . There are different interpretations, but the author has the right to demand that his play is performed and the parts played wholly according to his own interpretation. . . It is necessary that the particular atmosphere intended by the author is created."[10]

These intonational directions show how important the emotional key was for Chekhov, but they also show one more important thing: the

[9] K. S. Stanislavskij, *Sobranie sochinenij*, T. 1, Moskva 1954, p. 232.
[10] *Teatr i istkusstvo* 1904, nr. 28, p. 522.

rhythm of the emotional key. The Chekhov mood was, and perhaps still often is, interpreted as a dominating, all-pervading atmosphere of elegy and despair, an interpretation which threatens to make Chekhov plays boring and monotonous. But what Chekhov did want was to give an illusion of life on the stage, and life was for him both laughter and tears, both hope and despair, both longing and triviality. It is certainly true that the emotional scale Chekhov works with is of no very broad register. The poles do not lie very far from each other. But in the middle register he uses, Chekhov has been able to capture very subtle nuances—the hasty glance we had at the intonation in "The Cherry Orchard" above clearly shows this.

And in this middle register he works with perpetual changes and contrasts. It is as if he were keen that no one key become too dominating or last too long. There must be change and rhythm if his plays are really to give a picture of everyday life. His striving towards this is most obvious in "The Cherry Orchard." Here Chekhov marks it very clearly, underlines it, presumably because he thought that not suffcient attention had been paid to it in his previous plays. As I said before, there are not many intonational directions in "The Cherry Orchard" that appear more than once. The only ones that occur more often are those that intimate that a line is to be spoken "happily" and "laughingly" or "sorrowfully" and "in tears." In the play there are some 15 of each type which in its own way thus shows how he tries to keep a balance between the contrasting keys.

Some of Chekhov's most usual contrasts are the contrast between a lyrical or elated and a banal, everyday atmosphere, the contrast between a sad, serious and a comic atmosphere, the contrast between a lively, active and a resting, pensive atmosphere. It is characteristic for Chekhov that these keys not only succeed each other but are also to be found in balance in the same scene.

It is often said that there are many "indifferent" lines in Chekhov's plays. Apart from the self-characterising monologues so typical of him, monologues whose syntactic construction — often without directions from the author — intimate their lyrical key, there are long passages with markedly colloquial lines. But these are only indifferent in that the semantic content of the words is at this point transferred to the background. Instead it is the way the words are intoned that is functional, the voice expressing what a person thinks or feels.

These indifferent remarks, I think, give the most obvious examples of how intonation and rhythm work in Chekhov's plays. I will use some of them here to clarify what I mean.

There are several types of indifferent remarks in Chekhov's plays. Let us begin with Gaev's billiard terms in "The Cherry Orchard". The real meaning of the words has no relevance in the context where they are used. Gaev resorts to them on occasions when he is disturbed or embarrassed and does not know what to say. Chekhov always gives clear directions for intonation. The words are either to be spoken "disconcerted" (*skonfuzhenno*) or "in deep thought" (*v glubokom razdum'e*) or "despondently" (*unylo*).

Thus the semantic content is of no interest here, what matters is the intonation: it reveals the emotional state of mind behind the words. Chekhov works this type of "indifferent" words to the limit in "Three Sisters" where Masha and Vershinin hold their strange dialogue:

> Masha. *Tram-tam-tam* . . .
> Vershinin. *Tam-tam* . . .
> Masha. *Tra-ra-ta* . . .
> Vershinin. *Tra-ta-ta* . . .

And the second time:

> Vershinin. *Tram-tam-tam.*
> Masha. *Tram-tam.*

The third time, Vershinin's voice is heard offstage: *Tram-tam-tam.* And Masha answers him with a: *Tra-ta-ta.*

It is understandable that a "dialogue" such as this would puzzle the actors: what was its function in the context, what intonation was one to use here? Ol'ga Knipper wrote to Chekhov and asked about the passage. Chekhov replied: „Vershinin speaks his ‚Tram-tam-tam' as a question and you as an answer, and you think that it is such an original joke that you speak this ‚tram-tam' with a smile" (XIX 24).

It is clear that these lines together form a dialogue of mutual understanding between Masha and Vershinin, a sort of love duet without words. One is reminded of the well-known scene in *Anna Karenina* where Levin and Kitty declare their love for each other without words, using only letters of the alphabet which they are able to interpret with the peculiar intuition of lovers.

And here another type of "indifferent" exchange. In the second act of "The Cherry Orchard", Epichodov crosses backstage playing on his guitar.

> Ljubov' Andreevna (pensively). Epichodov is coming.
> Anja (pensively). Epichodov is coming.

Ljubov' Andreevna thus states that she hears and sees her bookkeeper pass by. It is a statement, i.e., the semantic content of the words is not completely to be disregarded as in the above examples. But it is no normal statement; if such were the case Chekhov would not have marked that the line were to be said "pensively". It must therefore have a different contextual function. If this function is to be looked for in the semantic content of the words, a possible interpretation to these lines may be given with reference to the earlier conversation between Trofimov and Lopachin, Lopachin saying that giants would be necessary to solve the problems in Russia. Now when Epichodov appears on the scene perhaps Ljubov' Andreevna and Anja come to think that there are no giants to be found in Russia but all the more such tragi-comical figures as Epichodov, "thousand and one misfortunes" as he is called.

But I think it is of no use here to stress the semantic content of these words, trying to find some hidden meaning behind them. The scene is first of all conditioned by the rhythm in the emotional key. After the serious conversation between Trofimov and Lopachin the appearance of Epichodov comes in marked contrast, as a change in the emotional key. It communicates something comic and trivial, concepts connected with the figure of Epichodov. And further, after the lively, active conversation, a contrast of rest: Ljubov' Andreevna's and Anja's pensive, abstracted lines.

In this connection it is worth remembering some words which Chekhov wrote to Ol'ga Knipper in 1901 while rehearsals for "Three Sisters" were in progress. "Do not look sad in any of the acts", he wrote. "Angry, certainly, but not sad. People who have long borne grief inside them and have become used to it only whistle a little and often become lost in thought (zadumyvajutsja chasto). So you too must now and again lose yourself in thought on the stage" (XIX 10.). Most of Chekhov's characters are certainly such people who have long borne a grief or a longing within them. They often shut themselves from the outside world for a moment, letting some indifferent words communicate their abstracted state of mind.

There is another similar passage in "Three Sisters." Chebutykin, who usually sits reading the paper, noting down the various curiosities he finds there, suddenly reads aloud: "Balzac was married in Berdichev". And Irina meditatively repeats his words as she plays patience: "Balzac was married in Berdichev."

Chebutykin's words follow on a conversation between Vershinin and Tuzenbach where Vershinin propounds his favourite theory that life in two or three hundred years will be better and happier but that the generations living now have not the right to think of happiness. Chebutykin's words come when the discussion has reached a dead point and Tuzenbach says that "it is difficult to argue with you both."

Some scholars have chosen to give Irina's repetition of Chebutykin's words a special meaning. That Balzac, a great poet, marries in Berdichev, a little village in the country which no one might have heard of before, perhaps starts Irina thinking that happiness is possibly to be found where one least expects it. Perhaps their Moscow dream, their great dream of finding happiness in the city, is only an illusion? It may be that happiness is also to be found in the small town where they now live?

But I am very doubtful about this interpetation. If Chekhov had wished to include this idea in his play it would have needed further support, and one can hardly say that the thought is developed in other

passages in "Three Sisters". In fact this scene is a direct parallel to
the scene in "The Cherry Orchard" which we have already looked at.
It is above all an example of the rhythm which Chekhov works with in
the intonation and the emotional key. After the serious conversation
between Vershinin and Tuzenbach, Chebutykin's trivial line follows as a
marked contrast, a return to everyday life. And afterwards, a moment
of rest and meditation: Irina's abstracted, dreamy repetition of Chebutykin's indifferent words.

In the last act of "Uncle Vanja", Astrov goes over to a map of Africa
hanging on the wall and says a few words about how terribly hot it must
be in Africa just then, to which Vojnickij replies: "Yes, I suppose so."
This remark about Africa is like the one we have just spoken of; its
effect is also abrupt, unexpected, without any visible function in the
context. As with other indifferent lines, a hidden meaning has been
sought in it.

Stanislavskij, who played Astrov in the first performance at the
Moscow Art Theatre, for instance, gave it a definite emotional content,
let his voice give meaning to the words. Ol'ga Knipper told of this:
"How much bitterness and experience of life he put into this phrase.
And how he pronounced these words with a sort of bravura, challenging
almost." [11] It appears as if one ought to understand by Ol'ga Knipper's
remark that Astrov, with his words, brought out a sort of contrast to
Russian life where everything is indifferent, dull and apathetic; in
other countries, far away, there is heat, there is something that burns
and consumes.

Yet it is characteristic that the words may be interpreted in many
other ways. A Soviet scholar, Prof. Ermilov, for instance, writes thus:
"Astrov is ready to leave, his carriage is waiting for him at the door.
And this remark about Africa conclusively transports everything that
has happened here a moment before far far away: Africa, it is a sort of
scale, it is the impossibility of being able to measure the distance which
now separates the heroes in the play from the dramas they took part in
not long ago. . . After the remark on Africa everything that has taken
place on the property becomes conclusively as distant as Africa is distant
from here." [12]

As Chekhov himself said: "There are different interpretations. . ."
But if one is to judge by the author's own words, this was not at all his
intention with the remark. In a letter to Ol'ga Knipper he wrote about
this scene: "You write that Astrov in this scene turns to Elena as a
passionate lover, clutches for the emotion as a drowning man clutches
for a straw. But this is wrong, absolutely wrong. Astrov likes Elena,
she appeals to him strongly because of her beauty, but in the last act

[11] *O Stanislavskom*, Moskva 1948, p. 266.
[12] V. Ermilov, *Isbrannye raboty v trech tomach*, T. 3, Moskva 1956, p. 175.

he knows already that nothing will come of it, that Elena is going away from him for ever — and he speaks to her in this scene in the same tone as he speaks of the heat in Africa, and he kisses her simply like this, because he has nothing else to do" (XVIII 235).

Thus we see that according to Chekhov himself there is no use of seeking a hidden meaning behind these words. What matters here is the intonation, the words merely form a backcloth for Astrov's resigned tone of voice.

Another illuminating example of how Chekhov tries to create rhythmic variation in the emotional key is to be found in the scene between Ljubov' Andreevna and Trofimov in Act III of "The Cherry Orchard", a disturbed scene full of emotion which is unexpectedly and abruptly turned into something comic when Trofimov, rushing in agitation from Ljubov' Andreevna, falls downstairs with a crash. Here, as in several of the earlier examples, a contrasting note come in afterwards, braking the foregoing serious atmosphere of the scene. Chekhov is also capable of the opposite. In Act III of "The Cherry Orchard" Lopachin has his great scene, a dramatic entrance and monologue similar to the climax which the drama before Chekhov usually worked up to in the third or fourth act. When Lopachin does make his expected and prepared entrance, however, it is in by no means the same effective way as it would have been made with one of Chekhov's predecessors. Varja thinks it is Epichodov who had just been teasing her who has returned. She waits at the door with a stick and smites Lopachin when he comes in. The new owner of the cherry orchard thus makes rather a ridiculous entrance. It is clear that Chekhov inserted this mode of entry to contrast with the coming monologue, that it might not be too "dramatic" in the old meaning of the word.

But Chekhov also works with rhythmic variations in the middle of a monologue or a scene. An obvious example of this is to be found at the beginning of "Three Sisters". Ol'ga's and Irna's lyrical scene, where the atmosphere of the house as it was a year ago at their fathers' death is brought back, is interrupted in the middle by a conversation between Solenyj, Chebuytkin and Tuzenbach in the background. Only a few words are heard: "Chebutykin: Damned silly (*Cherta s dva*). Tuzenbach: Utter nonsense, of course (*Konechno, vzdor*)". It is clear that Solenyj has said something to make them indignant. These short exchanges occur just in the middle of the lyrical conversation between the sisters. It is obvious that they are intended to break the lyrical atmosphere, that it shall not become too monotonous, by introducing a more trivial one.

The final monologue of the three sisters is also constructed in a similar way. Right at the very end Masha's husband appears, in company with Andrej, pushing a pram at the same time as Chebutykin is humming his everlasting "Ta . . .ra. . .ra. . . boomdee-ay, nothing matters." Against the lyrical atmosphere, against the poetic structure of the sentences, Chekhov inserts the mute appearance of Andrej and Kulygin in contrast, a reminder of everyday life (compare Epichodov's appearance in "The Cherry Orchard") and Chebutykin's philosophy of hopelessness. He is anxious about the monologue, that the lyrical intonation shall not become too dominant and thus brings in contrasting tones.

It is characteristic of today's Chekhov scholars that they look for new meanings in the "indifferent" remarks. "It is said that Chekhov taught us scenic simplicity, but his words are not simple", Nemirovich Dancenko said during rehearsals for "Three Sisters" in 1939. His words seem to have left their mark on the modern scenic interpretation of Chekhov's play in the Soviet Union and on Chekhov's research as well. It is, of course, quite right to say that Chekhov's simple words are not simple in that they are not inserted at random; there is always a reason for them in the context. But I think that one may often go too far in seeking hidden meanings behind the "indifferent" lines. I do not believe that Chekhov tried to fill his plays with secret connotations which must be pieced together like a jig-saw puzzle. The most obvious reason for indifferent remarks is always the rhythm, the variation in the intonation, in the emotional key. Certainly in their context these remarks at the same time often evoke certain associations, but these associations are always of a general character. I consider it difficult to narrow them down by indicating one of them as being that which Chekhov intended. . . .

FROM *THE BIZARRE ELEMENT IN CHEKHOV'S ART**

Charles B. Timmer

I

A study in literature, whether on Gogol', Dostoevskij or Chekhov is bound to involve a study in anti-reason: it cannot limit itself to a study of aesthetic laws only, unless we are prepared to assume that the grotesque, the bizarre, the absurd elements in the works of these authors are unexplainable phenomena.

The grotesque, the bizarre, the absurd, — by using these words I realize that I am bringing to the foreground certain aspects of Chekhov's art, which to my knowledge did not thus far have the attention they undoubtedly deserve. It is certainly not my ambition to exhaust the subject in these notes; my purpose is merely to outline it and to make an attempt to trace the difference between the technique of the bizarre in Chekhov's last works ·and his use of the bizarre element in his early stories; for example, between a little scene like this in "The Cherry Orchard" (1903–04):

> *Varja:* The estate will be up for sale in August.
> *Anja:* Oh dear!
> *Lopachin:* (*puts his head through the door and bleats*) M-e-e-e . . .
> (*Disappears*)" [1]

and 'bizarre' stories like "On Christmas Eve" (1883), "At Sea" (1883), "Oysters" (1884), "The Mistress" (1882), "In the Home for Incurables and the Aged" (1884) and many others from Chekhov's early period, stories that are bizarre either in style or theme, or both. When we consider Chekhov's literary output as a whole, we cannot fail to notice one remarkable fact, namely, that the bizarre element is abundantly represented in the early, the 'Chechonte' stories, that it gradually disappears in his later and riper work, but reappears, more profusely than ever, in his plays.

---

* Charles B. Timmer, "The Bizarre Element in Chekhov's Art," *Anton Chekhov 1860–1960, Some Essays*, ed. T. Eekman (Leiden, E. J. Brill, 1960) pp. 277–284. Reprinted by permission of E. J. Brill, Leiden.

[1] Anton Chekhov, *Three plays*, transl. by Elisaveta Fen, London 1953, p. 30.

But what really is the meaning of the bizarre in art and what is its function? When do we call a certain phenomenon, a situation, a statement *bizarre*?

The word defies precise definition. However, it is possible to mention one inherent quality: — its irrelevancy, and one typical effect: — its capability of producing bewilderment. In this it differs from the grotesque, which really is nothing but comical exaggeration, showing us the ludicrous side of 'extreme situations'; it likewise differs from the absurd, which lies already wholly in the realm of the irrational. The *bizarre* is not necessarily absurd: it is, as it were, a statement, or a situation, which has no logical place in the context or in the sequence of events, the resulting effect, being one of sudden bewilderment; the bizarre brings about a kind of mental 'airpocket': one gasps for breath, until the tension is relieved by laughter. The *absurd* is contrary to reason and does not necessarily contain this element of playful, whimsical strangeness, which is so characteristic for Chekhov in the youthful wantonness of his art, a strangeness, which comes so strikingly to light again in many characters and situations in his plays. It is difficult, if not impossible to draw a distinct line between such conceptions as 'the absurd', 'the bizzare', 'the grotesque'; they often overlap and flow together. And besides, in all these matters the factor of personal appreciation by the reader or spectator and therefore of subjective interpretation influences the definition. A few examples by way or illustration, taken from Chekhov's Notebooks—this rich fund of grotesque, bizarre and absurd fancies and observations — , may throw some more light on the matter. Thus the following situation might be called simply 'grotesque': "A shy young man came on a visit for the night; suddenly a deaf old woman of eighty came into his room, carrying a clyster-pipe and administered a clyster to him; he thought that this must be the usual thing and so did not protest; in the morning it turned out that the old woman had made a mistake." [2] Here my contention that the characteristic quality of the grotesque lies in the exaggeration, in the hyperbolism of a *possible* situation, is clearly demonstrated by the English translation of this passage,[3] in which, possibly for reasons of modesty, the clyster-pipe is replaced by a cupping glass and the victim is bled. Suppose another translator would go one step further and change the syringe for a cup of tea — then the grotesque element would have disappeared altogether. The bizarre element can be found in a statement like this: "When I become rich, I shall have a harem in which I shall

[2] *The Personal Papers of Anton Chekhov*, New York 1948, p. 104. The translation of the Notebook is by S. S. Koteliansky and Leonard Woolf and quoted here with some corrections.
[3] The passage referred to reads in the English translation: "Suddenly a deaf old woman came into the room, carrying a cupping-glass, and bled him". Cf. A. P. Chekhov, PSSP XII 284: "Vdrug voshla starucha let 80, gluchaja, s klistirnoj kruzhkoj i postavila emu klistir."

keep fat naked women, with their buttocks painted green." This is a good example of that particular kind of 'mental leap', so typical of the bizarre, with the clear-cut caesura in the logical sequence after the third section of this statement. Finally, the absurd is demonstrated in a note of the following kind: "N., a singer; speaks to nobody, his throat muffed up — he takes care of his voice, but no one has ever heard him sing." Which, in my opinion, is a good example of irrational behaviour.

In the beginning of his career as a writer the bizarre element in Chekhov's work comes very close to the grotesque; wherever it appears in his later prose-writings and in his plays, it has more in common with the absurd. This is important and fully in harmony with the wellknown fact that the laughter in Chekhov's stories gradually dies down. In his early period it seems hardly likely that Chekhov used the bizarre deliberately as a consciously worked out technique: it rather appears that bizarre thoughts, statements, situations found their way in his work quite naturally, as the fruit of unbridled inspiration; they arose understandably from a youthful *brio*, playfulness and boldness in the author himself; they are, if I may quote Dylan Thomas, "A portrait of the artist as a young dog". More often than not the stories, in which the bizarre element is very evident, can be found in that group of narratives, which Chekhov himself did not include in his collected works and which form a part of his literary inheritance. The genuinely grotesque-bizarre stories are published under the penname Chechonte', a pseudonym rather bizarre in itself, at least for Russian ears.

Quite frequently the stories, containing bizarre elements, are written in the first person singular or plural, e.g. "The Crooked Mirror", "At Sea", "The Confession", "The Only Remedy", "At a Spiritualist Seance", "The Ninny", "A Charitable Publican", "The Guardian", "From the Reminiscences of an Idealist", "The Dream", etc. They are often provided with a sub-title in the way of "A Christmas Story", or "A Psychological Etude", or "Lament of a Ruined Man". In all these cases the bizarre character of the story is evoked by a peculiar blend of mystification, exaggeration and the deadly serious tone of the story-teller. A story like "At Sea" for instance, bearing the sub-title "A Sailor's Story", deals with anything but life at sea; this tale gives a perfect demonstration of the method of disguise and it leaves a peculiar impression of bewilderment and oppression with the reader, who at the same time feels inclined to laugh the whole thing off. The bizarre in stories of this kind, as also in "On Christmas Eve", an early story, written in a pseudo-romantic vein, and in quite a few others is realized by way of a subtle mockery of the 'terrible'; the element of horror is played with, rather flippantly sometimes, with the effect that horror becomes funny. Most of these stories have a definite point, with a surprising denouement, which does not however solve a problem or a mystery, but intensifies the comical effect of the narrative. Upon finishing his play "Ivanov", Chekhov wrote in a letter to his brother Aleksandr: "This is the first play I wrote, ergo—I was bound to make mistakes. The subject is complicated and not stupid. Every act I end just like my stories: throughout the whole act everything goes on peacefully and smoothly, but toward the end I give the spectator a punch on the nose." [4] It is in this "punch on the nose", in this sudden uncovering of "green-painted buttocks", that the typical bizarre element in Chekhov's early work is revealed and it is not without reason that his second collection of stories, which Chekhov published in 1886, bore the title "Motley Stories". Nor is it fortuitous that Chekhov did not include in his collection any work of his hand that had appeared under his own name in the literary magazine "New Times", work that he wanted to save for 'a more important publication'. Seen against the background of Chekhov's later, much more complicated and serious output, we can understand that the author at the height of his creative powers felt rather reluctant to include certain of his bizarre 'trifles' (as he calls them) in his collected works, although Chekhov's harsh judgment seems to us unwarranted: in their class these stories are priceless.

As I pointed out, the bizarre gradually disappears in Chekhov's later work, or rather, it loses its grotesque aspect and approaches more and more that particular attitude towards things, which we call the absurd. Here it must be stated at once, however, that the absurd as such in Chekhov's art is always treated merely incidentally, never programmatically, dogmatically or from the platform of a certain philosophy. For Chekhov life as such (existence) is neither absurd nor intelligible. The absurd elements in his stories should therefore not be confused with the absurd as idea. The absurd is the confrontation with the irrational; it is, what in relation to human judgment is considered as unreasonable. If we think of a scientist, whose knowledge in a certain field of science is unique and of immeasurable value to mankind, who suddenly dies in a car-accident, we may speak of an absurd occurrence, the absurd in this case consisting in the fact that such a tremendous wealth of knowledge and experience can be destroyed within a fraction of a second. Death in its finality is bizarre in so far as it causes bewilderment, it is absurd in so far as we consider it unreasonable. Chekhov had a wonderful feeling for the whole scale of subtle shades between the bizarre and the absurd in life and death. The long standing controversy, whether Chekhov was an optimist or a pessimist, with ardent partisans on both sides, loses its meaning, when we realize that Chekhov, like every sensitive artist, was torn between two contrary insights: that the world, or life as such, is unreasonable and at the same time, that man cannot leave off trying to find a reasonable explanation for this world, or, in the words of Albert Camus, this philosopher of the absurd (whose own death can stand as an example of absurdity); "Ce monde en lui-même n'est pas raisonnable. . . Mais ce qui est absurde, c'est la confrontation de cet irrationnel et de ce désir éperdu de clarté dont l'appel résonne au plus profond de l'homme." [5] Chekhov's dithyrambic dreams of a better life in the future, expressed in his last plays and in some of his stories, are no proof of his "optimism", but only of his desperate desire to find a solution to the problem of the antagonism, existing between absurd reality and rational ideality, his desire to bring about a peace between life as it is lived:—an apparently bizarre and senseless undertaking,—and life as it could be projected in the mind:—beauty, justice and harmony. On the other hand, if Chekhov were convinced that such a peace would a priori be impossible, that the search for a reasonable explanation of the world is an enterprise, foredoomed to failure, then we might be justified in calling him a pessimist; but he never made such a statement, on the contrary: somewhere, at some time in the future the solution will be found, he says. This is not optimism, but the firm conviction that life itself generates hope. Converted to secular values, we may compare Chekhov's faith with the 'Credo quia absurdum' of Tertullian, philosophically speaking the most optimistic statement ever made, if we put the stress on the 'credo', but at the same time the most pessimistic one, if we realize that we can never overcome the absurd, that we, as long as there is life, shall never be able to say: we believe in it, because it is reasonable. In other words: that faith can never be replaced by knowledge, Chekhov's dream of happiness 'after two hundred years' is nothing else than this désir éperdu de clarté, of which Camus speaks. In fact, hope and expectation are blended so masterfully in Chekhov's art with hopelessness and despair, the technique of evoking bizarre effects by letting hope clash on despondency is handled so skilfully, that we can say without hesitation that here we find the clue to that unique fascination, which emanates from his work and the spell it exercises on the reader. A perfect demonstration of this we find in stories like "Dreams" (1886), or "Happiness" (1887), in "Peasants" (1897), "In the Ravine" (1900) and many others. In the story "Happiness" an old shepherd is telling about the treasures, hidden, according to legend, somewhere in the vast Russian steppe. A young shepherd listens attentively to the old man's stories. "But, if you find the treasure, what are you going to do with it?", he asks in the end. The old man does not know; all through his long life he has dreamed of finding one of these legendary treasures, but the thought, what to do with it, has never occurred to him: that was not important. The young man also starts to wonder at the curious fact that only old men and women were so interested in these treasures, only the old kept constantly talking about them. At last the young shepherd falls silent and thinks about all the things he has heard in the course of the summer-night. "He was not interested so much in happiness in itself, which he

---

[5] Albert Camus, Le mythe de Sisyphe, Paris 1942, p. 37.

did not need, and which he could not comprehend, as in the fantastic, the fairytale side of human happiness. . .", concludes Chekhov.

One of Chekhov's notions of the bizarre,—and probably one of the most important ones,—is that in an apparently hopeless life there is still hope, that, as I said before, life itself generates hope. That, if there is seemingly no way out,—there *is* nevertheless a way out: by being interested, fully, humanly interested in "the fantastic, fairytale side" of every situation. To the question of what life *means*, Chekhov had no other answer than: it is what it is, as in "Three Sisters," when Masha asks: "Isn't there some meaning?" and Tuzenbach answers: "Meaning? . . Look out there, it's snowing. What's the meaning of that ?"[6] In the same play the final conclusion of Andrej, when Chebutykin asks him: "What about your wife?" is: "My wife is my wife".[7] But even if every life is condemned to end in failure, even if it has many terrible aspects, it still is hopeful, because it is life, because it can be seen and felt and tasted and experienced, because it can be told. In the story "Peasants" this hope, this life, this Chekhovian conception of indestructible continuation is impersonated in the little girl Sasha, who as an innocent witness of poverty and misery wanders through the whole story with eyes to see and to bear witness. The little girl is not a judge, she just observes and sees. The fact that in life there are eyes to see the injustice, the absurdity, is enough: this is all the hope there is. Well, and this is precisely the case with Chekhov himself: *he just sees.* And to see, really to see, with inquisitive, childlike eyes, means to discover the hidden relationships in life, to reveal its fairytale side. In many of Chekhov's stories it is the child, or the grown-up with the childlike mind that sees in this manner: it is the child and the artist, who possess this talent for discovering. And again, it is children and artists who have the genuine taste for the bizarre, the feeling for the absurd; it is they also, who can recreate it, because playfulness is an intrinsic part of their being, they represent the *homo ludens* with his taste for freedom. In Chekhov's first long story "The Steppe" (1888) it is through the eyes of the little boy Egorushka that the steppe and life in it are recreated. In the story "In Exile" (1892) it is the poor, illiterate Tartar with the mind of a child, who understands and grasps the 'hidden relationships' and stammers the truth in his broken Russian: "The gentleman is a good soul, very good, and you are a beast, you are bad! The gentleman is alive and you are dead. . . God made man that he should be alive, that he should have happiness, sorrow, grief, and you want nothing, so you are not alive, but a stone! A stone wants nothing and so do you. . .".[8]

---

[6] Anton Chehov, *Three Plays*, transl. by Elisaveta Fen, London 1953, p. 126.
[7] Id. p. 162.
[8] The Stories of Anton Tchekov, ed. by Robert N. Linscott, N.Y. 1932, p. 180.

When comparing the bizarre in Chekhov's work with the bizarre in Dostoevskij, we find some striking differences in their approach, both in technique and its application. In the great novels of Dostoevskij the bizarre element is mainly demonstrated in some of the secondary characters and they are always slices of enlarged humanity. Mentally, intellectually, the reader believes in a captain Lebjadkin ("Evil Spirits"), in a Lebedev ("The Idiot") and queer characters like these, although they possess a reality, built up out of isolated psychological components and the bizarre in them lies in their psychological hyperbolism. Lebedev in "The Idiot" is a vulgar scoundrel and a drunk, but at the same time a man, who prays at night for the salvation of the unfortunate comtesse Du Barry; he is a specialist in the exegesis of the Apocalypse, and in some casual, enigmatic remarks he gives a clue to the main theme of the whole novel. In the hundreds of characters in Chekhov's stories not one is in this sense 'enlarged' and hyperbolic; they always stay human in every respect; the bizarre with them,—even with the queerest characters we meet in his plays,—does not appear so much in what they are, as well in what they do. Looking for the bizarre in Chekhov's work, we do not find it in the characters, but in their situation, in their mutual relationships. The reason for this may be found in the fact that Chekhov's characters nearly all are 'whole', while Dostoevskij's characters are practically all 'split personalities', or combined doubles; they are dramas, tragedies in themselves, while Chekhov's people through their interrelationship create tragedies and dramas amongst themselves. Chekhov's characters long for things they do not possess (Moscow, talent, love, gooseberries), or for what they are not and cannot be (famous, active, energetic) and the author knows how to uncover the bizarre element in such hopeless longing: in this respect the epithet of "a cruel talent" could be given to Chekhov also! But Dostoevskij's heroes are both mean and noble, both evil and good, both vulgar and highminded; alternatively the one or the other quality breaks out and suppresses the opposite impulse. Therefore the bizarre with Dostoevskij is one of inner conflict and of being; with Chekhov of outer conflict and of situation. In 1886 Chekhov wrote in a letter to his brother Aleksandr: "Heaven forbid that we indulge in the use of commonplaces! The best would be to avoid in your stories the description of the mental state of your heroes altogether. You must try to develop this state out of the actions of your heroes." [9] This is exactly the opposite of Dostoevskij's method, where the action is rather a result, the outcome of the mental state of the hero, of what I call his 'inner conflict'. Nikolaj Chikildeev in the story "Peasants" had to give up his job as a waiter in a Moscow hotel because of ill health and returned with wife and child to his native village, where he slowly withers away. In the famous description of a night at the peasant-cottage Chekhov relates,

[9] PSSP XIII 215.

how "Nikolaj, who had not slept all night, got down from the stove. He took his dress-coat out of a green chest, put it on, and going to the window, stroked the sleeves, fingered the coat-tails—and smiled. Then he carefully removed the coat, put it away in the chest, and lay down again." [10] There is no question in Nikolaj's bizarre behaviour in the middle of the night of a description of inner conflict: Nikolaj is quite an ordinary man, but he is placed in an extraordinary situation, a man beyond hope and help, who attires himself at night with the only remaining attributes of his former happiness and dignity. In the given situation the bizarre lies in the fact that the ex-waiter, placed in the position of a parasite on the village-life, caresses as a symbol of liberty and human dignity an object, a waiter's dress-coat, which in fact should stand as a symbol for human servitude and humiliation. [11] It will be clear, from an example like this, that the technique of the bizarre, as used by Chekhov in this passage, is quite a far cry from the overt and wanton caprices in his 'Chechonte'-period; now the bizarre comes to us as a technique, subtly handled by a masterhand and only recognizable as bizarre through the intellectual cooperation of the reader. . .

[10] *The Portable Chekhov*, ed. by Avrahm Yarmolinsky, N.Y., 1947, p. 339.
[11] Cf. A. Derman, *Omasterstve Céchova*, Moskava, 1952, p. 42.

PART FOUR

☼

☼

THE CHERRY ORCHARD IN THE THEATRE: Selected Reviews

GERTRUDE BESSE KING*

Who is Chekoff? I knew that he had been a favorite in Russia for a decade, accorded place beside Pushkin and Turgeniev as one of the three mountain peaks of Russian literature, that he had reached England in virulent form about five years ago, and that he would in all probability strike America some few years hence, although one of his plays was given in Boston last winter. As to why he had been invested with such apparently secure immortality I was quite ignorant, and I waited with eager incredulity as the great brown curtains of the Moscow Art Theater swung open upon "Cherry Orchard."

I soon became aware that his was hardly a "play" at all. Here were people behaving in a most human sort of way, not at all as those who exhibit extravagant emotions before the footlights. They were not even keyed up, quite off-guard, as it were, not taking part in "situations" or talking in aphorisms. They were not even attempting, as in our own so-called "realistic" drama, the tricks, mannerisms, and telephone verisimilitudes that produce such artificial naturalness. They seemed to be living along, entirely unconcerned that a well-trained audience expects a catastrophe and a climax within two hours.

You would hesitate to call the enforced selling of "Cherry Orchard," the old family estate of a woman and her brother, and its effects upon the household and the neighbors, a plot. There is no denouement, for there are no complex threads to be extricated. An ex-peasant whose fathers before him were flogged in the kitchen has become wealthy and wishes to buy the place. The woman, who has lost her money through the extravagance of her lover, does not wish to part with it. But neither she nor her brother makes any effort to postpone the inevitable auction. This auction, the only real action of the play, takes place off stage, while a little village party is making merry for the last time through the old rooms. The successful bidder, the peasant, returns, insolently takes possession, and orders the cherry trees cut. During the last act the family pack and leave, forgetting an old retainer, who is locked within. The windows are boarded up, and you hear resumed the dull sound of the axes in the orchard.

But if you have practically no plot, only an unframed picture of the deep-rooted life that centers about the estate, you do get an acquaintance

* Reprinted from *The New Republic*, III (June 26, 1915), 207.

with that family and a feeling of having lived in its atmosphere since the members of it were children. The people are not manneristic or easy to characterize, they are not even vivid personalities beyond those one meets in an ordinary day's run, but they are livingly real. You don't think of asking whether Chekhoff conceived them well or whether the actors portray them convincingly; there they are, as much a part of the world as any of us. You may not have seen anyone just like them, but that only adds to their actuality. You might have met them somewhere, anywhere, before or after they had left Cherry Orchard. But you wouldn't have felt quite the same comprehending fondness for them, for they animate Cherry Orchard and it is part of them. Whether the little girl, the daughter, is running through the rooms to find her bag, or the governess is doing tricks to amuse the neighbors, or they are all sitting out on the newly gathered hay talking with the peasant about the coming sale, you feel the firm and delicate roots that have wound themselves for generations into the soil of Cherry Orchard.

To feel their relentless uprooting is painful tragedy, and tragedy without poetic mitigation. The sale does not point any moral, it is not the result of some weakness or wrong that has recoiled and struck back at the appropriate sense of justice. At the same time you feel thoroughly an identification with the sufferers. How then is it bearable?

Frankly, I am more conscious of the effect than of the method by which it was produced. For one thing, I suspect that the very frameless-ness of the picture, the absence of a nicely terminated plot, gives a feeling of space, of largeness, of perspective that is in itself corrective of petty rebellions. You look before and after, and so do not mourn for what is not. Hardly a detail that does not lead off suggestively. The rooms seem part of a house which a mere accident of vision prevents you from seeing in its entirety. The fields run away into illimitable distances. The problems concerning the estate reach back before the serfs were freed, and are bound up with the whole agricultural question of Russia. The acts of the people concerned are not isolated episodes, but carry you to what they have been doing previously, and will do long after the curtain has fallen. They are surrounded by an older generation, with its antiquated ideas and reduced sensibilities, and a younger that is joyously untouched by the prospect of calamity. Since the threads of an intricate plot are not present to be drawn together and tied up neatly at the end, you are not limited by that intense artistic economy which concentrates vital significance into the lift of an eyebrow, and which so thoroughly expurgates the irrelevant that there is little for the relevant to be relevant to. "Cherry Orchard" is not so, but is like the chaff that the wind driveth away, as like the wheat which remains. Effects are not dependent upon speed and heat, and, consequently, leisure and spacious-ness produce reciprocal amplitudes in the audience. Man no longer seems to strut a little hour upon the stage, but to play his part in the midst of centuries and in the presence of planets. By refusing to overdo the moment, Chekhoff invites eternity.

Here is an even greater puzzle. Why, for instance, should you like that newly rich peasant, even at the moment when, literally and figuratively drunk, he stalks through the house that has just been knocked down to him, shattering every sensibility you possess as he slams a plate to the floor? Yet you do like him, and when later he offers to send the tutor to the university, you knew he would. And if he fails to propose to the old housekeeper, which would have made it rather pleasant all around, you understand how he can't quite bring himself to it. The characters are not by any means lovable; some are coarse, some sentimental, others shallow or puerile; take them man for man they would probably average up about like the audience. Do you respond to them because they are so real? I doubt it, for since when have audiences reached that Whitman-like avidity for human beings as such? Rather you say to yourself: "Yes, people are like that, but I had no idea how attractive they were, with all their unattractiveness so apparent." It may be that Chekhoff and his producers have succeeded in stimulating the same sense of proportion in regard to character that they have as to plot: unattractiveness is never isolated, any more than misfortune is, and seeing beyond it as you do, you would no more object to it than you would object to a resolving chord.

I leave the dissection of the miracle to others, merely recording the achievement that makes you interested in the commonplace without changing it into something strange and new, that induces a tolerant kindliness quite foreign to your nature, that enables you to face sorrow, not because another such as you is receiving his deserts, but because pain is part of a larger reconciling experience.

VIRGINIA WOOLF*

Although every member of the audience at the Art Theatre last week had probably read Tchekhov's *The Cherry Orchard* several times, a large number of them had, perhaps, never seen it acted before. It was no doubt on this account that as the first act proceeded the readers, now transformed into seers, felt themselves shocked and outraged. The beautiful, mad drama which I had staged often enough in the dim recesses of my mind was now hung within a few feet of me, hard, crude, and over-emphatic, like a cheap coloured print of the real thing. But what right had I to call it the real thing? What did I mean by that? Perhaps something like this.

There is nothing in English literature in the least like *The Cherry Orchard*. It may be that we are more advanced, less advanced, or have advanced in an entirely different direction. At any rate, the English person who finds himself at dawn in the nursery of Madame Ranevskaia feels out of place, life a foreigner brought up with entirely different traditions. But the traditions are not (this, of course, is a transcript of individual experience) so ingrained in one as to prevent one from shedding them not only without pain but with actual relief and abandonment. True, at the end of a long railway journey one is accustomed to say goodnight and go to bed. Yet on this occasion, since everything is so strange, the dawn rising and the birds beginning to sing in the cherry-trees, let us gather round the coffee-cups; let us talk about everything in the whole world. We are all in that queer emotional state when thought seems to bubble into words without being spoken. The journey is over and we have reached the end of everything where space seems illimitable and time everlasting. Quite wrongly (since in the production approved by Tchekhov the birds actually sing and the cherries are visible on the trees) I had, on my imaginary stage, tried to give effect to my sense that the human soul is free from all trappings and crossed incessantly by thoughts and emotions which wing their way from here, from there, from the furthest horizons—I had tried to express this by imagining an airy view from the window with ethereal pink cherries and perhaps snow mountains and blue mist behind them. In the room the characters spoke suddenly whatever came into their heads, and yet always vaguely, as if thinking aloud. There was no "comedy of man-

* *The New Statesman and Nation*, XV (July 29, 1920), 446–447. Reprinted by permission of Leonard Woolf.

ners"; one thought scarcely grazed, let alone struck sparks from, another; there was no conflict of individual wills. At the same time the characters were entirely concrete and without sentimentality. Not for an instant did one suppose that Madame Ranevskaia was wrapping up a mystic allusion to something else when she spoke. Her own emotions were quite enough for her. If what was said seemed symbolical, that was because it was profound enough to illumine much more than an incident in the life of one individual. And, finally, though the leap from one thought to another was so wide as to produce a sense of dangerous dislocation, all the separate speeches and characters combined to create a single impression of an overwhelming kind.

The actors at the Art Theatre destroyed this conception, first, by the unnatural emphasis with which they spoke; next by their determination to make points which brought them into touch with the audience but destroyed their harmony with each other; and, finally, by the consciousness which hung about them of being well-trained English men and women ill at ease in an absurd situation, but determined to make the best of a bad business. One instance of irrepressible British humour struck me with considerable force. It occurred in the middle of Charlotte's strange speech in the beginning of the second act. "I have no proper passport. I don't know how old I am; I always feel I am still young," she begins. She goes on, "When I grew up I became a governess. But where I come from and who I am, I haven't a notion. Who my parents were— *very likely they weren't married*—I don't know." At the words I have italicised, Dunyasha bounced away from her to the other end of the bench, with an arch humour which drew the laugh it deserved. Miss Helena Millais seemed to be delighted to have this chance of assuring us that she did not believe a word of this morbid nonsense, and that the old jokes still held good in the world of sanity round the corner. But it was Miss Ethel Irving who showed the steadiest sense of what decency requires of a British matron in extremity. How she did it, since she spoke her part accurately, it is difficult to say, but her mere presence upon the stage was enough to suggest that all the comforts and all the decencies of English upper-class life were at hand, so that at any moment her vigil upon the bench might have been appropriately interrupted by a man-servant bearing a silver tray. "The Bishop is in the drawing-room, m'lady." "Thank you, Parker. Tell his Lordship I will come at once." In that sort of play, by which I mean a play by Sheridan or Oscar Wilde, both Miss Irving and Miss Millais would charm by their wit, spirit and competent intellectual outfit. Nor, though the quotation I have made scarcely proves it, have we any cause to sneer at English comedy or at the tradition of acting which prevails upon our stage. The only question is whether the same methods are as applicable to *The Cherry Orchard* as they are to *The School for Scandal*.

But there are four acts in The Cherry Orchard. How it may have been with the other readers I do not know, but before the second act was over some sort of compromise had been reached between my reader's version and the actor's one. Perhaps in reading one had got the whole too vague, too mad, too mystical. Perhaps as they went on the actors forgot how absurd such behaviour would be thought in England. Or perhaps the play itself triumphed over the deficiencies of both parties. At any rate, I felt less and less desire to cavil at the acting in general and more and more appreciation of the acting of Mr. Cancellor, Mr. Dodd, Mr. Pearson and Miss Edith Evans in particular. With every word that Mr. Felix Aylmer spoke as Pishchick, one's own conception of that part plumped itself out like a shrivelled skin miraculously revived. But the play itself —that was what overwhelmed all obstacles, so that though the walls rocked from floor to ceiling when the door was shut, though the sun sank and rose with the energetic decision of the stage carpenter's fist, though the scenery suggested an advertisement of the Surrey Hills rather than Russia in her wildness, the atmosphere of the play wrapped us round and shut out everything alien to itself. It is, as a rule, when a critic does not wish to commit himself or to trouble himself that he refers to atmosphere. And, given time, something might be said in greater detail of the causes which produced this atmosphere—the strange dislocated sentences, each so erratic and yet cutting out the shape so firmly, of the realism, of the humour, of the artistic unity. But let the word atmosphere be taken literally to mean that Tchekhov has contrived to shed over us a luminous vapour in which life appears as it is, without veils, transparent and visible to the depths. Long before the play was over we seemed to have sunk below the surface of things and to be feeling our way among submerged but recognisable emotions. "I have no proper passport. I don't know how old I am; I always feel I am still young"—how the words go sounding on in one's mind—how the whole play resounds with such sentences, which reverberate, melt into each other, and pass far away out beyond everything! In short, if it is permissible to use such vague language, I do not know how better to describe the sensation at the end of The Cherry Orchard, than by saying that it sends one into the street feeling like a piano played upon at last, not in the middle only but all over the keyboard and with the lid left open so that the sound goes on.

This being so, and having felt nothing comparable to it from reading the play, one feels inclined to strike out every word of criticism and to implore Madame Donnet to give us the chance of seeing play after play, until to sit at home and read plays is an occupation for the afflicted only, and one to be viewed with pity, as we pity blind men spelling out their Shakespeare with their fingers upon sheets of cardboard.

MARGARET MARSHALL*

Chekhov's plays are wrought with great skill and care. So complete and profound was his knowledge of the people and society he wrote about that the end product is distillation rather than document. But the live power of the plays, like that of lyric poetry, comes from a charge of emotion which sets up an infrangible arc of tension—and fills the simplest lines, the most casual remarks, the most quiet situations with light and meaning. The wonder is that he can sustain a dozen characters through two hours of at least seemingly ordinary, often colloquial, talk, and by means of it summon up a world which takes on for us so much reality and vested emotional interest.

At the moment the further wonder is that the iridescent, fragile web of "The Cherry Orchard" is so closely and firmly woven, so tough, that it even withstands the pulling and hauling it gets at the hands of its latest producers.

Most of the characters in "The Cherry Orchard" are eccentric. But their eccentricity, it seems hardly necessary to say, is all of a piece with the world they spring from. What is even more important, they are all encompassed in Chekhov's feeling about that world. He loved it, but his writing gets edge not only from the fact that he knew it was dying but that he could not, despite his love, wish it to survive. The fun he makes of his characters is made within this context. With the Epihodovs, the Pistchiks, the Leonids, the Charlottas he is very gentle. With the Yashas and the Lopahins he is more ruthless. They are pathetic because they are caught between two worlds, and they have worst traits of both, but they are firmly established in the new world and reconciled to it. With Trofimov he is again gentle because Trofimov *is* the perpetual student, the idealist who must commit himself to the future as idea yet will never be at home among "the villa residents" of any Cherry Orchard development.

This may seem too elementary to set down. But in the present production Yasha, Epihodov, Leonid, and Charlotta are made merely funny, sometimes grotesque—and therefore extraneous and really irrelevant. Yasha resembles a character that James Cagney might play—it would have been even more sensational of course if Cagney could have been persuaded. You might run across Epihodov in any musical show. Leonid

* The Nation, CLVIII (Feb. 5, 1944), 158. Reprinted by permission of The Nation, New York.

is simply made a fool of by Joseph Schildkraut—or is it vice versa? Charlotta is a clown. All are wrenched out of their proper place and proportion. Chekhov's wit is blown up into burlesque, the play pulled out of shape, its texture and tone violated again and again. In the worst scene of all the flirtation between Yasha and the eager Dunyasha is "modernized" into a cheap encounter that might take place in any park on any maid's day off.

Fortunately Madame Ranevsky (Miss LeGallienne), Anya (Lois Hall), Varya (Katherine Emery), and in lesser degree Trofimov (Eduard Franz) have been allowed to cleave to Chekhov. Among them they manage to preserve the spirit of "The Cherry Orchard" despite the chopping, with up-to-date axes, that goes on about them.

Joseph Wood Krutch has described Chekhov's mood as elegiac. I should underline that comment by adding that it is not nostalgic. Between these two moods lies the difference that makes Chekhov's plays endure. His particular world in decay takes on a generic dimension, and for all its local color "The Cherry Orchard" continues to be relevant as well as beautiful.

N. B.: Again I overheard the old remark that nothing happens in "The Cherry Orchard." Nothing happens—except that a world comes to an end.

STARK YOUNG*

The role of a dramatic critic is a sour thing at worst, though at best a critic—a creative critic as they say—may be constructive and of genuine use to the theatre. He may, at times, shall we say, both be useful to the theatre-going public and well worth his salt to the theatre, which as every worker in it knows needs salt, and sadly. A daily newspaper fares better in that it may for the nonce stick to sheer news, to be or not to be followed later on, as of a Sabbath article, by more abstract lucubrations. A journal, monthly or, like The New Republic, weekly, is supposed to follow matters through somewhat further and to invite a different consideration.

The news of this production of "The Cherry Orchard" is that to begin with it is an entirely honorable venture; that it is well worth seeing by everyone; and that for those who have seen this play before it is necessary, it must be seen. All of which having been said, we arrive here in these columns at perhaps a thankless moment. We have a season and a theatre, say, where nobody is wholly to blame for this or that, everybody all round is to some extent to blame, though those in the theatre profession are more to blame at that. Here we have a situation in which actors who are at the top, such as it is, on our stage, are afraid to take a chance, to do a young fresh drama, to enlarge the horizon of dramatic writing, et cetera. They sink into playing trash and hope it goes over, though they have the prestige, funds and financial backing to risk other considerations. They do very little for the theatre and nothing for the drama as such. There are some pleasant pieces running, but nothing—we might accept the "Othello," cut as it is and brought into a somewhat false readiness of comprehension—that does anything for the flight or evolution of dramatic writing or theatre art. And for most of our leading Broadway lights—for all the leading ones, in fact—I would say that they would not willingly, even in an endowed theatre where no money could be lost, take a chance on any drama they could not believe would be a hit, if need be a hit in the raw, as it were. Then along comes this clear venture of "The Cherry Orchard," taking a brave chance and, right or wrong, honest. Honest, sometimes innocent, but never fake.

* The New Republic, CX (Feb. 7, 1944, Feb. 14, 1944), 180–181, 211. Reprinted by permission of William McKnight Bowman, Literary Executor for Stark Young.

The translation of the play, credited to Irina Skariatina, is far above the published versions of "The Cherry Orchard" that have usually been adopted. In these versions Chekhov turns out to be that strange and dour creature that no Russian ever recognizes. A misty, moony, mucky author he seems, spiritually full of a strange squalor, and so subtle that only amateurish performers or performances were apt to come his way. In amateur art the amateurish is apt to be, as they say of foods, an extender, but not vital or life-giving. And in our Anglo-Saxon theatre the word "intellectual" is likely to paralyze us, exactly as, in the rhyme, the query about which foot came first checked the centipede, which up to then had been walking all right. This newest version of "The Cherry Orchard" lacks fluency now and then, as in the speeches of Gaev or Trofimov, but on the whole follows Chekhov's intelligent text with—I have compared it with the play in Russian—respect and accurate decency.

The one big point to stress in this discussion is that Chekhov's play seems fairly tricky unless the whole, general current is created, unless there is a unity of current and mood among all involved. These characters give and take life among themselves, they are happy in their vitality, they are tortured in their responsiveness, they shine, they weep, they move all together as, in St. Paul's great phrase, parts of one another's bodies. Only the silliest of stages can believe this will arrive overnight or over some months of nights. But it can be more and more approximated.

The performance, out of all the company, that was closest to Chekhov's intentions, was that of Miss Katherine Emery, as Varya, adopted daughter of the heroine, Lyubov, in love with the peasant rich man Lopahin, who finally buys the cherry orchard. Miss Emery understood and projected the inner pressure and outer torment that is implicit in Chekhov's method and presentation. Nobody else did so quite. Mr. Stefan Schnabel, for example, as Lopahin, protested too outwardly, in thought and gesture. Miss Leona Roberts in a small way gave a good perfomance for Charlotta, the governess, though, as a portion of the general taming of our wild Chekhov, her role was greatly and wrongly cut down. The taming of her tricks, of her ventriloquism and of her lacing herself tight, are all indications of what happens to Chekhov when we know better than he does.

Mr. Joseph Schildkraut, in the frighteningly famous role of Gaev, the family brother, approached the portrayal with a punch and vulgarity that must be mentioned no doubt but may otherwise be left aside save for the wretched bleeding of the play thereby.

Miss Eva Le Gallienne, looking very beautiful as the incredible Lyubov Andreyevna, in all her intensity, vagary and fascination, played well enough—though not well enough either for the Chekhov or Le Gallienne. She needs, in the first place, to get the right corset for that epoch, 1904, without which her excellent costumes look, especially from the back, quite wrong. In her speeches she needs to get a stream of continuity in the thinking, so that the lines flow and create a unified whole, tragic, comic and convincing. The trouble with this production—in toto —of "The Cherry Orchard" is the lack of complete unity and pressure of life. Such are words easy to say but present a need that is but partly solved with months of effort and playing together. And apart from this highly worthy occasion, the fact remains that very few of our players would take such suggestions as would Miss Le Gallienne. It is part of her gallantry and of her dear, heroic little figure in our theatre.

THE CHERRY ORCHARD AGAIN

By one of those miscarriages in the mail the corrected proof of my review of "The Cherry Orchard" at the National did not arrive in time for a missing paragraph to be restored to the text. It concerned the translation and directing of the play. And since these were both highly admirable in their intentions it does not seem fair to omit their mention, especially the direction by Miss Margaret Webster and Miss Le Gallienne.

I said that the version of "The Cherry Orchard" by Irina Skariatina on the whole follows Chekhov's text with respect, accuracy and an effect of naturalness. It is a considerably better version than that Miss Cornell used for "The Three Sisters." And it is also, on the whole, directed with more unity of method and consistency of approach.

I may take this chance to bring up some other points about this Chekhov production. The limitation in this most commendable directing of "The Cherry Orchard" lies— as is the case in Miss Webster's production of "Othello"—in the tendency toward simplification. I do not mean simplification that implies a firm repression of subtle values and a concentration of the main outline and the main themes. The simplification I speak of includes some of that process, of course, but it also implies— in the "Othello" very much so—a good deal of cutting and a frequent understatement of the dramatic values. The result is that hundreds of people will be telling you that this is the first time they ever understood and liked Shakespeare.

The trouble is it's not Shakespeare. It is something for them out of Shakespeare, something of them, plus something added over and above that is a great deal more of course. A useful thing to remember in all these popularizings—to remember, obviously, with considerable modifications for each case involved—is Shaw's remark that when you convert savages to Christianity it merely means that you have converted Christianity to savagery. In Chekhov it is very much misled indeed to cut his lines or stage directions in order to improve on him or make him easy. With repetition this whole performance of "The Cherry Orchard" should gain in flow and intensity, in innerness, in variety of touch and go, and in that intricate realism from which a kind of poetry emerges.

I will cite two instances in which the Chekhov quality and intention could be furthered—instances created by Chekhov with infinite care and subtlety or detail and motivation.

In Lyubov's scenes with Trofimov, the tutor, the many details and items and emotions are all one single state or situation. She mentions the impossibility of letting the cherry orchard go from the family, she kisses the tutor on the forehead, cries over the death of her little son years before, draws her handkerchief from her pocket and with it a telegram from her Paris lover, which falls to the floor. "My heart," she goes on (in the absence of Miss Le Gallienne's script, I take this from Chekhov's Russian) "is heavy today, you can't imagine how heavy. It is too noisy for me here, my soul trembles at every sound, I tremble all over and yet I can't go off to myself; when I am alone the silence frightens me. Don't blame me, Petya, I love you as one of my own. I should gladly have given you Anya's hand, I assure you, only, my dear, you must study and finish your course. You do nothing, Fate simply flings you about from place to place, and that's so strange—Isn't that so? Yes? And you must do something about your beard, to make it grow somehow—(Laughing) You look funny!" He picks up the telegram and from that she goes on into desperate words about the lover ill in Paris, worthless but beloved, about Petya's stern look at her, et cetera. Here the beard detail will serve for at least one illustration. The actress should not pause before the remark about the beard. The beard is in Lyubov's mind from the start, her dead boy's tutor such a failure, the perennial student, so motheaten, so distressing to look at, grotesque and so solemnly disapproving of her. All this co-exists in her mind along with the cherry orchard, the sad memory, the passionate recklessnes, and helps to set her off. This is Chekhov's method. The inconsistency and irony are far inward and profoundly human, and compose a single stream. Externally they are to be presented as one whole, lively and pressing. Any absence of this in the directing helps to create the effect of too much jumping from tragic to comic, comic to tragic, which troubles many critics—mistakenly—as unnatural on the part of both the performance and the Chekhov.

The other instance concerns the lines that Chekhov gives Trofimov, the tutor, to say. When the actor of this role is immersed in various emotional situations, and otherwise, that is one thing. But the long speeches about Russia, science, the arts and the future of mankind are close to Chekhov's heart. Mr. Eduard Franz should speak them as if for a moment perhaps the character were galvanized into more emphasis, point and energy. These ideas are a most important element in the play's content and original quality. The fact that they are put in the mouth of a theorizer in this world, a dreamer and failure, is but a part of Chekhov's listing the play as a comedy.

ERIC BENTLEY*

To my mind, Chekhov's supreme achievement is *Three Sisters*, but the fact that *Cherry Orchard* is more famous indicates that it has made easier contact with the public, which takes from an author what it craves and leaves the rest alone. What we call "the influence of an author" is likely to be the influence of one famous fragment of him. Chekhov survives in journalistic criticism as the founder of a type of drama in which "nothing happens" and little people drift in and out remarking that their lives are empty, a drama in which plot has been replaced by mood, and chiefly a mood of nostalgia and defeat. Now, though I wouldn't say that this notion of Chekhov derives from an adequate reading of *Cherry Orchard*, I would say that it derives from not reading his other works, and that *Cherry Orchard* provokes, if it doesn't quite justify, such a notion. When Chekhov composed it, he not only wrote about dying, he *was* dying, and neither his emotions nor his imagination, as it seems to me, retained their full force. His intellect he has preserved intact, and he is consequently able to carry his special dramaturgy to its furthest reach. The delicacy of his sensibility is unimpaired, and that marvelous sense of fun which was, so to speak, his sword in the struggle for existence is all the more gallantly employed as death approaches. Obviously, then, *Cherry Orchard* is a masterpiece, but, lacking the fullness of *Three Sisters*, it is a masterpiece more in the mode of Chekhovism as popularly understood—a Chekhovism of nuance and innuendo, muted lyricism, gentle pathos and gentler humor. The success of a performance of *Cherry Orchard* will depend upon an accurate subtlety.

Because the production at the 4th Street Theatre is both inaccurate and unsubtle, I adjudge it, in the main, a calamity. It has its points, of course. The whole text is there in another of Stark Young's trenchant translations (this one not so markedly different from other versions of the play.) And the technical standard of the show is higher than one is used to off Broadway; the axe sounds like an axe, etc. There are several good individual performances, of which the best is the most unobstrusive —Gerald Hiken as Trofimov. Mr. Hiken imposes himself upon an audience by an intensity born of concentration and an intelligence that has shown

* *The New Republic*, CXXXIII (November 21, 1955), 30. Also published in Eric Bentley, *What is Theatre*, (Boston: Beacon Press, 1956), pp. 90–93. Reprinted by permission of Beacon Press and Eric Bentley.

185

him the character as Chekhov wrote it, no more, no less. Nancy Wickwire was, so to speak, groomed to give the best performance in the show as Varya, though sometimes the grooming is more evident than the performance. She not only acts; she acts up. But the fact that Varya comes to seem the main part is a tribute to her power. (In nothing, by the way, is the greatest of Chekhov's dramaturgy more manifest than in the fact that *any* part becomes luminous and prominent by being well performed.)

If self-assertation is a slight blemish on the otherwise smooth surface of Miss Wickwire's portrait, it completely disfigures the Yasha of Leonardo Cimino. Here is a gifted young actor (and I have seen him in several roles) who seems unable simply to make his statement and is constrained to underscore, capitalize, italicize, and overpunctuate (using especially the exclamation mark), till his MS is unreadable. He pulls faces. He strikes attitudes. And, if anyone adds: "So does Yasha," I reply that Mr. Cimino has not convinced me of the fact.

And where are the two leading characters in the play? *Cherry Orchard* may, in itself, be small by comparison with *Three Sisters;* at the 4th Street, it is smaller still, being deprived of its two strongest presences: Mme. Ranevsky and Lopakin. Strong, in a moral sense, Mme. Ranevsky is not—rather, a classical study, à la Turgenev, of elegant, feminine, "romantic" weakness, a weakness that falls before the strength of the self-made man, Lopakin. She is the cherry blossom, and he the axe. Lopakin, it is true, is not the villain of a Marxist melodrama; his author was at pains to stress his humanity. Did this emphasis mislead George Ebeling, at the 4th Street, into forgetting the role's original premise and its part in the story? This Lopakin brings on stage at the outset all the warmth of a Methodist minister at a mothers' meeting; naturally, by the time he goes so far as to take over the orchard, he is shocked at his own audacity and suffering from heartbreak. Heartbreak! How many heartwhole characters in the older drama are being interpreted by our actors as heartbroken! The age of anxiety is the age of self-pity. Now David Ross, the director of the play, had intimated in the press that he was going to disencumber Chekhov of all the accumulated lies and evasions of two generations of "Chekhovism." This was very misleading of him, for there is a portentous air about the show, and a complete lack of simplicity. For example when Mme. Ranevsky makes big claims for the orchard, Lopakin retorts: "The only remarkable thing about this orchard is that it's big." Such a retort is shockingly reductive, and nothing if not prosaic. (It reminds me of Hemingway's remark that the only difference between rich and poor is that the rich are richer.) Yet, at the 4th Street, they try to make something wistful, inspiring, and "poetic" out of it. And if Mr. Ebeling reaches out towards a romance that is not there, Elizabeth Farrar fails to take hold of one that is. Certainly, Mme. Ranevsky is a failure but as what? As a mistress in a villa in

Mentone—that is, in a role with considerable social and, in a sense, spiritual pretension. When she pours scorn on Trofimov for having reached 26 without taking a mistress, we hear an echo of the pride she must once have felt in her feminity. . . . But why run on when none of this has been presented on stage?

I enjoyed *Three Sisters* last year at this same theatre. At a second visit, one enjoys Mr. Ross' use of his cramped central stage a good deal less. One becomes too aware of unnatural, unreal positions, moves, and groupings. One comes to feel that, after all, Chekhov requires something like a real room for dramas in which walls and furniture play so significant a part. Then again, a strong wind of emotion blows through even a rough-and-ready performance of *Three Sisters*, as through a Beethoven sonata played by a capable amateur. *Cherry Orchard*, it seems to me, is like some exquisite and exact bit of tone-painting by Debussy that makes no impression at all unless it receives from the performer an equal exquisiteness and exactitude.

RICHARD HAYES*

Mr. David Ross' production of "The Cherry Orchard" at the Fourth Street Theatre is the most distinguished and variously beautiful rendering of Chekhov's dramatic vision it has been my good fortune to encounter. That vision is recorded not alone in the nuance and suggestive ambience of the production—that flicker of light and shade which is so characteristic a feature of Chekhov's theatrical personality—but in its dramatic rhythm as well: Mr. Ross has imposed the play boldly not merely as portraiture, but as action and morality. Every value has its weight and proper balance in the dramatic scheme; the emphases are faultlessly placed and marked, the tempo securely controlled. From a solution of reality dense with implication, truth is distilled. Yet the production, for all its complexity, is fluent and direct, with great purity of line: one's attention is never solicited by the extraneous and the peripheral. Mr. Ross and his associates have even subdued the physical deficiencies of their theater, and fashioned out of the meager possibilities of its stage any number of dramatic images of singular beauty.

We stand, as Miss Lillian Hellman suggests in her introduction to the *Selected Letters,* in an ambiguous relation to Chekhov the dramatist. He has refined and extended the possibilities of dramatic form, and his methods (if not his intentions) dominate a large segment of the contemporary theater. In the four major plays, he has himself made one of the great statements about the nature of reality and the quality of being. Yet too often what we know, as theatrical spectators, is not so much Chekhov as it is "the Chekhovian": the muted and elegiac, the melancholy, the wistful. The modern temperament—so Mr. David Magarshack argues in his excellent study of Chekhov's dramaturgy—has responded disproportionately to those aspects of his personality, and stressed them at the expense of his total vision. What is more, Stanislavsky and the directors who followed him (for the theater of Chekhov belongs supremely to the director) have been responsible for systematically heightening the sombre colors of what are essentially plays of irony and effort and energy. Mr. Magarshack (supported by Chekhov's correspondence) is at pains to convince us that "The Cherry

* *Commonweal,* LXIII (Dec. 2, 1955), 223–225. Reprinted by permission of *Commonweal,* New York.

Orchard" is specifically "a comedy, and in places almost a farce";
Miss Hellman joins him in seeing the work as "sharp comedy."

The truth, perhaps, is a compromise of these antagonistic interpretations. I would myself prefer to call the plays comedies of persons
and tragedies of society. They are lyrical and social: their private
dramas are seen always in the perspective of a public fate, though
not obscured by it. To illustrate: the full light of Chekhov's discrimination obviously falls on Mme. Ranevsky and her brother Gayeff; he takes
their moral measure securely, and finds their spiritual soil too barren
to nourish the tragic seed. Yet he sees the pathos of their situation
as none the less genuine for that; however unable they may be to
salvage their ancestral pieties, they have yet the sensibility to feel the
loss. One need not read "The Cherry Orchard" as a sentimental melodrama of "traditional sanctity and loveliness" raped by a pragmatic
industrialism, to realize that it is still the supreme portrait in modern
world literature of the decline of the leisure class, and the advent of
the *entrepreneur*. And Chekhov would not be the first artist to com-
memorate in his work values which his conscious mind repudiates.

It is the special virtue of Mr. Ross' production to crystallize these
ambiguities, and delineate them firmly, in the terms of social class.
One has, in consequence, a sharper sense of the humiliations and
pretensions, the subtle antagonisms and loyalties which constitute the
dramatic web of "The Cherry Orchard." Miss Elizabeth Farrar, the
Mme. Ranevsky, for example, has been criticized for the extreme
stylization of her portrait, yet do not these vanities and affectations
reflect precisely the rather desperate, tatty elegancies of provincial
society? Miss Farrar seems to me to place the character of Mme.
Ranevsky at quite the right spiritual and dramatic depth, and her
performance is not being sufficiently honored. So too with Mr. Louis
Edmonds' resonant Gayeff. This is playing of a classical restraint and
discretion: the surface values—of breeding, of presence—are there,
but so is the judgment, embedded in the character. Because it is not
obviously accessible, the quality of Mr. Edmonds' contribution to the
performance has not been adequately recognized. I cannot imagine
this role played with more authority and abstinent severity and intelligence. Miss Nancy Wickwire's Varya seems to me to intrude
rather too heightened and shrill a note: should not the girl's suffering
be more mute and animal, and the anachronistic flavor of neurosis
subdued? Miss Wickwire's physical movement, however, is most
affecting, and no one would deny her her intensities. The visionary
student Trofimoff is placed by Mr. Gerald Hiken directly at the center:
again, Mr. Hiken distills the exact blend of diffidence and feeling, of
shabbiness and aspiration which, for Chekhov, characterized "the
eternal student." Finally, to pay only the major tributes, Mr. George

Ebeling's Lopakhin has in it the grittiness and homely texture of peasantry: he brings off the third act revelation *coup* with great power, and animates that act, indeed, with a momentum and urgency I had not known it previously to have. Under the tutelage of Mr. Ross, and with the assistance of their no less distinguished company, Miss Farrar and Miss Wickwire, Messrs. Edmonds and Hiken and Ebeling give full voice to the passionate lyricism of Chekhov's threnody for the lost illusions of youth. I have rarely been so stirred, or so continuously elated in the theater, as I was at this production of "The Cherry Orchard": there are passages in it brushed with the wing of perfection. (*At the 4th Street Theatre, 83 East 4th Street.*)

HAROLD CLURMAN*

London.

In less than three weeks, I saw twelve productions here, only to re-discover the wonder of the Moscow Art Theatre. The famous company, now celebrating its diamond jubilee (it was founded in 1898) and making calls on the great capitals of Europe, opened its London season at the Sadler's Wells Theatre on May 15. Its repertory for this tour consists of four plays—three of them by Chekhov—and one contemporary Soviet play. I saw *The Cherry Orchard* and *The Three Sisters*.

Many recent visitors to Moscow report a deterioration in the vitality of theatre production there. Although the caliber of the individual actors I saw in the two Chekhov plays was not up to the measure of such members of the original company as Katchalov, Moskvin, Leonidoff and Stanislavsky, I could discern nothing in the present performance which gave evidence of any deterioration. There was, in fact, an awe-inspiring mastery.

Here was theatre wrought with such a degree of discipline and dedication that it made productions elsewhere seem crude by comparison. I am not particularly sentimental, but I frequently found myself on the verge of tears during the playing of *The Cherry Orchard*, not alone due to the effect of the play's tenderness but to the fineness of the production's atmosphere and tone.

An extraordinary unity is the first characteristic which strikes the spectator. Each actor seems organically related to the others—and all are of a piece, though each has his own timbre as do the instruments of an orchestra. They appear to be the very stuff of Chekhov's plays.

The actors speak very quietly throughout, though they are always audible. The tempo is leisurely and natural. There is never the strain of a forced projection, yet we never feel that the show is "slow." Only at the end of the evening did I observe that, whereas in ordinary performances it takes two and a half hours to play *The Cherry Orchard*, the Moscow Art Theatre production took nearly four.

The performance never lags because the actors' complete concentration and absorption in the events of the play create an unbroken tissue of life, a moment-by-moment truth and meaning. We are all

* *The Nation*, CLXXXVI (June 7, 1958), 522–523. Reprinted by permission of *The Nation*, New York.

present within an experience in which every second is enrichingly human. We are not in a hurry "to get on with it," any more than the actors, for we, too, are living in and appreciating Chekhov's loving world.

It is still commonplace for many of our critics to indulge in saying that Chekhov is the dramatist of "frustration"—a word beloved among our own frustrated folk. But if it were not already clear through the plays' texts that it is stupid to speak of "frustration" in regard to people instinct with community of feeling, kindness, love of nature, yearning for a better life and an abiding sense of the preciousness of every second of experience, the Moscow Art Theatre's production makes it abundantly evident.

Chekhov's people suffer because they are so wholly human, and this suffering is significant. Chekhov, moreover, is always saved from bathos by his capacity for humorous detachment. This is a realism with no trace of meanness or coldness of heart. If Chekhov's characters rarely attain their ideals, the fault, we are led to understand, is not altogether in the people. What is more important is that the ideals themselves are so deeply rooted in fundamental human need that they make the people positive, ultimately hopeful characters, even in defeat. In many of our "optimistic" or "affirmative" plays, the characters' aims and ideals are either shabby or ludicrously empty of any general interest.

What is unexpected about the new production of the Moscow Art Theatre is that their realism is much more "subdued" than that of the original company. Stanislavsky, who acted in and supervised the first production, the "father" and symbol of modern theatre realism, was, it seems to me, far closer to the theatre theatrical, the theatre of an older tradition, than are his present heirs. And this holds true, I believe, not only of Stanislavsky himself but of the company he directed.

The older actors seemed to possess a more precise sense of individuality, a sharper talent for graphic characterization, a keener feeling for details of make-up, stage business, color and vocal grandeur, greater boldness in portraiture, a certain largeness of stroke with an affinity, paradoxically enough, to the theatre of great "stars." There was always the guiding principle of teamwork, of unity and ensemble, yet each actor somehow stood out, while at present, each actor seems to disappear in the whole. One feels, though this may not be literally true, that the present directors have molded each member of the company perfectly into the pattern of the production, but the actors have not been encouraged—and may not even desire—to invent or discover much on their own.

Let me cite a tiny example. In the scene of the fourth act of *The Cherry Orchard* when Gaev realizes that he and his sister are finally to take leave of their home and of each other forever, the present Gaev simply murmurs, "Sister, sister!" embraces her and turns sobbing against the wall. It is touching, no doubt, but without much nuance. When Stanislavsky played the scene, one observed that he was trying very hard to suppress his tears, his face turned crimson with the effort, he began to grope for a handkerchief which he never managed to find, and the sobs gushed forth, the sound of which he tried to bury by covering his mouth with his hand. The effect was not only memorably affecting but retained in its pathos the special ineptitude of Gaev's character.

I do not point out this contrast in style to praise one or to depreciate the other but to note a distinct difference. How conscious this is, I cannot say. It may be a matter of different generations, an altered social and artistic outlook. Oddly enough, it strikes me that the older generation—Stanislavsky's and Chekhov's—besides being more "theatrical" was also more analytic and more critical. Its performance was at once fuller in emotion and observation and less idealized, less "ennobled," than the present generation's interpretation. In my view, the earlier production was more arrestingly creative, the present one more polished.

In neither case are the results the accident of genius. Such consummate theatre as the productions of both generations represent can arise only from the special condition which the Moscow Art Theatre established. These are permanent companies, the actors do not play these plays eight times a week, none of the players appears at every single performance, rehearsal time may be as long as four months for a play, when a play or production fails, the company does not disband. The company has its own theatre; their jobs are never in jeopardy, except for incompetence or insubordination. The technical staff is permanent, etc.

We in America have actors, directors, designers, technicians of every sort who are as gifted, though not as mature or as well trained, as any seen in the productions I have described. But our theatre organization is anarchic when it is not nightmarish. The miracle is that we do as well as we do.

STUDY QUESTIONS

Chekhov's Letters
1. What seem to be Chekhov's basic premises about the nature and role of the artist as shown in his letters?
2. To what extent do Chekhov's ideas about culture expressed in his letter to his brother underlie any of his comments about The Cherry Orchard —or seem consistent with them?
3. Do Chekhov's comments on setting, characterization, etc. in The Cherry Orchard give us any clue as to the meaning the play might have had for him? Why? Why not?

Andreyev, *Tchekhov and the Theatre*
1. What does *panpsychism* mean and why does Andreyev feel it is so important in Chekhov's works?
2. What is Tolstoi's criticism of Chekhov, according to Andreyev? Does Andreyev answer Tolstoi?

Efros, *Tchekhov and the Moscow Art Theatre*
1. What, according to Efros, is Chekhov's distinctive contribution to Russian realism?
2. Are there any causal connections between Chekhov's realism as Efros defines it and Stanislavsky's basic ideas about acting and play production?

Gorki, *Recollections of Tchekhov*
1. To what extent do Gorki's descriptions of Chekhov corroborate any of Chekhov's ideas expressed in his letter to his brother? Are there any significant differences?
2. To what extent do you think Chekhov's attitude towards banality as described by Gorki seems evident in The Cherry Orchard?
3. On the basis of your reading of The Cherry Orchard, would you agree with Gorki's interpretations of the characters of Madame Ranevsky (Lyubov), Gaev, Lopahin, and Trofimov? Why? Why not?

Gerhardi, *Anton Chehov*
1. Why, according to Gerhardi, can we not call Chekhov a pessimist? What then can we call him?
2. What is Gerhardi's view of Chekhov's primary objections to logic?
3. Explain the statement (p. 92) "Therefore life is an equilibrium of transitory values, whereas what is absolute and static is perhaps its equilibrium." Do you think his statement could apply to The Cherry Orchard? Why? Why not?
4. To what extent does Gerhardi feel that Chekhov believes life has meaning?
5. What does Gerhardi mean (p. 94) when he says that the average citizen "if he saw himself in this clear light would be astonished and amused at the tragedy of his self-sufficiency?"

6. Explain Gerhardi's comparison between the structure of a Wagnerian opera and that of a Chekhov play? To what extent do you think this comparison applicable to *The Cherry Orchard*?

Bruford, *Chekhov and his Russia*
1. Why was the period from 1762–1861 almost a golden age for the Russian land owning classes? Is there any evidence of this in *The Cherry Orchard*?
2. What were the principal economic and social consequences of the Emancipation? Is there any evidence of these in the play?
3. What, according to Bruford, are the principal changes Chekhov dramatizes in *The Cherry Orchard* and what is his attitude towards them?

Fergusson, *The Idea of a Theatre*
1. What does Fergusson mean when he calls the play a "drama of pathetic motivation"? (p. 105) What does Fergusson mean when he remarks on the same page: "This he achieves by means of his plot, he selects only those incidents, those moments in his characters' lives, between their rationalized efforts, when they sense their situation and destiny most clearly?"
2. What, according to Fergusson, is the purpose of ceremonious social occasions in Chekhov plays?
3. What does Fergusson mean when he says (p. 108) ". . . but the form of the play as a whole is nothing but poetry in the widest sense: the coherence of the concrete elements of the composition." Relate this to the distinction between poetry in the theatre and poetry of the theatre.
4. Show how, according to Fergusson, the behavior of Firs, Anya, and Trofimov in Act II exemplifies poetry of the theatre.
5. What does Fergusson conclude is Chekhov's attitude towards change as shown in the poetic scenic structure of Act II of *The Cherry Orchard*?

Magarshack, *Chekhov the Dramatist*
1. What is Aristotle's definition of comedy that Magarshack quotes and why is it important in his discussion?
2. Why, according to Magarshack, do people fail to recognize the comic nature of the characters in *The Cherry Orchard*?
3. According to Magarshack, what is the play's theme? How is this shown in the portrayal of Lopahin?
4. Why are Trofimov and Firs comic characters in the play? Are there any characters to which Magarshack's analysis may not apply? Why? Why not?

Corrigan, *Some Aspects of Chekhov's Dramaturgy*
1. In Corrigan's view what is "the greatest reality of existence or truth of existence" for Chekhov?
2. What is the role of exaggeration in relation to the truth of reality for Chekhov?
3. What is the role of introspection in Chekhov's characters? What examples from *The Cherry Orchard* would you cite to substantiate Corrigan's thesis? Consider, for example, Act III.
4. How does Corrigan differ from Magarshack in his conception of Chekhov's comedy?
5. How does Chekhov manage to have an audience remain detached and yet sympathetic to his characters?

6. What does Corrigan mean by "the aesthetizing of life" as part of Chekhov's dramaturgy? What examples from The Cherry Orchard can you cite to substantiate this idea?

Deer, *Speech as Action in The Cherry Orchard*
1. What are the reasons why it is difficult to determine the dramatic significance of Chekhov's dialogue?
2. Explain how, according to Deer, Lopahin's first speech really is dramatic and functional in the play.
3. What is the relation between realism and daydream in the behavior and attitude of the characters in The Cherry Orchard?

Latham, *The Cherry Orchard as Comedy*
1. What, according to Latham, is Chekhov's attitude towards the passing of the old order in The Cherry Orchard?
2. In what ways for Latham is the cherry orchard a symbol in the play?
3. In what ways is Chekhov satirizing Gaev and Madame Ranevsky in the play?
4. What symbols, according to Latham, serve to define Lopahin as a comic character? Explain.
5. What is Firs' role in the play?
6. Why for Latham is Trofimov a comic character?

Timmer, *The Bizarre in Cechov's Art*
1. How does Timmer differentiate among the grotesque, the bizarre, and the absurd?
2. According to Timmer, is Chekhov an optimist or pessimist? How is this question related to the distinctions between the bizarre and the absurd?
3. Explain Timmer's statement (p. 167): "One of Chekhov's notions of the bizarre—and probably one of the most important ones—is that in an apparently hopeless life there is still hope, that, as I said before, life itself generates hope."
4. Do you think the preceding quotation could apply to The Cherry Orchard? Why? Why not?
5. How do Chekhov and Dostoevsky differ in their presentation of the bizarre?
6. With what critic would Timmer be most in agreement in his ideas about optimism and pessimism and the absurd in Chekhov? How would you differentiate this critic's views from those of Timmer?

King
1. What seems to be Miss King's interpretation of the theme of The Cherry Orchard?
2. What seem to her assumptions about the artistic effects of plotlessness in the play?

Woolf
1. What seem to be Mrs. Woolf's basic ideas about the play's theme?
2. To what extent do these differ from Gertrude King's?
3. With which critic in this anthology would Mrs. Woolf most agree in her interpretation of the play? Least agree? Why?

Marshall and Young

1. In what respects does Stark Young agree with Margaret Marshall about the meaning of the play and the quality of the production? Disagree?

2. What does Young's extended analysis of the scene between Madame Ranevsky and Trofimov reveal about his basic assumptions regarding the play's meaning and Chekhov's attitudes towards human nature?

3. To what extent do Margaret Marshall and Stark Young seem to feel that the play is a comedy?

Bentley and Hayes

1. According to Bentley, what is Chekhovism? Why is it so misleading? To what extent does he think it justified on the basis of The Cherry Orchard?

2. What assumptions about the meaning of the play underlie Bentley's criticism of the performances of Lopahin and Madame Ranevsky?

3. For what reasons is Richard Hayes' review more favorable to the production than Eric Bentley's? To what extent does Hayes differ with Bentley about individual performances in the play?

4. According to Hayes, what is Chekhovism? Does it differ from Bentley's definition?

Clurman

1. What assumptions about the play's meaning emerge from Clurman's criticism of the production?

2. To what extent does Clurman's recollection of Stanislavski's production corroborate Gertrude King's reaction? Stanislavski's own description of his production in My Life in Art?

3. Judging from Clurman's comments, would he call Chekhov an optimist or pessimist? Would he regard the play as comic or tragic? Why?

SUGGESTED QUESTIONS FOR PAPERS

1. Compare and contrast the treatment of change in The Cherry Orchard by four critics in this text. Which analysis seems most convincing and thorough? Why?

2. Compare and contrast the treatment of change in The Cherry Orchard, and in two other full length Chekhov plays.

3. Compare and contrast the treatment of change in The Cherry Orchard, Shaw's Heartbreak House (which Shaw regarded as his treatment of the same subject as Chekhov's play), and The Wisteria Trees (an American adaptation of The Cherry Orchard by Joshua Logan. New York: Random House, 1950).

4. Compare and contrast the treatment of change in The Cherry Orchard and two other roughly contemporary Russian plays, Leo Tolstoi's The Power of Darkness and Maxim Gorki's The Lower Depths.

5. Compare and contrast the nature of the comic (or the comic elements) in The Cherry Orchard, and two other full length Chekhov plays.

6. Compare and contrast the nature of the comic or the definition of comedy in at least three of the longer selections in Theories of Comedy, ed. Paul Lauter (Anchor, Doubleday, 1964) and the extent to which they may apply to The Cherry Orchard and/or other Chekhov full length plays.

7. Compare and contrast the nature of the comic (or the comic elements) in The Cherry Orchard, Oscar Wilde's The Importance of Being Earnest, and Bertolt Brecht's The Three Penny Opera (in The Modern Theatre, ed. Eric Bentley, Vol. 1, Anchor, Doubleday, 1955)

8. To what extent do Chekhov's letters (see bibliography for texts) corroborate Gorki's characterization of Chekhov in his Reminiscences?

9. To what extent do other historians corroborate Bruford's analysis of the Russian landed aristocracy? Are there any significant differences? Would they affect one's understanding of The Cherry Orchard?

10. Some drama historians have asserted that without Chekhov the Moscow Art Theatre of Stanislavski could never have developed as it did. Just what was Chekhov's influence on the Moscow Art Theatre and how important has it been?

11. Since The Cherry Orchard does not exactly view change in a Marxist framework, one might expect that Chekhov would not be in good standing in Communist Russia so far as the Soviet critics are concerned. To what extent is this true judging from Chekhov's position in Russian literature and criticism since the Revolution?

12. To what extent are Stanislavski's comments on The Cherry Orchard representative of his comments on Chekhov's other plays? Is Stanislavski fair to Chekhov—that is, does he properly understand and appreciate his particular kind of dramatic genius?

ANTON CHEKHOV: A Selected Bibliography

A. CHEKHOV'S WORKS

Best Plays, translated and edited by Stark Young. New York, 1956.

The Brute and Other Farces, edited Eric Bentley. New York, 1958.

Letters, translated by Constance Garnett. New York, 1920.

Letters on the Short Story, the Drama, and Other Literary Topics, edited by Louis Friedland. London, 1924.

Life and Letters, translated and edited by S. S. Koteliansky and Philip Tomlinson. London, 1925.

Nine Plays. New York, 1946 (includes the full length plays and the farces).

Plays, translated and edited by Elisabeta Fen. London, 1959 (includes *Ivanov*, an early Chekhov full-length play not found in the Stark Young).

The Portable Chekhov, edited with an introduction by Avrahm Yarmolinsky. New York, 1947 (includes stories and letters).

Selected Letters, edited by Lillian Hellman and translated by Sidonie Lederer. New York, 1955.

The Unknown Chekhov: Stories and Other Hitherto Unpublished Writings, translated and with an introduction by Avrahm Yarmolinsky. New York, 1954.

B. CRITICISM AND BIOGRAPHY

Bentley, Eric, "Chekhov as Playwright," *The Kenyon Review*, VII (1945), 266–250.

Bruford, W. H., *Anton Chekhov*. New Haven, 1957.

Bruford, W. H., *Chekhov and his Russia*. New York, 1948.

Corrigan, Robert W., "Some Aspects of Chekhov's Dramaturgy," *Educational Theatre Journal*, VII (May 1955), 107–114.

Deer, Irving, "Speech as Action in *The Cherry Orchard*," *Educational Theatre Journal*, X (March 1958), 30–34.

Eekman, Thomas, editor, *Anton Chekhov, 1860–1960*, Leiden, 1960.

Fergusson, Francis, *The Idea of a Theatre*. Princeton, N.J., 1949.

Gerhardi, William, *Anton Chehov*, New York, 1923.

Gorki, Maxim, *Reminiscences of Tchekhov*, translated by S. S. Koteliansky and Leonard Woolf. London, 1921.

Heifetz, Anna, *Chekhov in English: A Selective List of Works by and about Chekhov to 1949*. New York Public Library, 1949.

Koteliansky, S. S., editor and translator, *Anton Tchekhov: Literary and Theatrical Reminiscences*. London, 1927.

Latham, Jacqueline, "The Cherry Orchard as Comedy," *Educational Theatre Journal*, X (March 1958), 21–29.

Magarshack, David, *Chekhov: a Life*. New York, 1953.

Magarshack, David, *Chekhov the Dramatist*. London, 1952.

Mirski, D. S., *A History of Russian Literature*. New York, 1926, 1949.

Popkin, Henry, "Chekhov the Ironic Spectator," *Theatre Arts*, XXXVI (March 1952), 17, 80.

Simmons, Ernest J., *Chekhov*. Boston, 1963.

Stanislavski, Konstantin, *My Life in Art*, translated by J. J. Robbins. London, 1924.

Stanislavski, Konstantin, *Stanislavski's Legacy*, translated and edited Elizabeth Reynolds Hapgood. New York, 1958.

Wilson, Edmund, "Seeing Chekhov Plain," *The New Yorker*, November 22, 1952, 180–198.

Yachnin, Rissa, *Chekhov in English: A Selective List of Books by and about Chekhov, 1949–1960*. New York Public Library, 1960.